THE
UNSLEEPING EYE

SECRET POLICE AND THEIR VICTIMS

Robert J. Stove

ENCOUNTER BOOKS
SAN FRANCISCO

First U.S. edition published in 2003 by Encounter Books, an
activity of Encounter for Culture and Education, Inc., a nonprofit
tax exempt corporation.

First published in 2002 as *The Unsleeping Eye: A Brief History of
Secret Police and Their Victims* by Duffy and Snellgrove, Sydney,
Australia.

Encounter Books website address: www.encounterbooks.com

Manufactured in the United States and printed on acid-free
paper.

The paper used in this publication meets the minimum requirements of ANSI/NISO Z39.48-1992 (R 1997)(*Permanence of
Paper*).

Library of Congress Cataloging-in-Publication Data
Stove, R. J. (Robert James), 1961–
     The unsleeping eye : secret police and their victims / Robert
J. Stove.
        p.   cm.
     Includes bibliographical references and index.
     ISBN 1-893554-66-X (alk. paper)
     1. Secret service—History.   I. Title.
HV7961.S764 2003
363.28'3—dc21

                                                      2002192785

                    10 9 8 7 6 5 4 3 2 1

Robert J. Stove lives in Melbourne. His articles have
appeared in Australian and American
publications including *The Australian, Soundscapes,
The New Criterion* and *The American Spectator.*

The Unsleeping Eye is his second book. His first
was *Prince of Music*, a study of the
sixteenth-century composer Palestrina.

contents

In memoriam
JESSIE STOVE, née LEAHY
1926–2001

The ruling power is always faced with the question, 'In such and such circumstances, what would you *do?*'

George Orwell

foreword

SECRET POLICING – that is, governments' surveillance of their own subjects, as distinct from espionage, which concentrates on governments' surveillance of others' subjects – remains a topic about which almost everybody knows a little and almost nobody knows a lot. The names 'Gestapo' and 'KGB' are common currency in every European language; anyone conversant with Communist administration recognises, in addition, such terms as 'Stasi', 'Securitate', 'Cheka', and 'OGPU'. But outside these well-defined fields of attested political criminality, little information about domestic surveillance has penetrated the public culture.

One can easily read entire books on Napoleon – in the English language, at any rate – without encountering any serious acknowledgement of the immense debt that his administration owed to the secret police skills of Joseph Fouché. Similarly, entire books have been published on Elizabeth I which spectacularly minimise (even if they cannot omit altogether) the importance of the Queen's secretary of state, Sir Francis Walsingham, in keeping her alive: let alone alive and on her throne. This pattern of neglecting domestic surveillance activities is most obvious in conventional biographies, yet it can also be discerned in more ambitious tomes. Thus, although one might assume that the English-language

1

literature on secret policing is huge, comprehensive, up to date, and readily accessible, one would actually be wrong on all four counts.

When my publisher first raised with me the idea of secret policing as the basis for a book, I assumed that scores of historians in Britain and America had already ploughed this field. To my astonishment I discovered, instead, a remarkable reluctance on their part even to broach the matter in other than the vaguest terms: a reluctance all the more striking, given the vast literature that espionage has inspired. I had managed to stumble across that rare, that most profoundly cherishable (for the historian) thing: a genuinely under-researched topic. As to *why* it has been under-researched, I can no more dogmatise now that I could before I started the manuscript. I can, however, guess, in a way that I could not have hoped to do previously.

First of all, to examine secret police services is to appreciate the importance of individual human beings, who, unlike their espionage counterparts, resist all attempts at novelistic or cinematic glamorisation *à la* James Bond. Such emphasis threatens, at least implicitly, the pre-eminence of all those vast impersonal socio-economic forces which inspire from most present-day academic historians (whether Marxist or not) Pavlovian drooling. Until relatively recently, secret police forces were almost always answerable to one individual, and in many cases could only loosely be described as 'forces' at all: so much did they depend on personal contact between a functionary and his (often freelance) underlings. Even when active bureaucracies of terror emerged, the scope for an individual personality to alter events proved much larger than any determinist will want to admit. When Felix Dzerzhinsky took over

Bolshevik Russia's original secret police force, the Cheka, he operated in a very different manner from his predecessor and his successor. The Gestapo of Hermann Göring differed in crucial respects from the Gestapo of Göring's successor Reinhard Heydrich. And so on.

Secondly, no one can study secret police services for long without acquiring a healthy aversion to the very notion of Big Government. This aversion cuts so completely across the predominantly welfarist sentiments, employment conditions and atmosphere of academic tenure that it is unlikely to be common among such tenure's usual beneficiaries.

All of the above might serve as an explanation for the paucity of literature on secret policing. It does not even begin to serve as an excuse. The following chapters are meant merely to serve as a stopgap for the common reader. They attempt to synthesise information from an unusually wide range of sources: a passing allusion in a biography here or a panegyric there; on the one hand, the occasional wide-ranging one-volume history; on the other hand, monographs so specialised as to be largely unknown outside bibliographers' ranks. Sheer chance's role in pointing the way to relevant data – a role all too familiar to anyone who essays the historian's art – has been exceptionally large on this occasion.

· · · · ·

Obviously a book that sought to cover all national histories of secret policing, from its apparent origins (in Sparta during the fourth century BC) to our own age, would be unreadably colossal. This book therefore deals with five, and only five, areas in which secret policing has been of vital importance to

3

government. The factors linking all five are two: the existence
in each case of a recognisable, centrally administered *nation*, in
which alone a secular surveillance bureaucracy can flourish
(hence secret policing's comparative feebleness during Western Europe's pre-national Middle Ages); and the presence, in
each government described, of at least one outstandingly
accomplished individual bureaucrat who was *not* his country's
head of state. At times such a bureaucrat could not necessarily draw a dividing line where secret policing ended and
espionage began. But in most cases the former, not the latter,
remained his primary responsibility.

Chapter One assesses Walsingham's intelligence network:
how it prefigured, and how it differed from, modern totalitarian surveillance; to what extent its guiding principles
remained after Walsingham's own death and the rise of his
ablest successor, Robert Cecil, who worked for a different
monarch in a dramatically changed geopolitical situation.

Chapter Two surveys the tortuous career of Fouché, and
how this Catholic turned republican turned Bonapartist
turned Bourbon apologist constructed – with tools sometimes
provided for him by Cardinal Richelieu and other *ancien
régime* precursors – a surveillance machine of a recognisably
modern kind, with access to propaganda techniques and cynical doubletalk which Walsingham neither attempted nor
supported.

Chapter Three outlines domestic surveillance in Russia,
from its accepted beginnings with Ivan the Terrible's Oprichnina network, through its subsequent (and seldom effectual)
manifestations under Romanov Tsarism, to its apogee under
Soviet Communism: in which milieu it attained an exterminationist effectiveness that no other country or political

system within the European orbit has managed to match. To an extent still insufficiently perceived in the West, Soviet Communism *was* domestic surveillance. No domestic surveillance, no Soviet Communism. The money and manpower that Soviet Communist leaders lavished on acquiring foreign intelligence formed only a fraction – some historians would argue as little as one-fifth – of the money and manpower that went towards spying on their own countrymen at home.

Chapter Four deals with Hitler's Germany, and disposes of the widespread myth that the Gestapo was responsible for all, or even most, National Socialist surveillance. In reality the Gestapo constituted but part of that surveillance, and not always the leading part. Its similarities with its Communist counterparts will be, let us hope, clear from what follows; so will its divergences from these counterparts.

Chapter Five differs from the other four in two immediately evident respects. First, it deals (as they do not) with a recognisable modern Western democracy, however flawed: the America which shaped, and which was in turn shaped by, J. Edgar Hoover's Federal Bureau of Investigation. Second, its protagonist's police force devoted its main energies to fighting apolitical crime, political surveillance operations taking (at least in theory) second place. Without public acclaim as tireless foe of kidnappers and bank-robbers, Hoover the secret policeman would have feared to exist. Accordingly, themes like the separation of powers – which seldom troubled the cogitation of Fouché, and which would for Walsingham have been as incomprehensible as Sanskrit – unavoidably emerge in discussion of the FBI's origins and structure.

• • • • •

From the foregoing, spectacular omissions will be easily noticeable. Thus, nothing on the Stasi in East Germany, or the Securitate in Ceausescu's Romania, or 'Papa Doc' Duvalier's Tontons Macoutes in Haiti; nothing on the Venetian Republic, with its institutionalised practice of anonymous denunciations to the dreaded Council of Ten, during Venice's great epoch of the fifteenth, sixteenth and early seventeenth centuries; nothing on Israel's Shin Bet; nothing on BOSS in apartheid-era South Africa; nothing on the PIDE in Dr Salazar's Portugal (much feared by its enemies, but unable to forestall the deposition of Salazar's successor Marcello Caetano in 1974); nothing on monarchical Iran's genuinely formidable SAVAK (equally incapable of preventing the Shah's 1979 overthrow); nothing, perhaps most grievously, on East Asian surveillance at all. Had we but wood-pulp enough, and time, there would be room for each of these. Perhaps, in a sequel, there will be.

Meanwhile the present book seeks, after the manner expounded by Sir Philip Sidney (who as Walsingham's son-in-law has a bit-part in this drama), to please, to move, and to teach; to provide insights, however limited, into a crucial factor of modern governance that our masters themselves would sooner we did not think about; and to suggest by this emphasis on administrative detail, some long-overdue reorientation in historiographical priorities. The discipline of history will obtain conspicuous benefits if its leading practitioners are regularly reminded that the Big Picture issue worthiest of historians' attention is the one that Lenin famously encapsulated: 'Who whom?' Who gets to arrest, torture, imprison, whom? Who ends up sentencing whom to death? In some areas Lenin's dictum (pregnant though it has been, in modern times, with implications for the life expectancy of half the human race) can be ignored as a vulgar distraction from the main game. In any coverage of secret policing, it is itself the main game.

• • • • •

A note on foreign names
When in doubt, I have transliterated Russian names according to the most widely recognised Anglo-Saxon forms, which occasionally differ from the forms that specialists in Russian history prefer. Thus, this book speaks of Scriabin and not Skryabin; Grigori and not Grigorii; Lavrenti and not Lavrentii. Only when specific quotations and title-pages give non-standard spellings have I used those spellings. If I cannot always hope to have avoided inconsistency, I hope at least to have made a passable job at avoiding the appearance of wilful eccentricity.

Regarding German orthographic customs, Göring used the *Umlaut*-laden *o* when signing his name, but Goebbels did not. Hence my differing renditions of the same vowel sound in their respective surnames.

R.J.S.

most dangerous and desperate treason: ELIZABETHAN AND JACOBEAN SURVEILLANCE

A man exceeding wise and industrious ...
a diligent researcher out of hidden secrets, and one
who knew excellently well how to win men's affections
to him, and to make use of them for his own purposes.
William Camden (1551–1623),
schoolmaster and chronicler, describing
Sir Francis Walsingham

Intelligence is never too dear.
Walsingham himself

'Into Thy Hands, Lord!'

ON 8 FEBRUARY 1587 a tall, powerfully built woman of early middle age calmly entered the great hall of Fotheringhay Castle, Northamptonshire. Imprisonment and severe illness – both of which had lasted for most of her adult life – had left her corpulent and slightly stooped, with no remaining trace of the elusive, animated beauty that portrait painters once vied to capture and that poets once hymned. (Pierre de Ronsard, France's leading sixteenth-century poet, had called her *belle et plus que belle*.) Yet her pride and dignity remained untarnished. Beholding her from behind a rail was a crowd of nobles, gentry and clergy, around three hundred in number. At first they were silent. Then the Dean of Peterborough, standing on a dais in the centre of the hall, led them in prayer, hoping to drown out any 'papist' utterances the woman made. In this hope they failed; with a firm clear voice, she recited penitential psalms in Latin, then asked God's blessing on Pope Sixtus V, on her only son, and on Elizabeth I.

As was the custom, the headsman asked her forgiveness. 'I forgive you with all my heart,' she answered, 'for now I hope you shall make an end of all my troubles.' Her two ladies-in-waiting removed her black robe and her veil, disclosing thick auburn-gold locks and a blood-red velvet dress. Laying her chin upon the block, she called out three or four times the words *In manus tuas, Domine!* – 'Into Thy hands, Lord!' – and the executioner's assistant laid a hand upon her to keep her still. The executioner swung his axe, but merely gashed the back of her neck; her ladies thought they heard her whisper 'Sweet Jesus'. He struck again, this time bringing forth a great fountain of blood. According to several accounts, only at a third stroke did he decapitate his victim; and even then, 'her lippes stirred up and downe almost a quarter of an hour'.

The crowd remained mute with horror. No one dared speak till the headsman shouted: 'God save the Queen!' To which the Dean of Peterborough replied, 'Amen! Amen! So perish all the Queen's enemies.' As the executioner picked up the severed head and exhibited it to the spectators, the auburn-gold wig came away, to reveal closely cropped hair 'as grey as if she had been three-score and ten years old'.

When it was time to take away the corpse, there was found a small dog,

> which was crept under her clothes which could not be gotten forth but with force and afterwards could not depart ... but came and laye betweene her head and shoulders a thing dilligently noted.

• • • • •

Thus died Mary, Queen of Scots; thus Sir Francis Walsingham, secretary of state and spymaster to Elizabeth I, achieved his greatest triumph. For months, he had feared he would be deprived of it. Elizabeth, though admitting that Mary's intrigues against the English government deserved death, reacted with loathing to the very idea of an anointed sovereign being judged by commoners. She would far rather have had Mary quietly assassinated, than given the aura of martyrdom in a law court.

Alas, her underlings refused to kill Mary without legal sanction. Mary's gaoler, Sir Amyas Paulet, responded to the very idea of secretly murdering Mary with righteous rage: 'God forbid that I should make so foul a shipwreck of my conscience.' Thus a formal trial of Mary became inevitable; yet even after she had been convicted and condemned to death, it took three months to prevail on Elizabeth to ratify the sentence. In January 1587, the Queen's secretary, William Davison, placed the death warrant for Mary in the middle of a pile of otherwise ordinary documents requiring her signature, trusting (correctly as it happened) that she would sign the warrant without even realising the nature of what she was signing.

However concerned Davison and Walsingham were with having Mary done away with, others regarded the topic in a spirit of near-total indifference. One such largely passive spectator was Mary's son and successor in Scotland, James VI. With noticeable weariness, the Protestant James – then aged twenty – disclaimed all sentiment towards the Catholic mother whom he had not even seen since he was ten months old. On 15 December 1586 James wrote to Elizabeth's some-time favourite, the Earl of Leicester:

> How fond and inconstant I were if I should prefer my mother to the title [of Scottish monarch], let all men judge. My religion ever moved me to hate her course, although my honour constrains me to insist for her life.

Having thereby 'insisted' in tones of almost complete inaudibility, James let the matter rest. In a letter to James (written six days after the execution), Elizabeth tried to justify killing his mother, with breathtakingly sanctimonious language:

> My Dear Brother: I would you know (though not felt) the extreme dolour that overwhelms my mind for that miserable accident, which, far contrary to my meaning, hath befallen … I beseech you that – as God and many more know – how innocent I am in this case, so you will believe me, that if I had bid aught, I would have

abided by it. I am not so base-minded, that the fear of any living creature, or prince, should make me afraid to do that [which] were just, or, when done, to deny the same. I am not of so base a lineage, nor carry so vile a mind ... if I had meant it, I would never lay it on others' shoulders; no more will I not damnify myself that thought it not.

For all her piled-on double negatives, she need not have worried: James expressed no further public disapproval. But even James might have started seriously defending his mother, had he perceived the sheer trickery and forging of evidence which Walsingham, to ensure Mary's execution, had carried out.

Walsingham's Rise to Power

Francis Walsingham's emergence as a political giant proved steady and gradual rather than dramatic. In early youth he had little to distinguish him from many clever, middlingly success-ful lawyers, save the fact of being more honest and intellectually inclined than most. His father, also a lawyer, had done well enough from his profession to buy the manor of Foot's Cray, in Kent, where Francis himself was probably born. No one bothered to record with any exactitude his date of birth, but it definitely occurred in or around 1532. Thus, Walsingham belonged to the first generation of Englishmen too young to recall life in a wholly Catholic England, before Henry VIII's breach with the Pope. His father had accepted the new religious dispensation with every appearance of loyal enthusiasm, and with Francis himself Protestantism became the guiding force of his life.

Educated in law at Cambridge, Walsingham was called to the Bar in 1552; but the following year he fled to the Continent, after Mary Tudor had wrested the throne from the Protestant Jane Grey. This departure indicated much in itself about the moral character of the Walsingham whom all Europe's governments eventually came to know and to fear. Most young Englishmen who shared Walsingham's Protestant beliefs placed them discreetly in storage once Jane Grey had been deposed and the unflinching Catholic Mary had been installed. Not Walsingham: who, rather than violate his convictions by swearing allegiance to a Catholic sovereign, would willingly have perished. During his European sojourn he eagerly studied the history and differing legal systems of Continental states. (In after years he commanded a nephew of his to do likewise when on the Continent, to acquire a firm grasp of languages, and to let no day pass 'without translating somewhat'.) Above all, he waited: waited for Mary to expire, although as she was only in her late thirties when crowned, and still young enough to produce an entire dynasty of Catholics, he looked doomed to a lengthy, frustrating exile.

His banishment turned out to be shorter than he had dared hope: little more than five years. In November 1558 Mary died, her dreams of motherhood cruelly disappointed by a sequence of false pregnancies that were probably symptoms of ovarian cancer. Back in London within weeks of Elizabeth succeeding her sister as queen, Walsingham allied himself with William Cecil: a fellow Protestant of a much more obviously ambitious sort than Walsingham, who had become one of England's leading civil servants while still in his twenties. (Despite his firm opposition to Catholicism, Cecil had spent Mary's reign in England unmolested.) Thanks to Cecil's approval, Walsingham became a Member of Parliament in January 1559: first for the constituency of Banbury in Oxfordshire, then (1562–67) for that of Lyme Regis in Dorset.

While the connection between the experienced Cecil and the comparative novice Walsingham necessarily had much more of a master–servant relationship about it in the late 1550s and early 1560s than it possessed later, their subsequent political combination's essential elements emerged quickly. Each man had qualities the other lacked. Already Walsingham was the savant, the Puritan, preoccupied with theological questions, subordinating *Realpolitik* issues to his lifelong dream of a sweeping Protestant victory across Europe; and Cecil was the voice of caution. Both Cecil and Walsingham regretted Elizabeth's cultivation, in her reign's early years, of her own bet-hedging world view that combined Protestant scriptures with predominantly Catholic ritual. Yet Cecil understood this compromise, and showed tact towards the Queen about it, whereas for Walsingham it constituted a reprehensible display of theological cowardice. As Walsingham himself bluntly put it in later years: 'Christ and Belial can hardly agree.' To Elizabeth herself, when she characteristically vacillated on an important question of foreign policy, he complained in the most brusque terms:

> For the love of God, madam, let not the cure of your diseased state hang any longer on deliberation. Diseased states are no more cured by consultation … than unsound and diseased bodies by only conference with physicians, without receiving the remedies by them prescribed.

Such remarks as these understandably prompted a modern historian to call Walsingham 'the one wholehearted ideologue' of Elizabeth's régime. At one stage Elizabeth, goaded to wrath by Walsingham's incivility, threw a slipper at him. The differences between him and Cecil extended even to portraiture. Cecil's best known surviving likeness, now in London's National Portrait Gallery, reveals him in his gorgeous robes of state; it combines a self-satisfied look (noticeable above all in the small, deep-set eyes) with the limited but sincere geniality of a man who can make himself obeyed without needing to cajole or browbeat. The same gallery's depiction of Walsingham, by contrast, shows him clad all in black: his long melancholy face more like that of a priest as depicted by El Greco than like that of any politician. For all his activity in sponsoring poets like Spenser (who hailed him as an exceptionally generous patron), Walsingham seems to have been *born* harried and liverish: yet another respect in which he was the antipode to Cecil, who took so detached a view of his responsibilities that when doffing his cloak of an evening after work, he would say to the cloak 'Lie there, Lord Treasurer.'

'Serve God by Serving of the Queen': Walsingham as Administrator and Diplomat

The bureaucracy of which Walsingham had become a part would scarcely have been recognised by a Spaniard, Frenchman or Swede of the time as a bureaucracy at all: so few members did it contain, and so much did it depend on support from volunteers at the municipal level. True, it was somewhat larger than historians concluded until recently; it consisted of around 2,500 individuals, most of whom retained their jobs only at the monarch's pleasure. But compared to France only a generation later, governed by about 40,000 bureaucrats, this 2,500 remained an extraordinarily small total. That Elizabethan administration worked as efficiently as it did resulted from three factors: the contemporary example of strife-torn France, whose religious wars provided most Englishmen with a cautionary tale of what to avoid; the calibre of individual bureaucrats such as Walsingham and Cecil, who for all their faults had loftier principles than mere take-the-money-and-run greed; and the almost obsessive Elizabethan preoccupation – faithfully echoed by Shakespeare, who in turn perpetuated it – with the Wars of the Roses. Having ended less than fifty years before the Queen's birth, these conflicts remained an ever-present Elizabethan nightmare (out of all proportion, it must be said, to the impact they had actually left on day-to-day fifteenth-century English life); and they confirmed Elizabethans' widespread belief that even the most odious despotism was better than anarchy. Hence the 1553 failure of Jane Grey to survive on the throne for more than nine days: since even the average Protestant preferred to see orderly dynastic succession by a Catholic candidate, rather than usurpation by a Protestant one.

It followed from this happy combination of dutiful administrators and distorted folk memory that the first decade of Elizabeth's reign (1558–68) was in every respect her most peaceful. The Queen justified her initial reluctance to hound Catholics by boasting that she had no wish to 'make windows into men's hearts'; at this stage she might even have meant what she said, however absurd such remarks afterwards became, when she not only made windows into men's hearts but demanded that men's hearts be publicly removed with a butcher's knife from men's bodies. Moreover, there still existed a good chance that Elizabeth would marry. The one genuine crisis of Elizabeth's early years as sovereign came when, in October 1562, she caught smallpox and for days hovered on death's brink, all the while refusing to name an heir. Even this event, though, failed to inspire alternative candidates with an overt lust to seize the English crown.

But by the late 1560s Elizabeth's situation became far more perilous, and her measures for improving it far more obviously tyrannical. Hitherto she and most of her advisers had assumed – partly through the total absence of Catholic attempts to prevent her own succession on Mary Tudor's death – that Catholicism would simply fade out, as fewer and fewer Englishmen old enough to remember the pre-Henrician *status quo* remained alive. Why waste resources on killing off a creed already dying of inanition? In 1568 a development occurred which demonstrated how misguided this attitude was: Catholic exiles established a seminary at Douai, in what is now northern France (though it then lay within the Spanish Netherlands' borders). Among the most distinguished of Douai's early alumni was a former Anglican deacon of great intellectual brilliance and greater holiness: Edmund Campion, whom Cecil had hailed as 'one of the diamonds of England'.

A year after this disconcerting project began, England's north (which had remained so hostile towards Elizabethan Protestantism that Elizabeth herself, for all her much-vaunted fearlessness towards would-be assassins, never dared journey there) rose in arms. Led by two of England's richest magnates, the Earls of Northumberland and Westmorland, the northern rebels consisted of four thousand foot soldiers and 1,700 cavalrymen. They at first were unconquerable: upon capturing

Durham in November 1569, they proclaimed their allegiance to the recently deposed Mary, Queen of Scots, demanded that Catholicism be reinstated as England's official religion, and tore up the cathedral's Anglican prayer book. Yet the further south they moved, the fewer locals joined them, and the more numerous the desertions from their initial ranks became, once the troops realised that the Spanish aid which Northumberland and Westmorland had promised would not arrive in time, if ever. (At this period, for opposite reasons, both English Catholics and English Protestants greatly exaggerated Spain's willingness to intervene militarily in English affairs. Spain – and in particular its generalissimo, the Duke of Alva – had already begun to find its current campaign in the Low Countries so great a drain on men and money that the notion of subsidising a hazardous English adventure was unthinkable.) Besides, the rebellion's aims tended to cancel each other out: while all the leading rebels favoured England's re-Catholicisation, not all of them shared the two Earls' desire to see Mary restored to Scotland's throne, let alone set by violence upon England's. In December Cecil dashed the Earls' hopes of freeing Mary from her prison, by transferring her south from Tutbury to Coventry before the rebels had reached the former town. Once the rebel forces had been scattered, Westmorland fled to Catholic Flanders; while Northumberland, seized in Scotland and underestimating his captors' national genius for striking an advantageous bargain, was handed over to the English in exchange for £5,000, after which he died on the scaffold in York.

Cecil hired one Robert Constable to entice Westmorland and the other leading fugitives back to England. Initially Constable rejected this task, all the more passionately in that

Westmorland was a relative of his. He compared the duty Cecil asked of him with the role of Judas, only to abandon this line of self-reproach when Cecil offered him a generous reward, coupling this offer with the suitably menacing comment that 'Her Majesty is very desirous to have these noisome vermin.' Although Constable never succeeded in tracing Westmorland, he acquired a knighthood for his trouble, while approximately six hundred other rebels or suspected rebels were captured and hanged. 'Some few of them suffered,' was Cecil's curt description of the outcome.

None of this showed Walsingham's own talents in the most flattering of lights. Despite having been given substantial responsibility for secret intelligence back in 1568, Walsingham allowed the Northern Rebellion to take him, and the administration more generally, by surprise. His overriding obsession with Elizabeth's enemies on the Continent – and to a lesser extent in Ireland, where an informer in his service provided evidence to indicate dubious loyalty on the part of an Irish archbishop – blinded him to the strength of her enemies closer at hand. Perhaps illness had impeded his powers (as it indubitably did for the last months of 1571, forcing him to take sick leave). Had his life ended in the early 1570s, history would remember him as little more than an earnest but inept aide of Cecil's who let his Puritan convictions impair his judgement. He needed, for the time being, a position in which he could declaim Protestantism's glories to his heart's content, preferably in a locale where his hatred of Spain could serve some strategic purpose. Fortunately for him, a suitable opening was soon found: the English mission in Paris, to which he went in September 1570 as assistant to Sir Henry Norris, the current ambassador. When Cecil decided that Norris lacked the finesse to pursue England's best interests in the matter of a marriage between Elizabeth and the Duke of Alençon (brother to three French kings), he had Norris recalled in December 1570, and had Walsingham made ambassador in Norris' place. By this means Cecil showed exceptional – and, as subsequent events showed, justified – loyalty toward one whose career to date had revealed little sign of finesse in any form.

During October and November 1569 (shortly before the Northern Rebellion gave the Queen's ministers so instructive a fright), Walsingham's home had accommodated, as a prisoner, a bizarre and loquacious Florentine financier named Roberto Ridolfi. Resident in England since the mid-1550s, Ridolfi exemplified that character type – by no means as rare among ostensibly hard-nosed bean counters as those compelled to deal with them might think or wish – whose addiction to fantasising would shame many an opium eater. Ridolfi combined banking services rendered to Elizabeth with a passionately voiced enthusiasm, when on the Continent, for deposing her. Since at even the lowest estimate of his troublemaking gifts Ridolfi represented a remarkable nuisance to the government, Walsingham subjected his involuntary house guest to comprehensive interrogation. He carried this out (in the fluent Italian that he had acquired from sojourning in Padua during Mary Tudor's reign), but extracted no admissions whatever from the smooth-talking Ridolfi, and duly let him go. Once free again, Ridolfi resumed his contacts with known Continental malcontents; and after the Northern Rebellion had failed, he sought the foreign assistance which he now realised was imperative if a future Catholic uprising against Elizabeth had the smallest chance of triumph.

Why did Walsingham release Ridolfi at all? Exceptional naïveté, perhaps. Another possible explanation for his doing so – one several times propounded by historians, though never proven – is that Ridolfi's subsequent pro-Catholic intrigues were an elaborate sham, never meant to succeed. According to this theory, Ridolfi remained in Walsingham's pay all along, as a double agent. Yet while a Cecil could have practised such duplicity without compunction, the idea of Walsingham – with his stiff-necked, ostentious virtue – stooping to such fraud is far less plausible.

Whatever the case, it would not be long before the two men's paths crossed again.

• • • • •

The first true successes of Elizabethan secret intelligence occurred after Walsingham had left for France. As of 1570, the stakes in England (as well as in Scotland and on the Continent) had been abruptly raised by an event wholly unpredicted and almost universally deplored: Pope Pius V's excommunication of Elizabeth.

For the Queen's first eleven years on the throne, Vatican attitudes towards her had varied from indifference to considerable sympathy. Even supposing that Elizabeth did die unmarried or find herself overthrown, her likeliest successor would be Mary, Queen of Scots, who for years had driven the Holy See to despair by her unceasing toleration of Protestants. Better to deal (so consecutive popes reasoned) with an honestly heretical sovereign than with one cravenly lukewarm in her Catholicism. At least Elizabeth had made the occasional concession to Catholic sensibilities: by abandoning Henry

VIII's audacious title 'Supreme Head of the Church' in favour of the phrase 'Supreme *Governor...*'; by allowing the liturgical singing of Latin; and by favouring – even when she could not enforce – clerical celibacy.

All this changed under Pius V, who feared no man and no woman either. Before the Northern Rebellion's outcome had been confirmed in Rome, Pius issued (on 25 February 1570) the bull entitled *Regnans in Excelsis*. This document specifically freed English Catholics from any duties of obedience to Elizabeth, 'the Pretended Queen of England and those heretics adhering to her'. Proclaiming Elizabeth to be illegitimate both by birth and as ruler, Pius thus scandalised not only Protestants but also most lay Catholic leaders: Philip II, the Duke of Alva and the Austrian Emperor Maximilian II included. Their complaints to Pius were of no avail.

The earliest confirmation in England of Pius' astonishing pronouncement came only on 25 May, when a Catholic gentleman named John Felton took the liberty of nailing to the Bishop of London's door a handwritten copy of the bull. When the government discovered his handiwork it arrested him, put him to the torture, and sent him to the gallows: upon which Felton gave his captors a diamond ring, asked them to convey it to Elizabeth as a token of fealty, and in his last moments declared with more courage than sense that 'he meant [the Queen] no personal harm, but believed her deposition to be for her own soul's good and the country's'. Foreign residence no longer offered protection against the government's informers. Agents in Cecil's pay seized in Antwerp the elderly Catholic John Storey, a former parliamentarian whose power in Mary Tudor's reign as a harrier of Protestantism marked him down for death at Protestant hands. Publicly

disembowelled in June 1571, Storey met his fate in the presence of Cecil and other leading councillors, as if to proclaim
for all England Cecil's personal – rather than abstractly
bureaucratic – impatience to stamp out real or imagined trea-
sons. But in the hope of silencing all reservations as to such
punishments' justice, Cecil took care to gain statutory sanction
for them, especially after *Regnans in Excelsis* had become
known. The Cecil-controlled Parliament declared it a capital
crime to convert any English subject to Catholicism, or to
import 'any bull, writing or instrument obtained from the
Bishop of Rome'.

   While Walsingham remained in Paris, Ridolfi struck.
This time he acted in confederacy with Scotland's ambassador
to England: John Leslie, Catholic Bishop of Ross, who itched
to restore Mary Stuart to the Scottish throne, and who in early
1571 wrote rather unctuously to Philip II, urging him to overcome his previous coldness towards the Queen of Scots and
'take her under his protection'. Ridolfi wrote in a similar vein
to the Pope. Both Ridolfi and Leslie worked meanwhile on
the Englishman who had shown more willingness than any
other to be a go-between: the highest ranking English noble,
Thomas Howard, fourth Duke of Norfolk, nephew to one of
Elizabeth's stepmothers. Norfolk – who lived in a grey, nebulous, dim-witted terror of offending anyone – had given the
Northern Rebellion's organisers vague promises of support,
only to renege on these when push, literally, came to shove.
He now considered himself a suitable bridegroom for Mary
Stuart, whom he had never met, and whom he disgusted by
his refusal either to propose marriage to her or to abandon her
outright. (When Elizabeth twitted him with wanting to wed
Mary, Norfolk assured her that he 'preferred to sleep on a safe

pillow'.) As for Spain's government, the Duke of Alva's low opinion of Ridolfi persisted; but Alva reluctantly acceded to Ridolfi's suggestion that Spanish troops (only if not required elsewhere) invade England on Elizabeth's death, there to proclaim Mary Stuart the rightful queen, with Norfolk as her lawful husband. To more than this, Alva refrained from committing himself; yet Ridolfi, showing habitual optimism, regarded Alva's concession as a guarantee of victory. Showing still greater optimism, Ridolfi sent letters to Leslie and Norfolk, describing in full his dealings with Alva. Showing the greatest optimism of all, Ridolfi included with each letter instructions explaining how to read the cipher in which the missive had been written.

In April 1571 Ridolfi's courier, a headstrong Catholic servant of Leslie's called Charles Baillie (sometimes spelt Bailly), was arrested at Dover and found to be carrying Ridolfi's messages. Flung into the Tower, Baillie fell for the wiles of a fellow prisoner named William Herle, who spoke of himself as an innocent Catholic victim of Cecil's malice, but who was in fact Cecil's spy. With icy precision Cecil spelled out to Lord Cobham, Lieutenant of the Tower, the procedures to be followed when interrogating Baillie:

> You will ask him for the alphabet of the cipher,
> and if he shall refuse to show the said alphabet, or to
> declare truly the contents of the said letters in cipher,
> you shall put him on the rack ... you shall procure
> him to confess the truth with some pain of the said
> torture.

Even after several hours' racking, Baillie still refused to
tell all he knew concerning Ridolfi, so he received a visit from
a second spy: one William Parker, who in Antwerp had helped
to capture John Storey. With scarcely credible boldness, this
Parker now represented himself to the gullible Baillie as …
John Storey, 'come to administer spiritual consolation'. To this
impostor (the real John Storey, ignorant of his impersonator,
lay in another cell awaiting death), Baillie revealed everything;
and Parker straightaway passed on the data to Cecil and the
other ministers. Leslie, comprehensively implicated by this
new information, at first invoked the protection of his diplomatic rank. He then wrote to Baillie, sombrely warning him
that the game was up, and urging him to 'comfort himself in
God'; he sent this letter via a messenger who, instead of giving
it to Baillie, gave it to Cecil. Threatened with torture despite
his ambassadorial status (since English law, unlike Scottish,
refused to confer diplomatic immunity in treason cases), Leslie
locked himself in his room and went without food for three
days. Then, deciding that discretion was the better part of
hunger, he announced to Cecil's assistant, Thomas Wilson, that
he had become totally disillusioned with Mary Stuart. He
now insisted that everything rumour had maintained about
the Queen of Scots murdering two of her husbands was true.
'Lord!' Wilson observed in response to this revelation of Scottish home life, 'what a people are these, what a Queen, and
what an ambassador!' Leslie survived for another quarter of a
century, despised but undisturbed. Ridolfi was luckier yet: he
spent most of his remaining years in Tuscany, became a senator in Florence, and lived till 1612.

No such good fortune came Norfolk's way. Suspiciously
heavy bags, which Norfolk had ordered taken to sympathisers

of Mary Stuart, were found to contain both large sums of money and compromising papers, all of which ended up in the government's hands. Once lodged in the Tower, Norfolk, who seems to have had a death wish, continued to correspond with a fellow plotter on his domestic staff even while in his cell; the relevant letter was, in a pattern by now familiar, passed on to Cecil. After numerous reprieves – the Queen had great difficulty in believing that a duke of part-royal lineage could be as treacherous, or at any rate as stupid, as this one had turned out to be – Norfolk was beheaded on 2 June 1572.

• • • • •

Walsingham's mission to Paris ended in April 1573, having been ineffectual from all viewpoints. Nobody questioned his fundamental devotion to his monarch. He fully subscribed to the advice that Cecil encapsulated in one sentence many years afterwards: 'Serve God by serving of the Queen, for all other service is indeed bondage to the devil.' Walsingham's chief problem in Paris was that even when well enough for the job, he had needed to negotiate with not one but *two* hostile Catholic camps: the ruling House of Valois, which at least could be occasionally appealed to by invocations of national interest; and the explicitly pro-Spanish, pan-Catholic House of Guise, which could not. After more than a year's effort he did manage to extract from France's government (April 1572) the Treaty of Blois, by which France vowed to abandon its centuries-old alliance with Scotland in favour of a pact with England. He also kept open the possibility of Elizabeth wedding Alençon, a possibility that lingered until shortly before Alençon's death twelve years later. Yet his hopes of gaining

27

official protection for French Protestants collapsed ignomin-
iously with the St Bartholomew's Day Massacre of the
following August. Once the massacre had begun, Walsingham
laboured to protect individual Protestants from mob violence
(which claimed two of his own servants' lives) by giving them
refuge. Otherwise he remained powerless, and with cold rage
he vowed never to let himself be humiliated by Catholic
forces again. 'I think less peril to live with them [Catholic gov-
ernments] as enemies than friends,' he snapped.

Considering the contrast between his pre-ambassadorship
and his post-ambassadorship effectiveness levels, it is tempting
to posit a conspiracy theory: to argue that Francis Walsingham
I died in Paris, allowing someone else to assume the dead
man's identity and become Francis Walsingham II. A likelier
explanation for the contrast is the fact that in December 1573
Elizabeth appointed Walsingham secretary of state, thereby
allowing him to sit on the Privy Council with Cecil. (By this
stage Cecil, always sensitive to taunts about his lower middle-
class origins, had been elevated to the peerage. He chose the
title of Baron Burghley, by which he will be known hereafter
in this narrative, to avoid confusion with his son Robert
Cecil, who took a comparably important political role late in
Elizabeth's reign.) As a Privy Councillor, Walsingham could
order torture by special warrant: thanks to a loophole in
English common law, which declared torture to be under
normal circumstances illegal, but which considerately made an
exception in the case of Privy Councillors. (From 1574 he
combined his Privy Council membership with renewed
tenure in Parliament, this time representing Surrey. A tradition
already existed by which Privy Councillors who lacked titles
of nobility, and who therefore could not join the House of

Lords, were expected to occupy places in the House of Commons.) When his system of informers was operating at full stretch, it included – as well as snoopers on the home front, four of whom had the specific role of seeking out Jesuits – information-gatherers in twelve towns of France, in nine towns of Germany, in five each of Spain and Italy, and in three of the Low Countries: not counting individuals in Tripoli, Algiers and Constantinople. As David Lloyd, a seventeenth-century chronicler, noted:

> He [Walsingham] would cherish a plot some years together, admitting the conspirators to his own and the Queen's presence familiarly, but dogging them out watchfully: his spies waited on some men every hour for three years: and lest they could not keep counsel, he dispatched them to forraign [sic] parts, taking in new servants.

Aiding Walsingham in his choice of informers was the oversupply of young, well-schooled male unemployables. The Elizabethan age, like our own, had far more university graduates than it had jobs for them to fill; moreover, it suffered from what one historian has expressively described as 'demographic diarrhœa', compounded by the fact that Elizabeth possesed (as the same authority remarks) 'no standing army, to take on the younger sons and obligingly kill them'. Several of Walsingham's agents had bachelor's degrees from Oxford or Cambridge. One such agent, Bernard Maude, BA (Oxon), came to Walsingham's notice when serving three years' imprisonment for having blackmailed the Archbishop of York, and then compounding his rashness by admitting his guilt to

Burghley, who made him repay the sums he had extorted. The young Francis Bacon, newly emerged from his Cambridge studies, stumbled into the informer's trade when (while only in his teens) he needed to raise money for paying a £30 debt. Still, in many cases the single most important qualification for Walsingham's service lay, not in a piece of paper, but in a Catholic background. This enabled the informer to infiltrate Catholic circles from which even the most inquisitive Protestant would be debarred. A 1992 study of the subject comments: 'If there was a whiff of Rome about a spy so much the better.'

One quondam Catholic – Solomon Aldred, a tailor – earned prestige points in Walsingham's eyes through being locked up by Milan's Inquisition; Walsingham helped to obtain Aldred's release, and found him a loyal servant from then onwards. Aldred proceeded to recruit others to his calling, such as former seminarian Gilbert Gifford. Gifford bore a particular grudge against the authorities at Douai, who had expelled him for insubordination; after being enrolled by Aldred and Walsingham, Gifford made a great show of penitence, was readmitted to Douai, and enthusiastically reported on its staff and student populations to Walsingham himself. (From the 1570s onwards, informers like Gifford were a perpetual nightmare for Douai and its rector, Cardinal William Allen: how could Douai staff be expected to distinguish a sincere Catholic convert or Catholic revert from an *agent provocateur*?) Two other embittered ex-Catholics, George Eliot and Anthony Munday, provided tainted evidence against Father Campion when the latter returned to England on his Jesuit preaching mission; Eliot did so with such obvious rancour that he acquired the appellation 'Judas'. One Thomas

Rogers had actually endured time in the Belly of the Beast: Rogers underwent a prison sentence in Rome's Castel Sant'Angelo, after which he happily began working for Walsingham. Rogers' most notable finding consisted of a clandestine postal service that Catholic exiles had set up, via the good offices of the French ambassador in London at the time, who used his diplomatic privileges to forward their letters to the desired destinations. For correspondence in the other direction, Walsingham could rely on a Genoese-born merchant, Horatio (later, thanks to Walsingham, *Sir* Horatio) Palavicino, who in northern France served as 'distributor of funds and letters', and afterwards undertook a similar role in Frankfurt.

Yet despite all these successes, Walsingham's record in personnel management had its failures too. Edward Stafford – eventual ambassador to France – suffered from so severe a gambling problem as to be largely useless for covert activities requiring protracted absences from the card table. (In other respects, though, Stafford demonstrated a certain self-preservation. When Walsingham hired a courier to keep an eye on Stafford's wrongdoings, Stafford simply plied the courier with enough alcohol to knock him unconscious.) Another less than credible figure, Anthony Standen, saw nothing amiss in simultaneously gathering secret intelligence for Walsingham and for Philip II. A third operative securely inhabiting the 'could do better' category was one Ratcliffe, whom Walsingham commissioned to assassinate Philip II's half-brother, Don John of Austria; but before Ratcliffe could act, Don John had him arrested. Later in the same year (1578) Don John died from natural causes, making further enterprises of Ratcliffe's kind redundant.

In its achievements and in its setbacks alike, Walsingham's relationship with his agents remained a wholly personal one, with no intermediary in the form of established civil service procedure. Agents needed to be paid for out of Walsingham's own pocket, on the off-chance (it seldom amounted to more than an off-chance) that the Queen would reimburse him. Estimates of the amounts involved vary dramatically from historian to historian, but the sum of £2,000 *per annum* during the late 1580s represents something of a scholarly consensus. The sense of relish that has sustained many another secret police chief in later ages did not, therefore, suffuse the harassed Walsingham. Nor did any pleasure in deceit. No error in Elizabethan studies is more misleading than the widespread idea that Walsingham enjoyed intrigue for its own sake. When Walsingham ordered a Catholic priest's arm-sockets to be ripped in two upon the rack, or entrusted Ratcliffe with the task of murdering Don John, he did so only after having solemnly convinced himself that the national and religious interests which he served required these manœuvres. 'Intelligence,' he said, 'is never too dear'; how high the cost could become in terms of physical pain and mental torment inflicted for reasons of state, Walsingham well knew.

• • • • •

Until 1580 there remained some hope that the question of Catholics' position in England could be solved without too much mayhem. After that date all such hope died. The failure of a 1579 expedition to re-Catholicise Ireland – sponsored by Pope Gregory XIII, Pius V's successor, and devised in order to take military advantage of Irish loathing towards Elizabeth –

confirmed Gregory in his belief that nothing less than force of arms could secure safety for English Catholics. As a result, the following year he spelled out what Pius V in 1570 had drawn the line at suggesting: that Catholics not only owed no allegiance to Elizabeth, but could take her life without committing a sin. Gregory's intransigence had as its sole practical result the resumption of all-out war by Burghley and Walsingham: against not merely individual Catholics, but Catholicism itself.

Among the saintliest victims of this new war Father Campion achieved, through no fault of his own, pride of place. Back in 1573 Campion had actually expressed alarm in Rome about the increased dangers in which *Regnans in Excelsis* had placed Catholics in England. Seven years later, at the time of his arrival in England in the company of his friend and fellow Jesuit Father Robert Persons (pronounced, and sometimes spelt, 'Parsons'), he remained indifferent to political issues. Persons showed his own unconcern with such issues by specifically forbidding faithful English Catholics to take part in Anglican church services. As Evelyn Waugh pointed out, this singularly un-Machiavellian act is the very last thing Persons would have done if his purpose had *really* been to subvert the Elizabethan state:

> If the object in their [the Jesuit missionaries'] secret coming and going from house to house had been conspiracy; if, as was said by their enemies, they were using the confessional to prepare a concerted insurrection in support of Spain, they would have instructed their followers to equivocate with 'mental reservations', to lie low, to attend the services, take the oaths [of Protestant

fealty], and then at the appointed signal fall upon their unsuspecting neighbours; nothing would have been more recklessly imprudent, or fatal to their purpose, than to make their adherents advertise themselves publicly to the authorities.

But such scruples on Campion's and Persons' part failed to soften the hearts of their tormentors, for whom blurring the distinction between rendering unto God and rendering unto Cæsar was so deeply ingrained a mental habit as to constitute a first principle. Though Persons escaped the clutches of Walsingham's agents (and made his way back to Douai), Campion fell into their hands in July 1581. For many years during his youth he had, by his modesty, culture and intelligence, been a particular favourite of Elizabeth and Burghley; therefore, no disgrace or maltreatment was too severe to heap upon him now. Kept in solitary confinement in the Tower, he was immured in 'Little Ease' – a cell thus called because it was too small to let its occupant stand up or lie down – and thrice racked in the hope of extracting self-incriminating confessions from him. (He did reveal some minor details, but nothing that even the most cynical Elizabethan judge could place much evidentiary value upon.) As almost always with such occasions, a climate of emotionless bureaucracy prevailed. Every turn of the rack was duly noted in the records for Burghley's benefit:

It was the custom of the time for the clerk, seated beside the rack, to record all that the witness said; then, when he was released, as soon as his fingers could hold a pen, he was required to put his name at the foot of each sheet. The pitiful, straggling, barely recognisable signatures were then admissible as evidence.

Campion himself, after a trial significant mainly for its combination of desultory theological rancour on his prosecutors' part with tranquil clear-sightedness on his own – 'In condemning us,' he argued, 'you condemn all your own ancestors' – was sentenced to the death almost inevitable for one of his kind. The informer George Eliot, belatedly abashed at having borne false witness against Campion, crept along on one occasion to the cell where Campion prepared for the end, and implored his victim's (freely granted) pardon. Along with two other priests, Alexander Briant and Ralph Sherwin, he met his fate (1 December 1581) upon the same Tyburn gallows where John Storey had died a decade before. Even at the last he refused to oblige his oppressors with the admission of political treason that they craved from him. To demands that he beg the Queen's forgiveness, he calmly answered:

Wherein have I offended her? In this I am innocent. This is my last speech; in this give me credit – I have and do pray for her ... for Elizabeth your Queen and my Queen, unto whom I wish a long quiet reign, with all prosperity.

Accounts differ as to whether the executioner showed enough mercy to allow Campion to die from strangulation, or started the eviscerating process upon him while he was still conscious. What remains beyond dispute is the completely unexpected effect which the bloody spectacle created. Rather than terrorising English Catholics, it inspired in them renewed zeal. Walsingham himself lamented: 'It would have been better for the Queen to have spent 40,000 gold pieces than to put those priests to death in public.' Ballads among Protestants – impressed, sometimes despite themselves, by Campion's fortitude and gentleness – started to circulate, complete with lines like these:

If instead of good argument
We deal by the rack
The Papists may think
That learning we lack.

Convinced that Campion could never have achieved any popular following if the existing legal sanctions against Catholics had been properly enforced, the government passed (also in 1581) new legislation which for the first time explicitly forbade attending Mass. It imposed fines of £240 per year on anyone over the age of sixteen who eschewed Anglican services in favour of the Catholic rite. A single attendance at Mass would cost the culprit £66 13s 4d, plus a year's imprisonment. To assist in overcoming potential sneaks' misgivings about betraying Catholics, one-third of each fine went to the informer himself.

Neither Burghley nor Walsingham ever appreciated that in Catholic doctrine, 'the blood of the martyrs is the seed of the Church'. Personally brave (a coward would not have sheltered, as Walsingham sheltered, refugees from the St Bartholomew mob), Walsingham could not fully grasp the fact that his enemies might be brave too. Their valour was often better appreciated by those alumni of Walsingham's surveilliance procedures who had daily dealings with them, than by

Walsingham himself. Such alumni included Richard Topcliffe, a figure who came into his own during the 1580s, and about whom even four hundred years afterwards it is almost impossible to write temperately. Of the same Catholic and vaguely gentlemanly background that had become almost a *sine qua non* among Elizabethan narks, Topcliffe (born in 1532, and therefore Walsingham's own age) at first proved no better and no worse a human being than the average Walsingham secret agent. Subsequently, however, he revealed himself to be, in plain language, a psychopath. His masters, convinced that the Tower's repository of torture lacked a certain something in getting results – even with Little Ease, even with 'The Scavenger's Daughter', a large band of iron which forced its victims into a fœtal position, so 'that the blood sprouted out at diverse parts of their bodies' – sought Topcliffe's aid. In an early and fruitful example of privatisation, the government gave Topcliffe the unique privilege of torturing Catholics with the special instrumentarium available at his own home. This equipment, he boasted to anyone who wished to listen and to a great many who did not, made the Tower's rack seem like child's play. One Catholic victim of Topcliffe's ministrations discovered, in horrified amazement, that to his sadism Topcliffe added erotic fantasising. He would intersperse physical torments with preposterous but ornate discourses upon how he had enjoyed sexual favours from the Queen.

To console himself for those rare occasions when the torture business slowed down, Topcliffe developed a profitable but inefficient sideline as a contract killer: inefficient because his eagerness to take his clients' money failed to translate into comparable eagerness to finish the job. A certain Thomas Fitzherbert took Topcliffe to court, because though he had paid Topcliffe £5,000 to do away with relatives of Fitzherbert's, as well as with one Bassett, 'from whom he expected legacies', the relatives had eventually succumbed to ordinary disease: leaving Fitzherbert out of pocket 'and Bassett … in full prosperity'. Having clearly failed to uphold honour among thieves, Topcliffe was briefly sent to gaol, whining with characteristic good taste that this outcome was enough 'to make the bones of Father Southwell dance for joy'. (The Jesuit and poet Robert Southwell, yet another distinguished Catholic victim of Topcliffe's malice, had inspired in his torturer especial fury for *complaining* in open court about the manhandling he had suffered. Southwell testified to having been abused in 'such [bodily] parts, as is almost a torture to Christian ears to hear it'. Challenged by Topcliffe to reveal any marks of ill-treatment on his person, Southwell unforgettably replied: 'Let a woman show her throes.')

• • • • •

Yet no amount of punitive legislation or physical cruelty seemed capable of eliminating Catholicism. Despite the public executions of Catholics in every year between 1577 and 1603, one Puritan document of 1584 complained that 'three parts at least of the people are wedded to their old superstition still'. Nor could the government deter those who continued to devise plans for Elizabeth's downfall: plans such as the Throckmorton Plot. Young Francis Throckmorton belonged to one of Elizabethan England's most powerful clans; his cousin had married Sir Walter Raleigh, while his uncle had been Sir Nicholas Throckmorton, a long-serving diplomat. Living on the Continent during his late twenties, Francis fell in with members of the Guise family, who aimed (as the Northern Rebellion's leaders had done) to free Mary Stuart from prison and bring all of Britain under her rule. Also involved in the grand design were Spain's ambassador to England, Bernardino de Mendoza – whose London residence became a meeting-place for the conspirators – and Lord Northumberland (brother of the 1569 rebel). They reckoned, however, without Walsingham's suspicious mind and his long-attested refusal to recognise ambassadorial dignity as an excuse for escaping sur-veillance. (One of the French embassy staff reported regularly to Walsingham; it has been laboriously, though not conclu-sively, argued that this agent – who operated under the alias 'Henry Fagot' – was none other than the philosopher Gior-dano Bruno.)

In November 1583 Walsingham, whose agents had discovered in Throckmorton's house a list of potential sup-porters, as well as 'six or seven pamphlets against [the Queen]', ordered his arrest and torture: not without a sardonic obser-vation as to how long the victim's promises of silence would continue. 'I have seen as resolute men as Throckmorton stoop,' Walsingham sneered, 'notwithstanding the great show he has made of Roman resolution.' So it proved: after the usual pro-longed racking, Throckmorton confessed all, implicating Mendoza in particular. At a Privy Council meeting the nor-mally impassive Walsingham bawled Mendoza out (in Italian, since Mendoza spoke scarcely any English, nor Walsingham any Spanish), using language so haughty that Mendoza wrote to his master Philip II: 'You cannot overlook such insolence, though they offer you all the world to forgive them.' Walsing-ham gave Mendoza fifteen days to leave the country. As for the luckless Throckmorton, he alternated – after being

39

subjected to a formal trial of sorts – between amplifying and retracting his original confession; not that his changes of mind saved him from a traitor's death on 20 July 1584. Northumberland, fearing a similar end, shot himself through the heart.

Still, whatever inconsistencies marked Throckmorton's last weeks, his intrigue was plainness itself compared with the bizarre Parry affair. William Parry was a Welsh (his surname had originally been Ap Harry) parliamentarian, buried under a mountain of debt and burdened with an unenviable reputation for having deflowered his own stepdaughter. Burghley found him useful enough to hire as an agent for any undercover work that did not preclude advanced mental disturbance. From 1570 Parry had actually been employed at Her Majesty's court, until a near-fatal 1580 altercation with one of his creditors cost him his job and compelled him to abandon England. On his eventual return, Parry protested in the Commons (1584) against a proposed anti-Jesuit law, maintaining that if passed it would be 'full of blood, danger and despair to English subjects'. Accused by fellow parliamentarian Edmund Neville of inadequate loyalty to the Queen – indeed, of having wished to bring about the Queen's death – Parry found himself lodged in the Tower. There he poured forth to his three examiners – Walsingham; Elizabeth's court chamberlain, Lord Hunsdon; and her current favourite, Sir Christopher Hatton – a protracted and weird account of having been converted to Catholicism while in Italy (the better to ingratiate himself with discontented Catholic exiles from both England and Scotland) and of having become friendly with a distinguished ecclesiastic, the Cardinal of Como. From his dealings with these men he determined to do them the supreme religious favour by slaying Elizabeth. Neither the Cardinal nor

Gregory XIII placed much trust in him, but little matters like these could no longer deter his enthusiasm. He became (he now said) so carried away with excitement at the thought of stabbing the Queen that he came back forthwith to England. But once on English soil and confronted with the sight of his intended royal victim, his enthusiasm seeped away; and he could not bring himself to kill her, since she reminded him so much of Henry VIII.

At this point Parry dropped a further bombshell, accusing Neville of wanting to commit the very same crime that Neville had ascribed to him. Alas for Parry, he could produce no evidence to support this charge, whereas he had in his own belongings letters from the Cardinal of Como that confirmed his own regicidal inclinations. During his trial he at first pleaded guilty, then insisted that in spite of all his previous testifying he had never *truly* meant to murder his sovereign. Upon passing sentence of death, the judge – as puzzled by Parry's gyrations as everyone else who heard them – asked in the usual way if Parry could show any cause why the penalty should not be carried out on him. Parry gave the gnomic answer: 'I see I must die because I have not been constant to myself.' Requested 'to declare more plainly what he meant', Parry retreated still further into mystagogy: 'My blood,' he announced, 'be amongst you.' It soon was. On 2 March 1585, in the presence of his fellow MPs, Parry suffered the same mode of execution as Throckmorton and Campion had earlier done.

Parry's example having revealed that a freelance knife-wielding lunatic could come perilously close towards assassinating Elizabeth, the path for subsequent avatars of dottiness lay clearly ahead. One such feather-brained malcontent was a courtier, Anthony Babington, cursed with a romantic devotion to Mary Stuart that in the realms of fiction would seem crassly improbable. For Babington, freeing Mary from prison constituted a holy grail that justified any quest, however tortuous. From March 1586 he began associating with a dozen others, mostly fellow cradle-Catholics, who commissioned a group portrait of themselves to be painted, 'that the saviours of England might be so immortalised'. This sanguine band included a priest, John Ballard, and the poet Chidiock Tichborne. Mary Stuart, previously sceptical as to the likelihood of escape plans – so many of them had come to grief in the past – welcomed Babington and his friends as her likeliest deliverers. Unlike Parry, from whom she had completely distanced herself (going as far as to send Elizabeth formal congratulations on the failure of Parry's design), Babington overcame much of Mary's natural wariness. He was only twenty-four, good-looking, trusted by Elizabeth herself – who for several years kept him around her court as one of her token Catholics – and far from being a recent convert, had been from childhood 'inclined to papistrie': none of which did him any harm in Mary's view.

The Babington–Mary correspondence began in July, and by its nature it could not be entrusted to customary postal channels. Instead, letters to and from Mary were placed inside a leather packet which, in turn, was inserted into the bung of a beer barrel. Once the beer barrel had been left with Mary, her servants would remove the packet; she would read Babington's latest missive; she would put her reply in the same packet, the packet in the bung; and back the beer barrel would go. This presupposed two factors: wholly loyal servants of Mary; and a wholly loyal courier. Neither applied. What neither Mary nor Babington realised, until too late, was that their messages to each other were being intercepted *en route* by the go-between who transported the barrel: the ex-Douai student Gilbert Gifford, alias 'Pietro', 'Cornelys', 'Colerdin', and other names well known to those English Catholic circles in which he moved. Gifford's choirboyish prettiness belied the ruthless dedication with which he served Walsingham and kept his master apprised of Mary's writings as well as Babington's. (His original job application had not wasted words: 'I have heard of the work you do and I want to serve you. I have no scruples.')

To lull any remaining suspicions on Mary's part, Gifford had forwarded to her the preceding January a backlog of mail from Catholic exiles that had accumulated at the French embassy. After that she completely trusted him. He also ingratiated himself with Babington when, on 6 July, the two men first met (he simply turned up on Babington's doorstep, to announce Mary's interest in Babington's scheme).

Never conspicuous for prudence, Babington spelled out in his first letter his eagerness not just to release Mary but, if need be, to kill Elizabeth:

> Myself with ten gentlemen and a hundred of our
> followers will undertake the delivery of your royal
> person from the hands of your enemies. For the dis-
> patch of the usurper … there be six noble gentlemen,
> all my private friends, who for the zeal they bear
> to the Catholic cause and your Majesty's service,
> will undertake that tragical execution.

This was hair-raising stuff to be committing to paper, even in the ciphered format which both Babington and Mary used: all the more so in that every word of it was being monitored by Walsingham's newly established cipher department. Star of this department was one Thomas Phelippes, who boasted of being able to decrypt any cipher, however elaborate. Aged around thirty, and described at the time as being '[o]f low stature … eaten in the face with smallpox', Phelippes made up in efficiency for what he lacked in physical charm. With his analytic gifts – and a linguistic bent that made him fluent in German, French, Spanish and Italian – went a remarkable knack of imitating 'any man's hand[writing], if he had once seen it, as if the man himself had writ it'. He took only about a week to decode Babington's message, and straightaway informed Walsingham of the result. As yet, though, Mary had not matched Babington's self-incriminating mania. If Walsingham was to achieve his aim of bringing about Mary's execution – which Parliament was demanding more and more vociferously – he needed more evidence of her own complicity in Babington's purpose than he had so far acquired. He quickly got it.

Mary's note of 17 July to Babington expressed wholehearted approval of her would-be liberator's plot. It also pointed out the desirability of Mary's own release before or during Elizabeth's murder, so that no guard loyal to Elizabeth could seize the chance of doing away with Mary in the general confusion. Once Phelippes had deciphered this letter, he annotated it with the sign Π, which in Walsingham's private symbology meant the gallows. But still the conspirators had provided Phelippes and Walsingham with no clues as to which other plotters Babington had involved. Who exactly *were* these 'private friends' of whom Babington had written? And how to make Babington reveal their names? Despairing of even Gifford being able to achieve this, Walsingham instructed

Phelippes to add to Mary's letter a postscript in as good an imitation as possible of Mary's calligraphy: using, of course, the same cipher that Mary and Babington had employed. Thus, when Babington finally received Mary's missive, it contained the following addendum of Phelippes' own:

> I would be glad to know the names and qualities of the six gentlemen which are to accomplish the design-ment; for it may be that I shall be able, upon knowledge of the parties, to give you some further advice necessary to be followed therein, as also from time to time particularly how you proceed: and as soon as you may, for the same purpose, who be already, and how far everyone is privy hereunto.

The unsuspecting Babington not only wrote down the names of 'the six gentlemen' involved; he also went so far as to visit Walsingham's department, to obtain the passport that he required for a journey to see his allies on the Continent (including the tireless Mendoza, who had involved himself as deeply in this plot as he had done in Throckmorton's). At first Babington gave Walsingham the slip. The agent entrusted with his capture never expected that Babington would be stupid enough to call in at the office, and let himself be caught off-guard when Babington, having accompanied him to a tavern close by, stole out the back door. Over the next ten days Babington remained at large, frantically urging his fellow plot-ter John Ballard to assassinate Elizabeth while there was still time (Ballard refused, on the grounds that he needed an appropriate change of clothes), and wiping walnut juice over his skin to conceal his patrician pallor.

Arrested on 15 August, Babington at first denied everything: then, when he could no longer gainsay the evidence against him, placed all the blame upon his fellow conspirators and tried to plea-bargain his way out of trouble by offering Walsingham details of the others' doings. He might as well have saved his breath while it remained in his body, which it did not do for long. The Queen – bitterly recalling the kindness she had once lavished upon Babington – demanded that Walsingham and Burghley devise new and special forms of capital punishment for him and his confederates. Burghley, though, eventually succeeded in persuading her that the existing forms would engender sufficient public nausea, if the hangman carried them out to the letter of the law. Thus, on 20 September, Babington, Ballard and five others – Chidiock Tichborne, Edward Abbington, John Savage, John Tilney, and Robert Barnwell – met their ends, in such a manner as to be counterproductive. The staunch Protestant chronicler William Camden described the scene and its aftermath, which led to slightly less horrific treatment for the next batch of condemned criminals:

> [A] gallous [gallows] and a scaffold being set up for
> the purpose in St Giles his fields where they [Babington and his friends] were wont to meet, the first 7
> were hanged thereon, cut downe, their privities cut
> off, bowelled alive and seeing, and quartered, not
> without some note of cruelty. Ballard the Arch-plotter
> of this treason craved pardon of God and of the
> Queene with a condition if he had sinned against her.
> Babington (who undauntedly beheld Ballard's execution, while the rest turning away their faces, fell to

prayers upon their knees) ingenuously acknowledged his offences; being taken downe from the gallous, and ready to be cut up, he cried aloud in Latin sundry times, *Parce mihi Domine Iesu*, that is, Spare me Lord Jesus. Savage brake the rope and fell downe from the gallous, and was presently seized on by the executioner, his privities cut off, and he bowelled alive. Barnwell extenuated his crime under colour of Religion and Conscience. Tichborne with all humility acknowledged his fault, and moved great pity among the multitude towards him. As in like manner did Tilney, a man of a modest spirit and goodlie personage. Abbington, being a man of a turbulent spirit, cast forth threats and terrors of blood to be spilt ere long in England. The next day the other seven were drawne to the same place, and suffered the same kind of death; but more favourably by the Queenes commandement, who detested the former cruelty; for they all hung till they were quite dead before they were cut down and boweled.

At her own trial, Walsingham being among her judges, Mary attempted to disclaim all knowledge of Babington's intrigues: despite the genuine letters in her handwriting which the prosecution cited, as well as the forged postscript. Two of her own servants testified in court against her, and she was given no opportunity to cross-examine them: a violation of her legal rights that inspired some adverse comment at the time among pettifogging believers in the presumption of a defendant's innocence. It seems Elizabeth never did discover how Walsingham and Phelippes had tampered with Exhibit A.

Walsingham was only too happy to keep her blissfully unaware of it, since persuading her to do away with Mary presented enough of a struggle in itself, without questions of the prosecution's honesty arising.

For a few weeks in February and March 1587 it seemed (however great the lassitude of Mary's son) that Scottish ire at Mary's death would explode into all-out war against England: and that Scottish invaders could count on help from Mary's English sympathisers. Elizabeth and Walsingham soon dissipated this danger, thanks to a combination of financial wisdom and crowd control. James, always short of ready cash, depended very largely on subsidies from England. As for Walsingham, to take the populace's mind off Mary's fate – and to ensure that as far as possible no public sympathy for Mary would reveal itself – he staged a grand funeral for his son-in-law, Sir Philip Sidney: fatally wounded in battle the previous October against the Spaniards. Sidney (who had married Walsingham's daughter Frances, primarily because he needed Walsingham's money, which he spent at an astounding rate) displayed until his very last moments a gallantry that made him, in Elizabethans' eyes, the Protestant *chevalier sans peur et sans reproche*. Thanks to the superb, almost regal pomp of the public obsequies that Walsingham devised for Sidney (permanently impoverishing himself in the process), the death of Mary soon fell into public oblivion among all but a few irreconcilables.

• • • • •

After the events of 1586–88 – Babington's downfall, Mary's decapitation, and the Armada's defeat – little incentive remained to engage in further conspiracies against Elizabeth's life. European esteem for Elizabeth's survival skills reached even the Vatican, where once the 'invincible' Armada had proven thoroughly vincible, Pope Sixtus V exclaimed in terms guaranteed to astonish the Catholic faithful:

> What a wife she would make! What children we
> would have! They would have ruled the whole world.

Walsingham did not long survive the Armada's destruction. He died on 6 April 1590, either from the testicular cancer which he suffered or, as Camden's *Annals* state, from the medicine with which he hoped to cure himself. Undeniably he spent his last months in much pain, longing aloud for death to release him. From the Queen his passing inspired neither pleasure nor grief. What little capacity she possessed for disinterested affection centred, not on Walsingham, but on the now septuagenarian Burghley.

Meanwhile Burghley spent his later years in retirement on his estate at Hatfield, Hertfordshire: pottering around his beloved gardens, for all the world resembling a sixteenth-century precursor of P.G. Wodehouse's timid Lord Emsworth, rather than the pitiless administrator at whose frowns all Europe's chancelleries had once quaked. (In Burghley's last months – he died on 4 August 1598 – the Queen would not only visit him but feed him with a spoon held in her own hands, *his* hands being too much impaired by gout to be of use. No such kindness had marked her dealings with the dying Walsingham.) The quasi-prime ministerial role Burghley had once held, his son Robert Cecil now occupied. Dwarfish, severely hunchbacked, and abrupt in speech, Robert Cecil inspired in his Queen respect but never liking: 'little man', she habitually called him. Distinguished perhaps above all by his open loathing for Elizabeth's new favourite, the Earl of Essex – yet another son-in-law of Walsingham, one who had under duress married Sidney's widow – Cecil the Younger acquired something of his predecessors' political flair, but nothing of their publicity skill.

Admittedly, no one could have predicted the last grand plot, or alleged plot, of sixteenth-century England: the Lopez Affair, a business so muddled, so obscure even today, and so convoluted in its eventual part-emergence that whether it amounted to anything more than a governmental frame-up is still open to doubt. It bears no comparison with the Throckmorton and Babington cases. No historian can, to borrow Hamlet's words, 'pluck out its mystery'. At most it was a desperate throw of the dice rather than a sustained action. Its central figure, Rodrigo (or, in some accounts, Roderigo; in still other accounts, Ruy) Lopez, was an aged Portuguese Jew who had arrived in England well before Elizabeth had inherited the crown, who had been personal physician to Walsingham, and who probably knew less than almost anyone else about what transpired.*

The Lopez crisis arose from a combination of international and domestic concerns: Portuguese politics on the one hand; and on the other, the fact that Lord Essex had in his

---

* One theory, first propounded in the late nineteenth century by lexicographer and biographer Sir Sidney Lee, credits Lopez with being Shakespeare's model for Shylock. Jews in Elizabethan London were rare and conspicuous; Lopez undoubtedly maintained cordial relations with the theatre folk among whom Shakespeare moved; while the sheer number and ferocity of references to Lopez's end in The Merchant of Venice's Act IV might not be coincidental.

mulish way taken over management of Walsingham's surveillance system. In 1580, Portugal as an independent nation had ceased to exist. That year, once its last native-born king had died without legitimate male heirs, Philip II (whose mother had been the late king's sister) annexed it to Spain. His conquest resulted in the exodus of several thousand Portuguese patriots who, though nearly all Catholics, preferred life in Protestant London to possible death in Catholic Lisbon at Spanish hands.

Of the Portuguese émigrés' rights, Essex set himself up as the great English champion. Hence his interest in Lopez, who by this time had become personal physician to the Queen. Lopez's wide circle of acquaintances made him a particularly prized agent of Essex. And not of Essex alone: it seems that Lopez placed a punitive burden on his own nervous system by operating as a triple, if not a quadruple, agent. He maintained regular intelligence dealings with the large, prosperous Jewish community based in Antwerp. He well knew prominent courtiers in Madrid, to whom he expressed enthusiasm for the idea of murdering Elizabeth. He nurtured his friendship with the banished Spaniard Antonio Perez, King Philip's erstwhile secretary, now mortal foe. In addition, he continued to associate with the Portuguese diaspora's leaders. Besides, the Queen trusted him without reserve.

Regrettably for Lopez, he kept up his medical practice. His patients included none other than Essex, whose wenching had given him – strong circumstantial evidence argues – syphilis. In a world first for medical science, this malady killed, not its sufferer, but its diagnostician. While in his cups one evening among Spanish expatriates, the reckless doctor told his drinking companions about Essex's amatory illness. Word of Lopez's blunder quickly reached Essex, who to an innate vehemence of temper and a *nouveau riche* fear of public ridicule, added the wild swings of mood so frequent among those afflicted in a pre-penicillin age with advanced venereal disease. Loose-tongued Lopez clearly being of no further value as an operative, Essex wrote to his chief informer Anthony Bacon (Francis' brother) with heavy-breathing enthusiasm: 'I have discovered a most dangerous and desperate treason. The point of the conspiracy was Her Majesty's death. The executioner should have been Doctor Lopez; the manner poison.' Spain's government, Essex asserted, would pay Lopez 50,000 gold pieces once he had eliminated the Queen. Naturally Lopez denied the charge at his trial, over which Essex and Cecil presided. Equally naturally, his prosecutors could reveal nothing of his background and previous indispensability as official snooper. Elizabeth herself feared that a mistake had been made (she gave back to his widow the estates he forfeited as a traitor); but, like Cecil, she could or would do nothing to stop the law, or what Essex imagined to be the law, taking its course.

Whether Lopez's promises to the Spaniards of killing Elizabeth were more than the mendacious assurances of a fundamentally pro-English *agent provocateur* will never be known, but the chances are that they were not. Martin Hume, an early twentieth-century scholar of Elizabethan politics, explained why:

> It appears to me quite incredible that he, in high
> favour in England, should poison his benefactress to
> gain a reward from a king … who, moreover, was a
> notoriously bad paymaster. Lopez had made England
> his home for forty years, and if the Queen had died at

his hands, not only England, but every Protestant country in Europe would have been closed to him thenceforward, and he would have been ruined professionally. It would have been equally impossible for him to have trusted to the mercy of Philip and the Inquisition ...

On 7 June 1594 Lopez was executed, amid the jeers of spectators who might well have believed he was guilty, and who in any event had no love for Jews. His somewhat tactless declaration to the crowd that 'he loved the Queen as well as he loved Jesus Christ' met, therefore, screams of mirth.

'This Is No Time to Talk of Equivocation': The Gunpowder Plot

Essex's dreams of mastering all England did not last long. Within seven years of his triumph over Lopez, he disgraced himself twice: first by making a secret truce with Irish insurgents whom he was supposed to conquer, and then by stirring up a hopelessly ineffectual rebellion which aimed to oust Cecil. The latter indiscretion led him inexorably to the headsman's block on Ash Wednesday 1601. With Essex gone, Cecil's status as Elizabeth's most powerful subject continued unchallenged. After Elizabeth's own death on 24 March 1603, and King James' subsequent union of the Scottish and English Crowns, Cecil's power actually increased.

During Elizabeth's old age Cecil had corresponded with James behind the Queen's back: caution being vital, because not only had it been made a crime for Englishmen even to discuss the identity of Elizabeth's heir, but there were a dozen-odd candidates for the succession apart from James himself.

Though most of them were in practice ineligible by virtue of their Catholic faith, several true Protestants remained. With characteristic prudence, Cecil kept his correspondence with James firmly ciphered, using the number 10 to signify himself, 30 to indicate James, and 24 to mean Elizabeth.

Cecil aimed to restore English administration in general – and surveillance in particular – to the efficiency it had achieved under his father and under Walsingham: before it had been rudely interrupted by Essex's febrile arrogance. Efficiency, indeed, was Cecil's sole weapon. He had (save within his own family circle) no charm, no *presence d'esprit*. No amiable vices endeared him to the public, his sole character infirmity being undue fondness for letting his pet parrot strut around on his desk. An experienced, long-serving and conscientious parliamentarian, he wrote speeches full of epigrammatic bite, but possessed no oratorical panache. Jacobean England was not a good time to be physically handicapped, and Cecil's enemies never allowed him to forget his monstrously stooped spine. His cousin and antagonist Francis Bacon limned Cecil in the acid of his great essay 'On Deformity':

> ... all deformed persons are extreme bold. First, as in their own defence, as being exposed to scorn; but in process of time by a general habit. Also it stirreth in them industry, and especially of this kind, to watch and observe the weakness of others, that they may have somewhat to repay ... it layeth their competitors and emulators asleep; as never believing they should be in possibility of advancement, till they see them in possession ... Kings in ancient times (and at this present in

some countries) were wont to put great trust in
eunuchs; because they that are envious towards
all are more obnoxious and officious towards one.
But yet their trust towards them hath rather been as
to good spials [spies] and good whisperers, than good
magistrates ...

Under Cecil the anti-Catholic campaign continued
with rigour, although after the Armada's loss neither Spain nor
any other Catholic power possessed the strength to attempt
another invasion. Francis Bacon's bureaucratic rank obliged
him to attend torture sessions of Catholic suspects during the
1590s; Attorney-General Sir Edward Coke carried out such
tortures himself. Considerations of familial relationships mattered little or nothing: in June 1592 Cecil ordered the arrest
and imprisonment of a family friend whose ransacked home
turned out to contain rosaries, a hairshirt, scourges, and books
of Catholic devotion. But at this stage the overall calibre of
surveillance personnel had undergone some slight improvement, an improvement that became more marked after
Elizabeth had gone. Two of Cecil's chief assistants were Sir
William Waad (or Wade), Lieutenant of the Tower; and
Sir Thomas Challoner, an ex-diplomat who collated for
Cecil's consideration the reports submitted by agents in the
field. Neither man indulged in open criminality, or drooling
sadism of the sort that Richard Topcliffe had exemplified.
With James' installation in London, and the consequent influx
of brilliantly educated Scots on the lookout for English liveli-
hoods, the competition for state employment grew tougher
than it had been in the days when Walsingham had recruited
Bernard Maude in the latter's prison cell.

In one other, much more significant, respect Cecil broke with Walsingham–Burghley traditions. Hispanophobia, as the driving force of English policy, was halted before going into reverse. King James dreamed of a marriage between his son Charles and a Spanish princess; this dream, combined with James' innate dread of becoming involved in war on the Continent, ensured a steady outpouring from him of friendly noises in Spain's direction. Each year after 1605, Cecil received from the Spanish embassy a bribe of £1,000. Burghley had always rejected with polite chuckling the occasional sweeteners that Philip II's ambassadors offered him; but then Burghley lived under a Queen whose frugality was proverbial. His son enjoyed no such privilege, serving as he did a monarch afflicted with squandermania that manifested itself above all in dazzling presents for young boys.

At least Cecil knew how to get value for his pound. Before James had spent a year on England's throne, Cecil had ordered the arrests of rivals for his position: including George Brooke (his own brother-in-law) and Sir Walter Raleigh. Brooke aimed to depose Cecil, and to keep the King in close custody until he sanctioned this deposition. Raleigh, though probably disapproving of the scheme himself, knew about it and failed to prevent it. In planning thus, Brooke underrated the industry of Cecil's spies. He also misjudged the character of James. As Scotland's boy-king, James had so often escaped from captivity imposed on him by a succession of ambitious regents that in adult life eluding Brooke's desire to control came as easily to him as breathing. Both Brooke and Raleigh were beheaded: Brooke within six months of his arrest, Raleigh only after spending most of the next fifteen years on death row. (Three other conspirators sentenced to the supreme punishment, including Brooke's elder brother, received from the King last-minute reprieves.)

If James had doubted Cecil's expertise before, he ceased doing so once Cecil had trapped Raleigh and Brooke. He first made Cecil Viscount Cranborne, and then created him Earl of Salisbury, the title by which Cecil will henceforth appear in this chapter. But the greatest moment in the man's career came a little later, with the Gunpowder Plot's discovery.

· · · · ·

Those Catholics whom Elizabeth could not win over had hoped with all their hearts that with James' arrival, their situation would improve. In Scotland, after all, James had kept the Presbyterian Kirk (at least temporarily) in its place, through a mix of guile and leather-lunged talkativeness that surpassed even the Kirk's. As a pacific gesture after Brooke's downfall – since two Catholic priests had supplied Salisbury with information that helped bring about this downfall – James had released Catholics for one year from their legal obligation to pay fines for non-attendance at Anglican services. Moreover, once James had revealed his longing for a Spanish marital alliance, he gave Spain a good opportunity to make the alliance conditional on freedom of belief for English Catholics. Where these Catholics erred was in exaggerating Spain's enthusiasm for playing any religion card whatever, let alone that particular card. Philip III, Spain's king since 1598, bore no closer resemblance to his father Philip II than James bore to Elizabeth. Where the second Philip had thundered, the third Philip mewed. The third Philip's actual philosophy of life (as distinct from the motto on his coat of arms) was

'The meek shall inherit the earth, if that's all right with the rest of you.' He ruled – or rather, as his sire had predicted, was ruled by – a bankrupt nation: two bankrupt nations, if his Portuguese domain can be separately counted. Therefore he needed James at least as much as James needed him; and he dreaded imperilling an Anglo-Spanish bond by the appearance of stubbornness on the Catholicism issue. Now, more even than in the Duke of Alva's heyday, English Catholics were on their own.

When they realised the extent of their isolation, certain of them grew ever more enamoured of desperate measures. One such was Robert Catesby, who had supported Essex's 1601 uprising, and whose cousins included the more impoverished Thomas Wintour. In April 1604 Catesby instructed Wintour to sound out in Flanders a fellow Catholic, the Yorkshireman Guido (or Guy) Fawkes, then under contract as a mercenary soldier. Fawkes proved willing to join in Catesby's plan of blowing up Parliament, due to meet again in early 1605. Assisting the plan was the fact that another Catholic, Thomas Percy, had rented an apartment near Parliament House itself: thereby providing room to store explosives, and a hiding place for the schemers. Percy harboured a personal grievance against James, who sufficiently feared Percy's kinsman Lord Northumberland (nephew of the 1569 rebel, and son of the Throckmorton conspirator) to incarcerate him for more than a decade.

There remained, nevertheless, several Catholic occupants of the House of Lords – and numerous other nobles sympathetic to Catholicism – whose lives must not be risked by undue haste in the gunpowder department. One Catholic peer was Lord Monteagle, who on the night of 26 October brought to Salisbury's attention an undated and hastily scrawled note, addressed 'to the right honorable the lord mowteagle':

> my lord out of the love i beare to some of youer
> friends i have a caer of youer preservacion therefore i
> would advyse yowe as yowe tender yoeur lyf to devyse
> some exscuse to shift of youer attendance at this par-
> leament for god and man hathe concurred to punish
> the wickednes of this tyme and thinke not slightlye of
> this advertisement but reyere youre self into youre
> contri wheare yowe maye expect the event in safti for
> thowghe theare be no apparence of anni stir yet I saye
> they shall receyve a terrible blowe this parleament and
> yet they shall no seie who hurts them this councel is
> not to be contemned because it maye do yowe good
> and can do yowe no harme for the dangere is passed as
> soon as yowe have burnt the letter and I hope god will
> give yowe the grace to mak good use of it to whose
> holy proteccion I commend yowe.

Most historians from that day onwards have remained as bewildered as was Monteagle about the letter's authorship. Fawkes and Catesby put the blame on one of their own number: Monteagle's brother-in-law, Francis Tresham, who repeatedly protested his innocence and at last convinced his fellow conspirators that he spoke the truth. It is entirely possible that Salisbury himself, who promptly showed it to the King, concocted it: that while he stopped short of actually inventing the plot (albeit several historians have charged Catesby with being a double agent), he was happy to let it burgeon once his informers had notified him of its existence, the better to acquire the glory of suppressing it just in time.

Three arguments point to Salisbury's guilt as a forger. One is the regularity of English Catholics' socialising with one another; surely if Tresham or any of the other conspirators had really wanted to warn Monteagle, he would have chosen a less hazardous method of so doing than writing his advice down. (As the historian Alison Plowden bluntly observed, 'a few words muttered in the privacy of the jakes would have been enough'.) The crucial role which correspondence and handwriting expertise had played in sealing Babington's fate, less than two decades earlier, made it dangerous to assume that even anonymous letters could for long remain anonymous once in governmental hands. Secondly, if the letter to Monteagle was a legitimate tip-off, why did Salisbury wait more than a week – until 4 November – before even ordering a search of the parliamentary premises? Thirdly, why did both he and the King automatically conclude that *gunpowder* was the threatened method of destruction? The letter makes no mention of means, only of the anticipated end: and that in the vaguest language.

At any event, the week's delay in official action almost enabled Fawkes and the others to achieve their aim. Only on 4 November did Salisbury's fellow Privy Councillor Lord Suffolk lead a search party to the Parliament cellar. There Suffolk discovered Fawkes, who nevertheless ran away so fast as to obtain a few hours' freedom in the capital (using the alias 'John Johnson') before being captured by a local magistrate. Fawkes' accomplices escaped to Staffordshire; and there, in the struggle with the constabulary, Catesby was killed. Wintour, severely wounded, lived long enough to be dragged back to London with most of the others, whose foiled venture set London's ballad-sellers working overtime on their own claims to immortality:

> Please to remember
> The fifth of November
> Gunpowder, treason and plot:
> We know no reason
> Why gunpowder treason
> Should ever be forgot.

Yet before the full repertoire of judicial torment had been expended upon Fawkes and his fellows, Salisbury lacked what later ages were to call a smoking gun. Until January 1606 he could obtain no indication of the plotters having been anything more than a bunch of extremists with twisted notions of patriotism: for which they went to the gallows in two batches on, respectively, 30 and 31 January. (With one exception, Tresham, who had already died in his cell.) The Puritan majority in Parliament wanted more than mere local troublemakers. If a grand Jesuit conspiracy behind Fawkes and his accomplices did not exist, it would have to be invented.

To his relief, Salisbury discovered that one Jesuit had indeed been tangentially involved with the defendants' machinations: Father Henry Garnet, whom Fawkes' colleague Robert Bates had named in the hope of escaping further torture. Garnet had been surreptitiously active in Catholic proselytism since the 1580s. (His circle of intimate friends included the great composer William Byrd, whose spiritual allegiance Elizabeth – so often prepared to look the other way if an individual Catholic could be useful to her – loftily ignored when hiring him as organist for her Chapel Royal.) Yet the government had been unable to fasten any more specific misdeed upon Garnet than the suspected exercise of his religion. Even when its agents discovered – on the estate of Stonor House in Oxfordshire, where Garnet frequently stayed – a secret printing press used by the Catholic underground for disseminating homiletic literature, any involvement on Garnet's part remained conjectural. But Bates' admission revealed the Garnet connection with Fawkes and company.

Garnet, it emerged at his trial, had known of the intended mass murder plot from its inception. He knew it because the plotters told him of it; and the plotters told him of it because they introduced during confessions their desire to carry it out. From the first, he abominated it, and begged the conspirators to abandon it. But because Fawkes and the others had informed him of it under the seal of the confessional, he could not reveal to the authorities what he had been told. It is a testimony to the completeness with which not only Catholic rites, but basic Catholic thought-processes, had been expunged from the general English consciousness by 1605 that the very *idea* of confessions remaining secret struck Garnet's prosecutors as some sort of obscene novelty.

One word in particular, thanks to the Garnet case, entered into the English argot: 'equivocation'. As Garnet's judges employed it, 'equivocation' had no more precise a meaning than do its present-day counterparts 'racism' or 'sexism'. Like those terms, it became a catch-all epithet used to avoid the trouble of thinking: in this case, an epithet denoting (preferably but not exclusively Catholic) broken promises and general failure to meet Puritan levels of boorishness.* The diplomat Sir Dudley Carleton observed, in a letter of 2 May 1606, that Garnet had 'been found shifting and faltering in all his answers, and it looked he will equivocate at the gallows, but he will be hanged without equivocation.' In his last moments Garnet, executed on the day after Carleton's remark – near St Paul's Cathedral, to encourage baseless rumours that he intended a last-minute and life-saving conversion to Protestantism – allowed himself a sad rebuke which paid his hecklers back in their own linguistic coin. 'This', he said, 'is no time to talk of equivocation.'

• • • • •

The Gunpowder Plot's discovery was more than Salisbury's finest hour; it was his last truly satisfying hour. Perhaps no master as addicted to low cunning as James – 'the wisest fool in Christendom', France's Henri IV famously called him – would have protected Salisbury forever against those, inside and outside Parliament, who longed to see him powerless. What remains beyond dispute is that after 1610 Salisbury, who

---

* The term's most famous appearance is on the lips of the drunken Porter in *Macbeth*, whose longest speech Shakespeare crams end-to-end with allusions to Garnet's case. 'Faith,' babbles the Porter, 'here's a farmer who hanged himself on the expectation of plenty': Garnet's pseudonyms included the surname Farmer. 'Much drink,' the Porter continues, 'may be said to be an *equivocator* with lechery': Garnet's enemies charged him (accurately) with excessive toping, and (falsely) with debauching a Catholic spinster named Anne Vaux. And later: 'It [drink] sets him [the drunkard] on, and it takes him off': 'taking off' was established Jacobean slang for 'being hanged'. Near the play's end, Macbeth laments his earlier willingness to believe 'the equivocation of the fiend,/That lies like truth'.

once had not put a foot wrong, could not put a foot right. When he died on 24 May 1612 – still only forty-eight years old – it was merely the ghost of a successful administrator who departed. The Salisbury who ruled England had perished two years earlier, traduced again and again by the House of Commons as the grovelling servant of a spendthrift master, and increasingly unattractive to the master himself. James, after all, had fallen hopelessly in love with a pretty and brainless youth named Robert Carr. Clever little crookback Salisbury could get nowhere against James' drivelling expostulations on the need to pile up money and real estate for Carr's benefit: 'I maun hae [must have] the land, I maun hae it for Carr,' James would lament in his much-mimicked Scots accent. At least Salisbury, like Banquo, fathered a line of politicians likely to 'stretch out to the crack of doom'. Salisbury's direct descendants played indispensable roles in politics until well into the twentieth century (they included two British prime ministers, one of them our Salisbury's namesake, the other Arthur Balfour).

That said, seldom has any leader's administrative apparatus collapsed so totally after him as Salisbury's did. Like Walsingham, like his own father, Salisbury had aspired to the Platonic ideal of surveillance voiced by Macbeth against his opponents:

> There's not a one of them but in his house
> I keep a servant feed [hired].

After Salisbury's death this whole notion became meaningless. Not till Cromwell had seen off Charles I did it even regain the status of a desire, never mind approach a reality. To quote Alison Plowden again:

It was not until [Cromwell's] government ... began to feel menaced by dissidents at home and exiled royalists abroad that a secret service, on anything like the scale of that operated by Francis Walsingham, began to re-emerge under the able and energetic direction of Cromwell's spymaster, John Thurloe.

Monomaniacal lovers of freedom will consider the non-existence of England's secret police between Salisbury and Cromwell as a total blessing. The historian's verdict must be more mixed. Even as he feels some relief at the governmental debility which did away with well organised tattle-tales, he is forced to entertain a grudging respect for the trio of surreptitious tyrants that Walsingham, Burghley and Salisbury constituted. They graduated, after all, with first-class honours from the university of Elizabethan political science: a hard school, and often enough a bloody school, but at least one that refused to encourage in its students any traces of cowardice, anarchism, inverted snobbery, or cant.

the birth of the modern:
FRENCH SURVEILLANCE FROM RICHELIEU TO FOUCHÉ

> A man who minds his own business and
> goes on to mind other people's.
>
> *Talleyrand on Joseph Fouché*

'Vice Leaning on the Arm of Crime'

ONE OF THE MOST admired passages in nineteenth-century French prose comes from the autobiography of François Auguste René, Vicomte de Chateaubriand. To understand this passage's import, it should be remembered that Chateaubriand had spent most of the French Revolution and much of the Napoleonic era in self-imposed exile. Only when the Bourbons under Louis XVIII had regained lasting control of France did Chateaubriand come politically into his own, when a grateful king appointed him foreign secretary. He felt understandable disgust at the monarch's lenience towards those intriguers who had spent most if not all of their lives destroying everything monarchy stood for.

Hence his horror when, on waiting in one of King Louis' anterooms in July 1814, he beheld two such intriguers on their way to profit from the royal clemency. One was Talleyrand – in full, Charles Maurice de Talleyrand-Périgord, Prince of Benevento – who now, having triumphantly survived every political twist of the previous two decades, enjoyed the powers (though not the title) of prime minister. The other was Joseph Fouché, Duke of Otranto, Napoleon's police minister: who had not only signed the death warrant for Chateaubriand's own brother, but back in 1793 had cast one of the crucial votes that sent Louis XVI to the scaffold. 'Suddenly,' Chateaubriand recalled,

> a door opens; silently there enters vice leaning on the arm of crime, M. de Talleyrand walking supported by Fouché; the infernal vision passes slowly in front of me, reaches the King's study and disappears. Fouché had come to swear allegiance to his lord; on bended knee the loyal regicide placed the hands which had caused the death of Louis XVI between the hands of the brother of the royal martyr; the apostate bishop stood surety for the oath.

Few men can boast the ability to inspire equal terror in sovereigns and in France's most pitilessly effective revolutionaries, the Jacobins; Fouché belonged with those few. Napoleon himself, in his final exile, admitted Fouché to be 'certainly the most cunning of the lot'. Yet still Fouché's name remains surprisingly obscure in the English-speaking world. If only because of Fouché's genius for anticipating twentieth-century dictatorships' methods in what his fellow Jacobin, Louis de Saint-Just, cheerily called 'the eye of surveillance', such ignorance is regrettable.

In the Beginning:
Richelieu and the *Ancien Régime*

Like so many developments in France's history – including the first French newspaper, the first French colonial empire, the first French codification of weights and measures, a fully-fledged French navy, and the *Académie Française* – the first recognisably modern sort of national secret police owes its existence to one man: Armand Jean Du Plessis, better known as Cardinal Richelieu. The obsession that haunted Richelieu's life, and more particularly his eighteen-year tenure (1624–42) as First Minister to King Louis XIII, was fear of anarchy: fear that the weakness which had paralysed French government during the sixteenth century's religious wars would return, redoubled. Within scarcely more than fifty years, between 1559 and 1610, three out of five French monarchs had met violent ends.

In best French style, Richelieu supplied elaborate justifications for infringing on subjects' liberties. By so doing he was, if not breaking new ground, then at least making a significant departure from the outlook of most pre-Richelieu European rulers, who disavowed any such intention. Elizabeth I's professed reluctance to make windows into men's hearts merely echoed that of other monarchs in her time and earlier: including Sigismund Augustus, King of Poland 1548–72, who defended his refusal to arbitrate and persecute on religious issues with the comment: 'I am the King of the people – not the judge of their consciences.' No comparable 'don't ask, don't tell' approach guided Richelieu.

The Cardinal established a stable of sycophantic pamphleteers, who spent their working lives writing for such government-funded magazines as *Le Catholique d'Estat*. Like many another quasi-absolute ruler, Richelieu appreciated that having a posse of tame intellectuals was almost as desirable a state of affairs as having no intellectuals at all.

A less publicised aspect of Richelieu's authority consisted of the so-called *Cabinet Noir* that he founded. This department's main jobs lay in intercepting suspicious-seeming letters, and quelling both local and foreign-based conspiracies before they could do their worst. His chief subordinate was the Capuchin friar François le Clerc du Tremblay, alias Père Joseph: history's original *éminence grise,* thus styled because of the coarse grey habit his order compelled him to wear. Père Joseph's uses – not only as spymaster, but as leader of diplomatic missions to Vienna – included deflecting public reproaches aimed at the Cardinal's person. One pamphleteer complained in Latin, *Huic ille tegendo sceleri cucullum præbet* ('He [Père Joseph] offers him [Richelieu] a friar's hood to hide his crimes in'). When the much-feared Capuchin died in 1638, Richelieu more keenly than anyone mourned the loss to French administration: '*Où est mon appui?*' ('Where is my prop?'), he would disconsolately ask. By later régimes' standards the *Cabinet Noir* was tiny; Richard Deacon, a leading modern expert on France's secret services, states that even at its height of influence it never employed more than fifteen individuals. Not so tiny, though, as to have been overstretched. Its master's conviction that guiltlessness should not, of itself, be allowed to save subjects' lives has a decidedly modern ring. One of Richelieu's French biographers, Auguste Bailly, emphasises that

> His [Richelieu's] secret service kept him informed of
> all that went on, even, it seemed, about the thoughts of

his enemies … he acted in order to show those whose fidelity might waver that even innocence was no safeguard, and that there was no law in France for those who revolted against the King, or by their sympathies made common cause with factions.

Dozens of bereaved aristocratic families – whose leaders had paid with the executioner's axe, simply for daring to defy the Cardinal's will – concurred with such assessments.

· · · · ·

No individual Frenchman in the century and a half following Richelieu's death (Louis XIII outlived the Cardinal by only six months, his successor Louis XIV ascending the throne when still a child of four) showed the Cardinal's single-mindedness concerning domestic surveillance. Indeed, the actual necessity for it had diminished. The sheer drama and decisiveness of Louis XIV's victories on the battlefield from the 1670s till the early eighteenth century – so unlike the inconclusive, seemingly endless slugging matches that had dominated European warfare in Richelieu's lifetime – helped guarantee his government's survival. What the Sun King's cannon could accomplish, eavesdropping did not need to duplicate. Moreover, the Sun King's extremely well attested *personal* force of will (repeatedly eyewitnesses tell us of his talent for generating dread by nothing more than a resentful look or an icily murmured monosyllable) lessened the requirement for a *bureaucratic* dread-generating apparatus.

The question remains, whether heavy enough and disciplined enough hands in the French censorship and police sectors, during the reigns of Louis XV (1715–74) and his grandson Louis XVI (1774–92), could have ensured for the *ancien régime* a longer life than it enjoyed. Surprisingly, for all the billions of words that the French Revolution has inspired in historians, this question was seldom asked before the 1970s, and has never been conclusively answered. In recent years, though, a few gleams of light have begun to shine on the topic. It emerges, for example, that the future revolutionary leader Jacques-Pierre Brissot acted as a police spy for the monarchy when his authorial production alone could not save him from bankruptcy courts. Brissot's surveillance sideline followed a risky period in 1784, when he found himself imprisoned in the Bastille for having mocked government officials in various pamphlets.

'Everything's Going to Change for the Better Now': The Revolution and the Rise of Fouché

Once the French Revolution's early stages had put the monarchy on the defensive, domestic political policing began at last to be taken seriously. The Marquis de La Fayette, as head of the National Guard under Louis XVI during the years 1789–91, exercised much of the political strength that First Ministers in previous French kings' reigns had wielded. He ran a team of agents sufficiently disciplined and alarming to force fanatics like Jean-Paul Marat into seclusion. These agents even broke into the printing shop where Marat set the type for his unfailingly vituperative magazine *L'Ami du Peuple,* and smashed the presses. Over a period of months, Marat spent his days and nights hoping to keep one step ahead of La Fayette's police, at one point being required to hole up in a cell so tiny that it forced him to spend six weeks 'crouched down on one buttock'. Marat's luck improved in October 1791, when public outrage at the trigger-happy National Guardsmen's antics against republican protesters forced La Fayette to step down, and before the end of 1791 to leave France altogether.

That same year, for the first time, the phrase 'Ministry of the Interior' began to be used of a bureaucratic institution. For most of the monarchy's brief remaining life, the department's minister was Jean-Marie Roland de la Platière, a moderate belonging to the Girondin movement, so-called because most of its members hailed from the Gironde region of southern France. Roland (he ceased to employ 'de la Platière' as soon as aristocratic usages became unfashionable) took over the ministry in March 1792. Harshly but accurately described by one historian as 'a pedant and a bore of such proportions that even to read about him 170 years after his death is enough to deplete the room of its air', Roland quickly set up a network of domestic informers: to little effect, when it came to his own survival. (Whether through active mischief-making or pure laziness, the *commissaires* reporting to him grossly exaggerated his popularity with the masses. Ordinary Frenchmen were improbably described as overwhelmed with gratitude for Roland's emergence: as saying 'Everything's going to change for the better now that the patriotic Minister has been installed', and as being moved to tears of thankfulness for the advent of 'the virtuous Roland'.) In June 1792 Louis XVI, weary of Roland's nagging, dismissed him from the cabinet.

When a mob directed by the Paris Commune – the capital's municipal government – forced the Royal Family out of its accommodation in the Tuileries on 10 August, and butchered the Swiss Guards who stood between the Bourbons and popular vengeance, Roland regained his ministry. If anything, he achieved still less in office after the monarchy's downfall than he had before it. Like most of the Girondins, he suffered in an extreme form from the liberal delusion that life is a debating society. This left him at an incurable disadvantage against serious revolutionary leaders who, whatever their sins, had the priceless gift of knowing what they wanted. While Roland treated the National Convention to his brand of unctuous rhetoric, the hard men simply seized *de facto* control of the Paris militia from Roland's nerveless hands: meanwhile allowing him to keep his ministry, and therefore the illusion of power. How little the illusion pertained to the reality became clear when *Père Duchesne*, the wildly successful scandal sheet – estimated readership 200,000 – published by extremist Jacques-René Hébert, made Roland and his wife (by this time widely suspected of adultery) its main targets. From *Père Duchesne,* readers of adequately strong stomachs could learn that

> It was past midnight and the 'virtuous' Roland slut was relaxing in the arms of the nigger Lathenas from those pleasures which her bald old husband has to procure for her.

(Some notion of Hébert's habitual taste levels can be gained from his subsequent public insistence that Marie Antoinette sexually abused her own son. The falsity of this accusation moved even the normally unpitying Robespierre to protest: 'It's not enough that Antoinette should be a Messalina. That idiot [Hébert] must make her an Agrippina.')

Roland had little leisure to relish his continuing fantasies of personal influence. In April 1793 the uniformly regicidal

Jacobins, all by this time loyal to Robespierre, seized Roland's papers; and when these proved too boringly uninformative to reveal any genuine treason, the Robespierre-controlled Committee of Public Safety decided to concoct some. Most of Roland's fellow Girondins were sent to the guillotine on 31 October. Mme Roland met the same fate on 8 November, not before acquiring permanent residence in *Bartlett's Familiar Quotations* through her final pronouncement, 'Oh Liberty, what crimes are committed in thy name!' Two days afterwards, on hearing the news of his wife's execution, Roland himself – who had fled to Rouen – stabbed himself to death.

More skilful than Roland in exercising terror was François Héron, a mysterious figure who so well covered his tracks that many accounts of Revolutionary administration omit him entirely. After the killing of Louis XVI in January 1793, Héron attained control of the security police (or rather, of much of it; individual revolutionists maintained their own spying networks, independently of official snooping). Allied with the Hébertists, Héron nevertheless retained enough *Realpolitik* to display a finesse far exceeding Hébert's own. Nominally responsible to the foreign ministry, Héron appeased Robespierre's leadership by sending him and the Committee of Public Safety reports on actual or potential troublemakers, not among 'counter-revolutionary' groups alone, but also within a rival Revolutionary organisation, the Committee of General Security. Those *commissaires* who had the function of spying on 'enemies of the Revolution' listened, we are told, in a hundred cafés, in every club and *assemblée*, on the *quais*, on the terrace of the Tuileries, in public baths, in swimming-baths, in laundry boats, in billiard rooms, at the hairdresser's (an excellent listening post), among the spectators at the guillotine or at its provider, the Revolutionary Tribunal, in queues, in … the villages on the slopes above the Seine, in the markets, at the fairs, and in public lavatories.

The same chronicler informs us that notwithstanding the spies' ubiquity, 'even at the height of the Terror … people talked loud and clear. One is constantly amazed at their impudence and their imprudence.' That death and disgrace could, and regularly did, result from a single slip of the tongue seemed never to prevent gossip: much of which duly went into the *commissaires*' files, with whatever embellishments appeared fitting. An agent who covered reams of paper with descriptions (however fictional) of suspects' height, weight, voices, faces and speech would always go far; an agent who contented himself with recording the bald fact that a suspect had said *Merde à la Convention* was firmly reprimanded.

• • • • •

If Héron was the father of well-organised French republican surveillance, then the man responsible for perfecting it and brilliantly adapting it to subsequent Napoleonic exigencies was Fouché: already celebrated from 1793 for his aptitude in causing terror, despite formidable competition in the mass murderer department. It is typical of one who shunned the limelight wherever possible, and who preferred scuttling in the wings to occupying centre stage, that the very year of Fouché's birth has been disputed. Most historians since the mid-nineteenth century have settled for 1759, though some have attributed his arrival on earth to any year between 1754 and 1761. (The actual day of his birth seems beyond dispute: 21 May.) He hailed from Pellerin, a village near Nantes in France's west; his forebears were, for the most part, sailors and modestly successful merchants. This background suffused him with an outlook very different from the genteel origins that produced a Robespierre and a Marat. Until shortly before his death Fouché retained a countryman's shrewdness – a freedom from self-pity and from histrionics, a capacity for ruthless commonsense – that enabled him in even the wildest chaos to detect how many beans make five: this despite a tendency to ill-health that prevented him from going down to the sea in ships as many of his ancestors had done.

Conspicuously blessed with a powerful intellect, and of clear outward piety, young Fouché studied and then taught at Nantes' Oratory of Jesus. Taking holy orders made only a brief appeal to him, but even after abandoning this idea he continued to instruct Oratory students. It is even possible that his religious belief in these early days was wholly genuine, and that his subsequent atheist rages resulted from traumatic grief at his loss of youthful faith. In any event, Fouché acquired a justified reputation for cool courage through making one of history's first ascents in a hot-air balloon (still considered a dangerous fad, the Montgolfier brothers having pioneered balloon transport only from 1783) and met various well-born young bloods, several of whom he afterwards showed no compunction in persecuting. His circle of friends at this time included the future Empress Joséphine's first husband,

Alexandre de Beauharnais; and Napoleon's brother, Jérôme Bonaparte, eventual King of Westphalia. On moving to Arras, Fouché became friendly with two of the locals, both of whom would within a decade enjoy powers of life and death over their compatriots: Robespierre, then an unsuccessful lawyer of literary pretensions, and military engineer Lazare Carnot. He courted Robespierre's sister, Charlotte, whom he soon jilted, while with characteristic cleverness he ensured the continued esteem of Robespierre himself by lending the latter money to cover the costs of a trip to Paris.

Fouché's own progress to the capital occurred in September 1792, when the electoral district of Loire-Inférieure chose him as its deputy to the National Convention. That same month he married Bonne-Jeanne Coignaud, the notably plain daughter of a civil servant, to whom he remained faithful and devoted until her death in 1812. Once in Paris – typically, he delayed his arrival until the September Massacres and their resultant recriminations had subsided – he allied himself with the Girondin element. Deficient in the Girondin leaders' gift of speech-making (though he had previously spoken with enough force to keep mischievous schoolboys under control), Fouché tended to keep silent: always a wise course, as his later career demonstrated, and never wiser than amid the First Republic's birth-pangs. The more he witnessed of the Girondins' misguided eloquence – of their genius for weighing down even the most humdrum parliamentary speech with so many allusions to Roman republican heroes as to suggest that a classical education is a complete and suicidal waste – the more disgusted he became. When he realised that in the average Girondin's opinion, eloquence *was* political activity, his alarm grew. More than half a century later

Lord Macaulay would rebuke the Girondins for 'criminal irresolution'. Fouché, an eyewitness to their bungling, could not have put it better himself.

What confirmed him in his inference that the Girondins were travelling at lightning speed on a one-way ticket to nowhere was the spectacular Girondin failure to keep united on the issue of what to do with the ex-King. The Girondin party split in two between those who wanted to see Louis executed, and those who wanted to spare his life. When the Convention put the question to a vote on 16 January 1793, Fouché said in advance that he favoured letting Louis live. Instead he proceeded, when the time came, to advocate *la mort*. Louis was beheaded only five days later, various appeals by moderate deputies for a second Convention ballot having been rejected with the sanctimonious assurance that further delay in carrying out the execution would only aggravate the royal victim's suffering.

Not till the second half of 1793, however, did Fouché acquire the national and international notoriety that would be his lot for the next two decades. Among the Revolution's most vexing issues was the irreconcilable gulf between those who (most famously Robespierre) desperately wished France to retain some form of deistic religion – the vague doctrine of the Supreme Being – and those who, like Fouché, had abandoned all religious belief whatsoever. No one in revolutionary France took atheism more seriously than Fouché himself. When posted by the government to Nevers on the banks of the Loire, Fouché forbade the display of any religious symbols, either in Nevers itself or in nearby towns. Two epoch-making laws came into effect during October 1793: the imposition of a Revolutionary calendar, and (at Fouché's behest) a statute compelling gates of graveyards to bear signs saying *La mort est un sommeil éternel* ('Death is an eternal sleep'). Catholic priests, stripped of most of their rights as early as 1791, now had to promise to abandon their vocations, to marry within a month, and to adopt orphans. Fouché and his hoodlums commandeered churches for revolutionary pageants: robbing them of their Communion vessels and any other precious metal objects, melting those down, and sending them to Paris as trophies in the war against 'superstition'. Afterwards foes accused Fouché of having diverted some of this gold and silver for his own use; but the charge never stuck, and remains unconvincing. The Fouchés of this world love sheer power far too much to cultivate an undue taste for wealth.

Having established himself as undisputed boss of Nevers and its environs – while attempting to justify his confiscation of local property in language so imbued with class hatred that some historians have gone so far as to call him a proto-Communist – Fouché acquired from the Committee of Public Safety a still more important mandate: to smash counter-revolution in the city of Lyons. From May to October 1793, the Lyonnais had held off soldiery from Paris; their successes included overthrowing and beheading their own Jacobin mayor, Joseph Chalier, who in his last moments correctly prophesied: 'My death will cost this city dear.' The Convention's most bloodthirsty rabblerouser, Bertrand Barère (whose inexhaustible poetic imagery when demanding the judicial murders of all whom he disliked earned him the soubriquet 'Anacreon of the guillotine'), excelled himself on the theme of putting Lyons right:

Let the plough pass over her. Let her name cease

to exist … No mercy. Let everyone be smitten.
Two words will suffice to tell the whole. Lyons
made war on liberty; Lyons is no more.*

Fouché's appearance aided him in engendering fear; a
tall, gangly albino whose most lifelike portrait shows
grotesquely heavy-lidded eyes and thin smirking lips, he bore
a remarkable resemblance to what T.S. Eliot called 'the white
flat face of Death'. Once in Lyons, he and his troops accompanied a donkey 'housed in priest's cloak, with a mitre on his
head' through the city streets to the 'martyr' Chalier's tomb.
Robespierre's second-in-command, Georges Couthon,
entered Lyons in state: borne in a chair, a youthful disease
having left him almost wholly paralysed from the waist down.
Couthon ordered the guillotining of a mere two hundred citizens; this needlessly modest body-count earned him fierce
rebukes back in Paris, and a more efficient arbiter of mayhem
had to be despatched to Lyons in Couthon's stead. The arbiter
concerned was Jean-Marie Collot d'Herbois, a grossly untal-
ented thespian who had harangued voters into giving him a
seat at the Convention, and who later acquired a job on the
Committee of Public Safety. Having been laughed off the
Lyons stage, Collot d'Herbois took the revenge that every
failed actor dreams about: murdering his audience.

On 12 December Fouché and Collot d'Herbois began
their massacre. First, seventy locals were chained together, after

---

* This last phrase (in the original, *Lyon n'est plus*) became the title for a comprehensive and unpitying 1937 analysis of Fouché's Lyons activities, on which
the present account draws. The book's author, Édouard Herriot, served as
France's prime minister twice (1924-25 and 1932), combining this office with
a fifty-two-year tenure as Lyons' mayor.

which they were killed by cannon and by musket, and their bodies pitched into the river Rhône. Then another two hundred and nine died similarly, though the Rhône had become too foul-smelling and too clogged-up with cadavers to serve again as a gravesite, so these and subsequent victims were interred on land in a huge ditch, in response to olfactorily outraged locals' complaints. Even some members of the firing squad found their task unbearable; from one such squeamish marksman Collot d'Herbois snatched his musket, and, 'levelling it with unmoved countenance', showed him how a *true* Republican does his duty. Altogether 1,910 Lyonnais perished in the twelve weeks till late March 1794: 1,069 by shooting, 841 by decapitation. Shunning Collot d'Herbois' do-it-yourself work ethic, Fouché beheld the butchery from a safe distance, gazing at it as if it were but a mildly interesting instance of experimental theatre in the round.

In an era that placed some intrinsic value on human life, Fouché's enormities caused abhorrence throughout Europe. This disgust found a poetic voice through the embittered references to him in *The Anti-Jacobin*, a periodical that future British prime minister George Canning and other ambitious young Tories produced. (Incidentally, the 'her' in the fifth line refers not to a flesh-and-blood female, but to the literary muse of Rousseau.)

> Presumptuous Folly stood in Reason's form,
> Pleas'd with the power to ruin – not reform …
> Saw Persecution gnash her iron teeth,
> While Atheists preach'd *the eternal sleep of death* [italics
>   in original].
> Mark her fair votaries, prodigal of grief,

With cureless pangs, and woes that mock relief,
Droop in soft sorrow o'er a faded flower,
O'er a dead jackass pour the pearly shower,
But hear, unmov'd, of Loire's ensanguin'd flood,
Chok'd up with slain; – of Lyons drench'd in blood.

Not even Fouché could have hoped to carry out such slaughter within Paris, where memories of the September Massacres of 1792 still haunted political discourse. But this was regional France, which had persisted in harbouring Girondins and outright monarchists; in regional France, therefore, anything went. Asked by Robespierre to clarify the motives behind the shootings, Collot d'Herbois explained that mowing down two hundred 'conspirators' in a single session was not at all a crime; rather, it sprang from a deep philanthropic impulse. As Collot d'Herbois put it, with true revolutionary logic:

When twenty criminals are guillotined, the last to be executed has already died twenty times, whilst the two hundred conspirators die but once.

This seemed an entirely reasonable answer, and Fouché remained in the clear. His Parisian admirers piled compliment after compliment on him:

Citizen Fouché has brought about miracles ... The infirm have been succoured, the poor given fresh respect, fanaticism has been destroyed ... such is the summary of the achievements of the representative of the people, Fouché.

To cover all his options, nevertheless, Fouché disbanded the firing squads on 6 February, and thereafter resorted to the guillotine. Anticipating Chairman Mao's breezy epigram 'To execute one man is to educate a million', the former pedagogue Fouché henceforth chose his prey with some care, concentrating on specific ringleaders whose deaths would 'allow their followers to ruminate on their fate'. Victims included a twenty-six-year-old nun, whose 'treason' had consisted of praying to God in public, and whose guillotining was so botched that various local working women had to hack away at her neck with meat cleavers until outright decapitation occurred. Fouché ended his Lyons sojourn with an inspired gesture of totalitarian showmanship: among the last two killings he ordered were those of the executioner and his assistant, partly in revenge for their having done away with the former mayor Chalier, partly to show the world that his power over life and death extended even to professional killers.

If Lyons was (in its frightful way) a triumph for Fouché, Paris threatened to be a disaster. When he returned to the capital in April, he found himself in grave danger, largely because he openly scorned Robespierre's religious faith. Other public atheists, Hébert among them, had become dead public atheists. On 8 June – or 20 Prairial, as current usage had it – at a ceremony in the Tuileries, Robespierre held a Feast of the Supreme Being, where he proclaimed the evils of irreligion and actually burned an effigy representing Atheism. Fouché viewed all this as simultaneously ludicrous and dangerous. In this opinion he found supporters among other deputies, such as the general Paul Barras and the Convention's young president, Jean Tallien, both of whom (like Fouché) considered Robespierre well launched on the road to making himself personal dictator. At a Jacobin Club meeting Robespierre lambasted Fouché for the very villainies in Lyons that the government had earlier condoned; and after this chastisement, the Jacobin Club expelled Fouché from its ranks. He appeared destined for the tumbril; every few days he changed his lodgings for fear that the police would capture him, and each night he crept round from door to door, warning other deputies: 'Robespierre is preparing another proscription. You are on the list.'

When Robespierre set up a new internal surveillance bureau under the Committee of General Welfare's legal jurisdiction, several Committee of Public Safety members opposed it on the grounds that it impinged on their own group's turf. (The spies under the Committee of Public Safety's own auspices made only 250 arrests during the years 1793–94, whereas during the months of June and July 1794 alone the Committee of General Welfare's spies made no fewer than 1,814 arrests.) Spurred by fear that the list of 'traitors' which Robespierre bragged of possessing contained their own names, the Convention's most influential leaders struck on 27 July. They drowned out Robespierre's oration with screams of 'Down with the tyrant!', and clapped him under arrest. Fouché, for all his involvement with the intriguers, took care to absent himself from the Convention that day; after all, the anti-Robespierre plot might fail, and then where would he be? As it happened, his worries had no basis: Robespierre was executed, along with Saint-Just and Couthon, only a day after being apprehended. More even than usual, Fouché – readmitted to the Jacobin Club on 31 July – felt good to be alive.

He felt even happier when, once the dismantling of Robespierre's Reign of Terror had started, his own cynicism contrasted with the Terror's outright maniacs. Maniac *in excelsis* was Jean-Baptiste Carrier, who in a later age might have found his true niche directing snuff movies on a Cecil B. de Mille-sized budget. Deprived of this vehicle for artistic immortality, Carrier cultivated such pastimes as repeatedly flinging himself on the floor 'howling and snapping like a madman', and committing mass infanticide (he called children 'little whelps ... they must be butchered without mercy') by ordering the shooting and clubbing to death of five hundred peasant boys and girls. Most famously, Carrier organised in and around Nantes gigantic *noyades*, which claimed approximately six thousand lives. He forced his prisoners into boats and then had the hulls cut away, so that the victims were trapped till the inrushing waters drowned them. Whenever a particular batch of captives demonstrated the misfortune of an evenly balanced sex ratio, Carrier had the prisoners stripped naked, lashed together in pairs, and hurled into the river. These divertissements he named 'Republican marriages'. Yet whilst such high jinks occurred with impunity under Robespierre's rule, they met with no favour once Robespierre had perished; and Carrier went to the scaffold in December 1794, helped thither by Fouché's enthusiasm for denouncing him. Collot d'Herbois fared somewhat better: his eventual desertion of Robespierre saved his neck, but could not save him from banishment to Cayenne, French Guiana, where in January 1796 he died of yellow fever.

• • • • •

One belief alone united those who toppled Robespierre: a determination that whatever atrocities continued outside the capital, Paris itself would remain free from Jacobin terror. Such a determination increased the need for surveillance. Thus, in late 1795, France's Directoire government – consisting mainly of republicans who shunned Robespierrian radicalism – founded a new, politically motivated surveillance organisation as a separate police ministry, rather than as a part of an existing government department. In this ministry the Executioner of Lyons at first had no function. Estranged from President Tallien, who with good reason considered Fouché an unreconstructed Jacobin at heart, Fouché dwelt in a garret. When he could earn a living at all during most of this period, he did so by smuggling, dubiously legal banking transactions, and occasional snooping for the Directoire's *de facto* ruler, Barras. These jobs afforded him little satisfaction: 'I was resolved,' he afterwards wrote, 'to accept a brilliant mission only.'

Meanwhile the Directoire soldiered on as best it could without Fouché's advice. It nearly collapsed in May 1796, when the communistic journalist François-Noël Babeuf conspired to bring it down. While Babeuf somewhat disingenuously denied being anything more than 'a director of public opinion', the Directoire took no chances with him, and in May 1797 it sent him to the guillotine. So alarmed did the Directoire become by the threat of Babeuf and similar figures – as well as by the persistent fondness for Jacobin ideology shown since 1795 by France's quasi-parliament, the Council of Five Hundred – that between 1796 and 1799 the post of police minister changed hands nine times. Nor, to the Directoire, was Jacobinism the only danger. Once Louis XVI's ten-year-old son 'Louis XVII' had obligingly died in prison (June 1795), the restoration of an adult Bourbon did not seem at all impossible, and in 1797 Lazare Carnot – Fouché's old friend from his days in Arras – fled France under suspicion of royalist sympathies. During the spring of 1797 no fewer than one hundred and eighty-two royalists had won Council seats: a phenomenon that represented nothing more than a protest vote, but also nothing less.

It increasingly seemed, then, a waste of good resources on Barras' part to let Fouché go on frittering his skills away: whether in his piecemeal spying, or in the high-sounding but impotent post of ambassador to the Cisalpine Republic to which the Directoire kicked him upstairs in 1797. (The Cisalpine Republic consisted of most of northern Italy, conquered for France by the young – not yet twenty-eight – Bonaparte.) At the same time, Fouché remained a Jacobin to end all Jacobins; and the thought of giving him power in his own right, perhaps to stage a repeat performance of 1793-94 with the Council of Five Hundred's help, inspired in the Directoire cold dread. Only one solution offered itself: if Fouché could somehow be turned against the Council's Jacobin contingent, he could do it and Jacobinism permanent damage.

Accordingly, on 20 July 1799, Barras appointed Fouché to the job which he had craved all along: the police ministry. In this role Fouché enthusiastically met Barras' and the Directoire's requirements. The Jacobins' leader in the Council of Five Hundred, who optimistically assumed that in Fouché he now had a friend at court, found himself bawled out by the new minister.

> Imbecile! What are you doing? What do you expect to accomplish? Just remember, as of tomorrow, when I deal with your club, if I find you still there at its head, yours will fall from your shoulders. I give you my solemn word on it, and shall keep it, I warn you.

Fouché's police paid many an individual Jacobin what they coyly described as 'domiciliary visits', until not only the Council's Jacobin contingent but the Council itself had been closed down. Newspaper proprietors insufficiently sycophantic towards the régime similarly found themselves locked out of their own property. To subsidise this administrative productiveness, he persuaded Barras and the Directoire to impose taxes on prostitution and gambling. When he took over as minister, he had discovered his department to be ruinously in debt; and, as he later put it,

> ... without money, no police is possible. I soon had money in my treasury by making vice, inherent to all great cities, tributary to the police of the State.

But *whose* State? Increasingly Barras looked like yesterday's man, his indolence, debauchery and pointless intrigue contrasting with Fouché's efficiency and vigour. General Bonaparte, though at this juncture by no means the popular or administrative favourite that subsequent legend made of him, was already well disposed towards the idea of shovelling Barras and the Directoire itself into history's dustbin. Even more so was Joséphine Bonaparte. She found herself cultivating Fouché's society, not through any personal attraction between the two (Fouché, as far as is known, never cheated on his wife), but because Joséphine always seemed short of money, and Fouché always knew where she could get more, provided that she did the right thing by giving him secret information as to Bonaparte's schemes.

In November 1799 Bonaparte achieved his chance, less because of his own bet-hedging performance than because

Fouché had decided Barras had to go. This decision entailed no love by Fouché for the Corsican parvenu. On the contrary, once Fouché succeeded in making an appointment with the General, he found himself compelled to wait in Bonaparte's anteroom for an entire hour. This indignity did not prevent Bonaparte from speaking well of the older man: 'He [Fouché] is the sort of man we need in an affair like this.' When the legislature met in mid-November – not in Paris but in nearby Saint-Cloud – Fouché ordered all roads connecting Saint-Cloud and Paris to be sealed off by special troops. To cover every possible contingency, Fouché even hobnobbed more and more with the royalist and Catholic underground. Many an aristocrat cooling his heels in England was not only allowed to come back to Paris, but actually invited back with Fouché's approval. Many a priest secretly saying Mass, and hauled before Fouché expecting the death penalty, found in his interrogator a surprisingly tolerant audience. The very fact that neither blue blood nor Catholic belief guaranteed execution during the late 1790s indicates how skilful Fouché had become at disciplined alliance-building.

Thus, when the Directoire formally collapsed on 9 November 1799 – the *Coup d'État d'18 Brumaire*, as it quickly became known to historians – Bonaparte furnished Fouché with an IOU on which the police minister had every intention of claiming. For so epochal an event, the formal end of the French Revolution, it proved remarkably bloodless. Barras, who under any earlier republican government would have found himself guillotined merely as a loser, underwent no worse punishment than being arrested in his bath. A handful of Jacobin generals were held prisoner by troops loyal to Bonaparte and to the latter's brother-in-law, the cavalry commander Joachim Murat, then let go on condition that they ceased further political meddling. Bonaparte himself, appointed First of the French Republic's three Consuls on 13 December, remained too conscious of his elevation's suddenness to seek wholesale revenge in a Robespierrian manner.

'Where Three Are Met Together, I Have Always One Listening': Fouché as Police Minister

Napoleon, in his first years of rule, moved with a caution unthinkable during his later life. Perhaps he still genuinely believed in his old republican ideals; certainly he behaved as if he did. When increasing his own authority he took, at first, care to do so within the law and with regard for public opinion. On 7 February 1800, less than three months after seizing power, he won backing at a plebiscite for constitutional change. Yet this change, while ensuring a ten-year term for each of France's Consuls, gave the First Consul near-dictatorial rights. Conscious that his government could continue only if fortified by military conquest – of the sort that France had sadly lacked since his run of Italian and Egyptian triumphs ended in 1798 – Bonaparte craved extra glory.

When news came that the Austrians had invaded the Cisalpine Republic, the First Consul left France and joined battle in northern Italy at Marengo. The first reports from the battlefield terrified Fouché: they spoke of crushing defeat for Bonaparte's men. Although anxious that Bonaparte had outlived his usefulness for France, Fouché decided to wait and do nothing: which was just as well, since only days later the news came that Marengo had actually been a Bonapartist success. The episode taught Fouché two things: the gimcrack nature of Napoleon's rule; and the vital significance of Plan B thinking. Never again would Fouché let himself be caught without an alternative power base, and preferably an alternative government, at the ready. Meanwhile he had to make the existing government work better than it was doing.

Since at this stage Bonaparte remained too much of an unknown quantity to inspire much hatred – even most of the exiled Bourbons regarded him, and still more Joséphine, with a tolerant eye – conspiracies against Bonapartism seldom occurred. This lacuna merely spurred on Fouché, who divined that if conspiracies did not yet exist in significant numbers, they must be invented. Accordingly, when Bonaparte went one evening to the opera, he became the target of an alleged assassination attempt. In fact the 'assassin' had been primed by Fouché, who years afterwards unblushingly observed:

> Every government at its dawn usually takes advantage of a danger it has created, either to make it more firm, or to extend its power; all it needs is to escape a conspiracy to acquire more strength and influence.

The detection of real intrigues proved almost as easy to Fouché as the invention of fake ones. On Christmas Eve 1800, Bonaparte – on his way to hear Haydn's oratorio *The Creation* – only just survived an assassination attempt that killed nine innocent bystanders. Impressively calm at the time of the incident, Bonaparte subsequently yelled abuse at Fouché for having let Jacobins come so close to killing France's ruler. Fouché, who unlike Bonaparte had been fully apprised of the murder plot well beforehand, replied that no Jacobins had been involved: that it had been a royalist stratagem, and that he could prove as much within a fortnight. The vital clue for Fouché came from a blacksmith, who recognised a horseshoe on one of the slain animals as having been made in his own shop. Eventually this information led to the arrest and execution of the royalist ringleaders.

• • • • •

As to how Fouché's police ministry worked in practice, something of its style emerges from the following mid-nineteenth-century account by Macaulay. Too young himself to have witnesssed it, he knew in his childhood various émigrés who suffered from Bonapartism at first hand. The typical secret policeman at this time was, we are informed,

> … a well-dressed person, with a soft voice and affable manners. His opinions are those of the society in which he finds himself, but a little stronger. He often complains, in the language of honest indignation, that what passes in private conversation finds its way strangely to the government, and cautions his associates to take care what they say when they are not sure of their company. As for himself, he owns that he is indiscreet. He can never refrain from speaking his mind; and that is the reason that he is not prefect of a department.
>
> In a gallery of the Palais Royal he overhears two

friends talking earnestly about the King [Louis XVIII, still stranded in England] and the Count of Artois [Louis' brother, the future Charles X]. He follows them into a coffee-house, sits at the table next to them, calls for his half-dish and his small glass of cognac, takes up a journal, and seems occupied with the news. His neighbours go on talking without restraint, and in the style of persons warmly attached to the exiled family. They depart; and he follows them half round the boulevards till he fairly tracks them to their apart- ments, and learns their names from the porters. From that day every letter addressed to either of them is sent from the post office to the police, and opened. Their correspondents become known to the government, and are carefully watched. Six or eight honest families, in different parts of France, find themselves at once under the frown of power without being able to guess what offence they have given. One person is dismissed from a public office; another learns with dismay that his promising son has been turned out of the Polytechnic school.

Next, the indefatigable servant of the state falls in with an old republican, who has not changed with the times, who regrets the red cap and the tree of liberty, who has not unlearned the Thee and Thou [Jacobinism had actively discouraged the polite second-person *vous* in favour of *tu*], and who still subscribes his letters with 'Health and Fraternity'. Into the ears of this sturdy politician our friend pours forth a long series of complaints. What evil times! What a change since the days when the Mountain governed France! What is the

First Consul but a king under a new name? What is this Legion of Honour but a new aristocracy? The old superstition is reviving with the old tyranny. There is a treaty with the Pope, and a provision with the clergy. Emigrant nobles are returning in crowds, and are better received at the Tuileries than the men of the 10th August. This cannot last. What is life without liberty? What terrors has death to the true patriot? The old Jacobin catches fire, bestows and receives the fraternal hug, and hints that there will soon be great news ... The next day he is close prisoner, and all his papers are in the hands of the government.

Fouché himself bragged, 'Where three are met together, I have always one listening.' Understandably, he took particular professional pride in having foiled a plot wherein he was approached by *every single one* of the conspirators separately betraying the others. Bribery, so important in oiling the machinery of surveillance under Louis XV, much diminished in overall importance under Fouché. It had its uses, and Fouché made sure that his department paid the perpetually extravagant Joséphine a thousand francs per day in exchange for information on her husband's private doings; yet he greatly differed from his eighteenth-century predecessors in keeping bribery under strict control.

For Fouché, a much more appropriate model than anything the eighteenth century offered was Richelieu's policing, of which Fouché's own service constituted a hypertrophically efficient version. He avoided the crippling obsession with foreign affairs, at the expense of domestic security, which had so weakened Louis XV's government. Not that he ever ignored events outside France; after all, the cook at Louis XVIII's expatriate court was on Fouché's payroll, and told his master of every significant event involving the exiled Bourbons. But the notion of making France's rulers feared abroad while they turned into a laughing-stock at home contradicted Fouché's entire policy.

In any event, French control of Europe under Napoleon (both as First Consul and, from 1804, as Emperor) increased so much that the dividing line between external and internal affairs thinned almost to invisibility. Foreign cities such as Turin, Antwerp, Geneva, Mainz and Ostend all counted, at this period, as part of France: to be subjected to French law, and in particular to Fouché's surveillance. Within France proper, Fouché instigated a prefecture of his own, parallel to the system of prefects that the *Code Napoléon* set up. Fouché's prefecture concentrated on maintaining loyalty to the government in the main cities and, above all, the principal seaports. Beginning in March 1800 the Parisian police answered, in their avowable public functions, to an ex-magistrate named Louis Dubois. As for underhand political surveillance within Paris, Fouché's second-in-command for that function was a man after his own heart: renegade priest Pierre Desmarest, in whom Fouché must have recognised something of his own youthful enthusiasm for extirpating religious belief. To report on subversion within the nation's capital, Fouché hired three hundred additional staff – many of whom had done time in prison – for his secret police: or, as he blandly preferred to call the organisation's members, *regulateurs de l'opinion à Paris* ('controllers of Parisian opinion').

Almost every day – usually around eleven o'clock in the morning – Fouché and Napoleon met. Even when they could not meet, such as when Napoleon was leading his armies, Napoleon insisted on receiving each day the *Bulletin de la Police* that Fouché wrote, and ordered printed, on the basis of his underlings' reports. Each week, generally on a Wednesday, Fouché discussed the political situation with Desmarest and other high officials. Partly on the basis of his underlings' reports, Fouché obtained his *Bulletin* information. So conscious did Fouché remain of the need to keep data confidential that only two copies of the *Bulletin* ever emerged from the printer's. Fouché kept one locked away in his office – in which he would habitually work until approximately ten o'clock at night – and passed on the other to Secretary of State Huguès Maret, who gave it to Napoleon in person. Since Napoleon's favourite colour was green, Fouché always had Napoleon's copy bound with a green silk ribbon.

One characteristic above all determined Fouché's dealings with his chief: total immunity to the Napoleonic Legend. The dazzling charm by which Napoleon made most other courtiers his abject slaves never touched his police minister. In Fouché, Napoleon brought out the didactic element that never sank far below the surface. Like Talleyrand (but unlike the average Napoleonic administrator), Fouché viewed Napoleon with the same indulgence that a pedagogue feels towards a brilliantly overachieving, unreliable and faintly ridiculous schoolboy. He failed to thrill with pleasure at Napoleon's military exploits; he even obliged the humourless Napoleon to serve as straight man for his own witticisms. Once Napoleon twitted Fouché for having voted in favour of Louis XVI's execution. 'That,' Fouché responded, not missing a beat, 'was the first service I was able to render Your Majesty.' Many years later, when both men were nearing their respective careers' end, Napoleon burst out: 'I ought to have you hanged!' Even this threat could not disconcert Fouché, who merely answered, 'I am not of the same opinion.' When his master accused him of having tolerated unpardonable police laxity, Fouché took some pleasure in replying that the 'lax' police had spied on one of Napoleon's paramours two-timing him with a violinist.

· · · · ·

On 14 September 1802 Fouché, to the astonishment of political observers, lost his job. Why Napoleon dismissed him remains unclear. The most prominent explanation offered at the time was that Napoleon had deplored Fouché's endeavours to talk parliamentarians into opposing Napoleon's self-proclamation as Emperor (a self-proclamation which did not, in fact, take place for almost another two years). But this cannot be accurate, since so many opponents of a monarchical restoration existed in 1802 that if Napoleon had treated all of them with similar severity, he would have had precious few bureaucrats left. Still less convincing is Napoleon's own statement that Fouché had proven so efficient in repressing opposition as to have eliminated all further need for his own services. Perhaps Fouché really had been accusing his master – as others indubitably did – of incestuous relations with his sister Pauline, and had been caught out doing so. Yet on other occasions Napoleon made the selfsame charge, when voiced by others, the subject of raillery. In any event he showed no overt resentment towards Fouché, whom he consoled by a promotion to the (largely toothless) Senate, and to whom he awarded a golden handshake of one million francs.

How much Napoleon's administration relied on Fouché became all too clear once he had departed. To an extent that under Fouché had become unthinkable, royalist intrigues against Napoleon's government and against his very person resumed. What is more, they came surprisingly close to success. The chief conspirator, Georges Cadoudal, had been a Chouan: that is, one of those agrarian royalists to whom Fouché refused to extend mercy. 'Once a Chouan,' Fouché said, 'always a Chouan' (*qui a chouanné, chouannera*). Cadoudal, built like an ox and recognisable at a hundred paces by his sheer bulk, made an improbable exemplar of secrecy; but the post-Fouché police were too inefficient to stop him making regular contact with General Charles Pichegru. A hero of the Directoire, Pichegru had been largely responsible for bringing Holland under French rule in 1795, but afterwards had fallen out with his revolutionary paymasters and had become increasingly amenable to royalist approaches. In 1797 he had been banished to the French West Indies, from which he soon escaped; he later associated above all with royalist expatriates in England, Cadoudal among them. Both Pichegru and Cadoudal endeavoured to recruit another general, Victor Moreau (a Breton, like Cadoudal and like Fouché himself), whom Joséphine had denounced to Napoleon as a possible traitor. It appears that although Moreau remained too much a republican in his soul to join the royalist plot, he did nothing to oppose it. Only in February 1804 did the authorities learn about the scheme, and then they arrested its main agents. Pichegru died mysteriously in his prison cell, asphyxiated with his own cravat (whether by suicide or by an obliging gaoler's ministrations has never been determined); Moreau, despite Fouché's efforts to save him, suffered exile (most of which he spent in America); and Cadoudal was guillotined. In the con-demned cell Cadoudal proved capable of jesting. On hearing the news that Napoleon had hoped to deter future coup attempts by elevating himself to the purple, Cadoudal com-mented, 'We have done better than we hoped. We intended to give France a king and we have given her an emperor.'

Others, less guilty than these three plotters, suffered from Napoleon's rage. For most of Napoleon's reign the thirty-one-year-old Duke of Enghien, among the few Bour-bons whom the revolutionaries ignored, had lived quietly in Baden. Despite having served with monarchist troops during the Reign of Terror and the Directoire, Enghien had no polit-ical ambitions himself, and seemed happy to be left alone. His Baden idyll remained undisturbed until a mendacious police report implicated him in Cadoudal's conspiracy. Thereupon Napoleon had Enghien arrested by French military police, subjected to a court martial of sorts on French territory, and on 21 March shot dead. With Enghien perished any hopes that moderate Bonapartists retained of reaching an alliance with the Bourbons. Not since Fouché's Lyons adventures had any single act by France scandalised Europe as much. Fouché, when told of this judicial lynching, deplored it as much as the next man. Curiously, the celebrated words he uttered on hear-ing the news – *C'est plus qu'un crime, c'est une faute* ('It's more than a crime, it's a blunder') – have almost always, ever since Napoleon's downfall, been misattributed in print to Tal-leyrand: an injustice which none lamented more heartily than Fouché. At least Napoleon, having realised how lucky his own escape had been, gave Fouché his old position back on 10 July.

• • • • •

In many respects Fouché had an easier time after 1804 than he had ever experienced during 1799–1802. For one thing, royalist conspiracies no longer threatened the empire. Bourbon supporters, after the Cadoudal–Pichegru enterprise's failure, ceased placing their trust in specific individuals hoping to bring Bonapartism down; they realised that only total military defeat could weaken Napoleon's hold on France. Newspapers lost all their independence and became mere propaganda vehicles of the police ministry. An especially significant source of income for Fouché was the levy he charged foreign diplomats, who could not possess passports unless they bought them from his office. Napoleon demanded splashy demonstrations of vengeance against enemies of his régime; for the most part Fouché ignored these demands, arguing that a steady application of quiet police terror against the régime's opponents did far more good than any number of bloodbaths.

Besides, the longer Napoleon stayed in charge, the greater his air of legitimacy: even if he never attained the effortless monarchical self-confidence that the Romanovs – or, above all, the Habsburgs – enjoyed. Few Frenchmen went on record as objecting to Napoleon's dictatorship while it notched up victory after victory on the battlefield. Fouché's honours continued to accumulate. In 1808 he became a Count of the Empire, and the following year Duke of Otranto (or Otrante, as the French called it): although, despite his titles of nobility, he continued to be usually known as Monsieur Fouché. (Similarly, Talleyrand continued for the most part to be called Monsieur de Talleyrand, despite having been created Prince of Benevento.)

With increasing distinction in his public life Fouché combined firm contentment in his private life. The man who carried out interrogations, authorised torture sessions, and signed death warrants without a trace of compunction metamorphosed, at his home on Paris' Rue du Bac, into a beguiling family man. At a time when most middle- and upper-class males avoided their own offspring whenever possible, Fouché would take endless delight in dandling *his* children on his knee, rejoicing in their prattle, and letting them create childish havoc even when visitors were present. He called his children (he and Bonne-Jeanne eventually had seven) 'the supreme joy of my life'. Their joyous innocence he guarded with a severity that would have done a monk credit. Fouché keenly deprecated permissiveness, and urged his sister to remind her own daughters at all times 'that a woman's empire in society is established by the firmness of her principles, spirit, and moral values'.

Only when the Spanish campaign dragged on did Fouché seriously suspect that Napoleon had overreached himself. Fouché's concern at France's failure to suppress guerrilla warfare in the Iberian Peninsula inspired him to renew his long-extinct friendship with Talleyrand, whose resignation from the foreign ministry Napoleon had obtained in August 1807. Reckless, brilliant, lazy, spendthrift and an erotomaniac, Talleyrand had little in common with the coldly efficient, superbly disciplined, workaholic, sexually conservative Fouché. (When Napoleon promoted Talleyrand to the high-sounding post of Vice-Grand-Elector, Fouché sneered: 'It was the only vice he lacked.') But shared panic at Napoleon's hubris brought the two men onto common ground, as mere temperamental affinity could never have done. Neither man had much time for Napoleon's Continental System, whereby European governments were forbidden to import English goods; indeed, Louis Bonaparte openly defied the blockade by letting his Dutch subjects trade with England unchecked. Posing as the champion of Spanish liberties against Bourbon oppression – for the Bourbons' cadet branch had ruled Spain since 1700 – Napoleon thrust upon the Spaniards Joseph Bonaparte, whom he compelled to give up the Neapolitan throne in favour of Joachim Murat.

And still the endlessly promised Spanish triumphs for France never came. Instead of the accustomed laurels, Napoleon won merely the chance for successive delaying actions. Napoleon himself described Spain as his 'running sore'. To Fouché, this stalemate meant one thing alone: a need to patch up some sort of Anglo-monarchist accord, whereby he could ensure the peace of Europe. Behind Napoleon's back, therefore – the Emperor was in Austria at the time, ingratiating himself with Habsburg monarch Franz I, whose daughter Maria Luisa he was to marry once his union with Joséphine had ended – Fouché ordered (July 1809) the National Guard's mobilisation without having consulted his master first. 'Let us prove to Europe,' Fouché announced, 'that while the genius of Napoleon confers glory on France, his presence is not necessary for driving back her enemies.' In addition, Fouché and Talleyrand sounded out Murat; both men talked of installing Murat on France's throne in Napoleon's absence. As if this behaviour were not arrogant enough, Fouché proceeded to do what Napoleon never dared do: tell Joséphine to her face that she should divorce her husband, since she had failed to bear him children.

The combination of Fouché's military intrigues, his hauteur towards Joséphine, and his surreptitious use of the Emperor's name in peace negotiations with London that he scrupulously avoided telling the Emperor about, left his boss with but one option. After a tirade from Napoleon at a meeting of the Council of State ('So it's you,' the Emperor screamed, 'who decides peace or war! You deserve to lose your head on the scaffold!'), Fouché learned on 3 July 1810 that he had once again been dismissed. This scandalised Maria Luisa, whose shrewd father had once cautioned her:

> If you find yourself in any difficulty, take the advice of Fouché – he is the one who will be most useful to you.

• • • • •

Regrets at Fouché's departure were by no means confined to the new Empress. The novelist, dramatist and critic Germaine de Staël, whom Napoleon had banished from France for her consistent opposition to his tyranny, had a soft spot for Fouché, who, she maintained, 'did no more wrong than necessity required'. Indubitably Fouché had pretended not to notice Mme de Staël's occasional visits to the capital; he had more urgent work to do than make life miserable for a harmless, talkative blue-stocking.

Jean Savary, former leader of Napoleon's shock troops, took Fouché's place as police minister. The Emperor admiringly said of him, 'If I ordered Savary to get rid of his wife and children, I am sure he would not hesitate.' Others alleged that 'If the Emperor told Savary to kill you, he would take you tenderly by the hand and would say to you: "I'm in despair at sending you to the next world; the Emperor wills it so" ' (*l'Empereur veut ainsi*). A much-prized, all-purpose bullyboy since the Consulate – he it was who had incarcerated Pichegru and Cadoudal, as well as organising Enghien's execution – Savary went on to provide an early demonstration of the Peter Principle. Menacingly effective in a subordinate role, he rose to the level of his own incompetence when compelled to take his own decisions and to run a whole department. Under Savary, morale decreased so much in the ministry that a joke began to do the rounds: 'Do you know what's going on in Paris?' 'No.' 'Ah, then you must be in the police.'

Not all Savary's problems were his own fault. Before leaving, Fouché had burnt some of the official documents in his office, and stolen others: a simple but useful technique for discomfiting rivals, and one which Fouché would employ again. When Savary told Napoleon of the missing paperwork, the Emperor demanded that Fouché give back what was left of it: which, reluctantly and at his leisure, Fouché did. As in 1802, so in 1810, Napoleon offered Fouché a face-saving sinecure. This time he announced that Fouché would take up the post of Governor of Rome: a largely ceremonial office that represented no challenge to any bureaucrat of Fouché's calibre. Yet once Napoleon had discovered how many valued files Fouché had taken with him, he forbade Fouché to take up the governorship: forcing him instead to remain, jobless and bored, in Aix-en-Provence.

When Napoleon did finally admit his need for Fouché's services, he went about it in a churlish way. He certainly had no intention of obliging Savary to make way for his predecessor. Savary, no matter how badly he erred, was safe. (He became even safer with the foundation of a separate police department, the Sûreté, in 1810. This development relieved him of the responsibility for combating non-political crime.)

Meanwhile Fouché, instead of being reinstated in the work he did best, had to content himself from July 1812 with the governorship of the Illyrian Provinces. This area, comprising the nations now known as Slovenia, Croatia, Bosnia and western Serbia, was legally and politically part of France. In awarding him this post, Napoleon wanted him far enough away from Paris to minimise his capacity for local mischief, but at the same time beholden to Paris for all except the most trivial decision-making. One anecdote alone lightens Fouché's Illyrian years. When urged to arrest a local bandit, who avoided violence whenever possible and who (as is the way of bandits) had become a folk hero, Fouché replied that the man should be offered a civil service post, since he was clearly more efficient than Napoleon's court had become.

Fouché's frustration in Illyria, aggravated by his grief at the death (9 October 1812) of Bonne-Jeanne, increased with the news of Savary's most spectacular blunder: his inability to prevent a bizarre, but at first unstoppable, conspiracy by General Claude Malet. In 1810 Malet had been locked up for his long history of treasonable activities, but by 1812 Savary no longer bothered to place adequate guards on Malet's cell. Such carelessness enabled Malet, on the night of 22–23 October, to bribe a warder, escape into the streets and, with troops from the Second Paris Guard who were loyal to him, commandeer the police ministry. Malet announced that Napoleon had died on the Russian campaign, and that he himself would run a provisional government. But after this impressive start, Malet proceeded to give time for loyal Bonapartist soldiers to overthrow him. At his trial, Malet was asked if he had accomplices; he rather poignantly responded 'Yes, the whole of France, and you too if I had succeeded.' His execution the same day failed to reassure Napoleon, who was appalled at how near Malet had come to toppling him from his throne.

Yet even this shock could not induce the Emperor to recall Fouché. Instead, once the Austrians had recaptured the Illyrian territories in October 1813 and forced Fouché to flee, Napoleon sent him to Naples: unaware of how good an opportunity he thus afforded Fouché to resume, which he did with considerable enthusiasm, his conspiring with Murat.

By this stage neither Napoleon nor Fouché was the political genius he had been. Much of Fouché's once all-consuming aspiration lay in the grave with Bonne-Jeanne; and instead of shaping events as he had hitherto done, he increasingly allowed events to shape him. On 2 May 1814, the day of Louis XVIII's triumphal entry into a Paris that he had not seen for twenty-three years, Fouché was nowhere in evidence. He did not actually get to Paris until the following June, by which time Louis had been formally recognised as king and Talleyrand was enjoying the position at Louis' side which Fouché would once have striven mightily to make his own. Consoling himself with the belief that 'we shan't have them [the Bourbons] for more than a year', Fouché turned down the offer of a cabinet position in Louis' service. From his paralytic philosophical equilibrium he emerged only when Louis' government interpreted his silence as evidence of treachery. Police visited his apartment, hoping to capture him; but he showed something of his old initiative, and proved too quick for them. 'In the best tradition of the French bedroom farce', Fouché climbed a ladder to the top of the wall that divided his home from that of Hortense Beauharnais, Joséphine's daughter by her first marriage. Falling into Hortense's garden, he lay low until the danger had passed.

His caution paid off in March 1815, when the escaped Napoleon made his way back to Paris amid the delirious acclaim of the same crowds that less than a year before had cheered Louis XVIII. For months the British had complained that Elba's proximity to Europe would encourage Napoleon's plans for reconquest; now their forebodings were proven right.

Napoleon no longer dared entrust the police yet again to the incautious Savary: Fouché's comeback could no longer be avoided. And so it occurred. Re-establishment in his old office revivified Fouché as the steely risk-taker of yore, with much of his old manipulative skill intact. He took the precaution of misfiling all the Ministry's crucial documents, so that whoever succeeded him (and Fouché had no illusions about Napoleon's restoration being permanent) would fare no better than Savary had done. He also resumed contact – partly via visits to Basle in Switzerland – with Austria's Foreign Minister, Prince Metternich, in whom he had perceived a figure able to dominate whatever New Order the Allies imposed. Since Fouché's high opinion of Metternich's international importance coincided with Metternich's own views on the subject, the two men esteemed each other as much as so congenitally distrustful a pair of time-servers could hope to do. So precarious was Napoleon's own rule during the Hundred Days that when the emperor in one of his shrieking rages – this one lasted for an hour – accused him of plotting with Metternich, Fouché disdained even to deny the charge.

After Waterloo on 18 June, deference towards Napoleon was a mask that Fouché no longer needed to wear. He dominated the last four recrimination-filled days of Napoleon's reign, finally securing the latter's abdication on the 22nd by an adroit blend of threats and superciliousness. For a man who could achieve this outcome, no reward in Louis XVIII's eyes seemed too great; and so the world was furnished with the grotesque spectacle of a restored Bourbon monarchy naming as its police minister the country's most notorious living regicide. Louis salved his conscience as best he could by the remarkably sanguine words he addressed to his martyred sibling: 'Unfortunate brother! If you saw me, you would pardon me.' But Louis' support had little value in itself; Fouché still needed to contend with a parliament dominated by the hard Right, the 'Ultras', as they were colloquially known. Louis' obeisance to the notion of constitutional monarchy meant that he had to tolerate, if not indeed to approve of, whatever his parliament demanded.

The Ultras' belligerence ensured that the indefatigable Murat met the supreme penalty of the law, though by this stage Murat's habit of running with the hare and hunting with the hounds had repelled so much of Europe that he was doomed anyway. For Fouché a different, in some respects crueller, fate lay ahead. Louis, left to himself, would probably have preferred to keep Fouché on; yet not only had the Ultras determined to ruin Fouché however they could, but the King faced intra-familial opposition to Fouché's presence from Louis XVI's only surviving child, Marie-Thérèse, the Duchess of Angoulême. Implacable and physically tough, the Duchess – who long outlasted her uncles, not dying till 1851 – had endured for her fellow Bourbons' sake imprisonment during the Revolution, in the same fœtid conditions that had ended her tubercular brother's life back in 1795. Napoleon had called her 'the only man in the [Bourbon] family'; now she showed her true strength, and on 14 September 1815 Fouché paid the price for it. On that day Louis, obeying her demands, made Fouché relinquish the police ministry for the final time. Palliated initially with the title of minister to Dresden, Fouché soon lost even that undemanding post. On 5 January 1816 he was formally indicted as a regicide, and ordered to quit France on pain of death.

Fouché in Retirement

A superb foul-weather captain of his soul, Fouché no longer possessed – if he had ever possessed – the spiritual strength required for survival during long years of the doldrums. Having lived on his nerve-ends for almost a quarter of a century, he needed the stimulus of constant danger. Sudden and enforced political peace demoralised him to an almost unbelievable extent. He who had once been the most terrifying man in France now became a querulous wreck, bewailing the misfortune by which fellow politicians had ceased to trust him. To the Duke of Wellington, Fouché fired off a 30,000-word diatribe against the Ultras: 'time, which destroys all, has not destroyed their prejudices'.

Once the Saxon sojourn ended, this most domesticated of politicians drifted from Prague to Munich, from Munich to Linz, from Linz to Trieste. Before leaving France he married a second time, unhappily. His new wife, Gabrielle-Ernestine de Castellane-Majastres, whom he espoused on 1 August 1815 in Louis XVIII's presence, was young enough to be his daughter; and she soon forsook her husband's bony caresses for younger and more hot-blooded male companionship. At least in Trieste, Fouché benefited from the hospitality of Jérôme Bonaparte. In his final term as police minister, Fouché had intervened with the King to save Jérôme from the long prison sentence Louis had wanted to inflict on him. Duly grateful, the former Westphalian potentate observed of Fouché:

> I wish I could divide that man into two persons, so that I could have the politician hanged and cherish the creature who rescued me.

In his glum mood Fouché took literary advantage of the new political calm dominating Europe: a calm that was (as historian Douglas Hilt has remarked) 'conducive, among other things, to the writing of exculpating memoirs'. Fouché's autobiography occupied him for most of his last years. Even at the time various commentators – Heinrich Heine for one – maintained that it must have been ghost-written, but though Fouché might well have received help from other hands in assembling and researching the book, its overriding tone of cynicism mixed with pomposity is nothing if not Fouchéan. In a style wholly typical of the man, all references to the slaughter in Lyons have been carefully omitted from Fouché's narrative: just as, when at the police ministry, Fouché had destroyed every document he could which pointed to his own guilt in that carnage. From his *Memoirs* Fouché emerges, if not as a plaster saint, then at least as a moderate constitutionalist, hoping that France would become a limited monarchy on the Hanoverian model across the Channel. How this hope squares with Fouché's actual performance never becomes clear. Perhaps Fouché's latter-day self-deception had actually left him sincerely convinced that ordering a nun's head to be chopped off with meat cleavers was somehow just the kind of thing George III would have done.

Death claimed the one-time Executioner of Lyons five

days before Christmas 1820, in Trieste. By this time even he had given up all self-assuring talk that Louis XVIII would somehow rebuff the Ultras and summon him back to power. On the 15th Fouché had unwisely gone for a walk, and had succumbed to a chill. Enfeebled though he was, he had one last surprise to spring upon posterity: on his deathbed he saw a priest, expressed his wish to be reconciled with the Catholic Church he had done his best to exterminate, and received the last sacraments. Trieste's ecclesiastical authorities permitted him to be buried in the city's cathedral.

Fouché's true memorial, however, was not the gravestone that marked the site of his interment. Nor was it the unexpectedly long procession of Continental plays, films and operas that perpetuated his name throughout not only the nineteenth century but the twentieth. Instead, Fouché is best remembered for the surveillance principles by which he left his ingenious, pertinacious, amoral mark upon twentieth-century government. If this is a legacy from which most men would recoil, it is not one which the thoroughly forward-looking Fouché himself ever gave signs of wanting to disown. Mussolini said: 'Everything for the State; nothing against the State; nothing outside the State.' However limited Mussolini's own observance of his doctrine, the uncharismatic Fouché had made it real. Small wonder that his biographer, Nils Forssell, in choosing a subtitle, hit on the words *The Man Napoleon Feared*.

the engineers of
human souls:
SURVEILLANCE UNDER
TSARISM AND COMMUNISM

Life has become better, life has become merrier.
Stalin, describing the Soviet Union in 1932

20 December 1936: Stalin's Jewish Joke

F OR JOSEPH VISSARIONOVICH DUGAZHVILI, alias Comrade Stalin – also known as 'Uncle Joe', the Hero of the Soviet Union, and (in Bertolt Brecht's phrase) 'the embodiment of [working-class] hopes' – 1936 had been an almost perfect year. He had enacted during that year the new Soviet Constitution, guaranteeing in theory all those individual and collective human rights that the USSR violated in practice. Besides, the first, and from his own standpoint the most successful, of the three Moscow show trials with which he liquidated so many of his most powerful enemies had recently concluded. He was therefore in the mood for what Carlyle (speaking of a far more innocent early eighteenth-century monarch) had called 'Brobdingnagian waggeries', at which the vodka flowed until almost all present

were paralytically drunk. On such occasions the entertain-
ment would often consist of Stalin's valet and court jester,
K.V. Pauker, who had risen from the unpromising background
of a servant at the Royal Opera House in Budapest before
World War I, to his present eminence as the first man allowed
to shave Stalin himself.

The *raison d'être* for this particular booze-up on
20 December was the nineteenth birthday of the USSR's
political police force, known by this time as the NKVD, but
in previous incarnations the OGPU, the GPU, and originally
the Cheka. Guests of honour included the NKVD's current
director, Nikolai Yezhov. Clearly, something extra in the way
of amusement would be required; and Pauker, 'the demon
barber', provided it. He made the subject of his drollery the
late Grigori Zinoviev, executed on 25 August after being tortured into pleading guilty to a fellow apparatchik's murder.
Like so many of Stalin's victims, Zinoviev had failed to realise
Stalin's enthusiasm for doing away with him. Stalin could
never pervert justice so. There must have been some mistake.
A telephone call to the great man would alert him to the
crimes being carried out in his name. This touching belief
Pauker made the subject of his present performance.

Displaying a sedulous realism that bespoke his theatrical
background, Pauker re-enacted the hapless Zinoviev's last
moments: moaning with panic, flinging himself at the feet of
the nearest NKVD warder, and shouting: 'For God's sake,
Comrade, call up Joseph Vissarionovich!' Stalin and his guests
greeted the brilliance of Pauker's imitation with frenzied
laughter: so frenzied, indeed, that they demanded an encore at
once.

This outcome Pauker had not anticipated. Its implications terrified him. Was he walking into a trap laid by Stalin, Yezhov, and the others? Could he get away with repeating his original impersonation syllable for syllable? No, surely a still greater theatrical coup from him would be expected.

With the inventiveness born of purest fear Pauker repeated Zinoviev's final pleas for help, but gave his monologue a new punchline. Instead of the plea to make contact with Stalin, Pauker ended his Zinoviev imitation by shrieking: 'Hear, Israel, our God is the only God!'

Everybody present knew that Zinoviev had been a Jew (as, incidentally, was Pauker himself). Everybody present also knew Stalin's feelings on the more general topic of Jews who had outlived their specific usefulness to him. Stalin's mirth at Pauker's mimicry, already great, now threatened to asphyxiate him. He laughed so hard that he 'clutched his belly in both hands, and had to sign to Pauker to stop'.

Thus Pauker survived his most inspired piece of acting. Within a year, as might be expected, he himself met the same fate as Zinoviev. But every comedian realises that, however great his own suffering, the show must go on.

'A Demeritocracy Open to All Talents': Russia's Secret Police under Tsarism

Historians usually date internal surveillance by Russian régimes from 1565, the year that Ivan the Terrible – who had already been sovereign for thirty-two of his thirty-five years – founded the Oprichnina. Its name roughly translatable as 'band of outsiders', the Oprichnina consisted of approximately six thousand cutthroats who, far from keeping their surveillance capabilities a secret, gloried in the terror they inspired. Aptly described by one chronicler as constituting 'a demeritocracy open to all talents', the Oprichnina's members (one Oprichnik, two or more Oprichniki) made a fearsome spectacle, clad all in black and mounted on black horses. Their emblem, displayed on their saddles, consisted of a broom topped by a dog's head. The broom symbolised their eagerness to sweep Russia clean of treason; the dog's head possibly indicated their own indiscriminate obedience to the Tsar, but might instead have referred to the Tsar's long-standing enthusiasm for flinging opponents to the mercies of ravenous hounds. (One such opponent, an Orthodox archbishop, was pursued to the death by such hounds after having been sewn into a bearskin.)

Confronted by the spectacle of Oprichniki on the warpath, an English trader named Jerome Horsey wrote:

> This crueltie bred such a generall hatred, distreccion [distress], fear, and discontentment thorow [through] this kyngdom, that there wear many practices and devises how to distroy this tirant; but he still did discover their plotts and treasons, by inoiblinge [enabling] and countenancinge all the rascalest and desperatt soldiers he could seek owt, to affront the chieff nobilitie.

As with most later law enforcement – or, at any rate, fear enforcement – institutions in Russian history, the Oprichnina relied primarily on individual denunciations, whether accurate or wholly fictional. Foreigners marvelled at what one sixteenth-century German visitor to Moscow called 'a kind of innate malevolence [on Russians' part] that makes them … fume with hatred for one another so that they kill themselves by mutual slander'. When Russia's leading clergyman of the time, the Metropolitan Philip, publicly condemned Tsar Ivan's bloodlust, Oprichniki kidnapped him, and the Tsar rewarded Philip's betrayer with the office of bishop. Philip died in prison soon after his arrest: probably throttled, though the authorities blandly ascribed his death to his cell's 'airlessness'. Chief investigators within the Oprichnina included Malyuta (Russian for 'Babe') Skuratov and Alexis Basmanov: Skuratov being especially notable for his presence at Philip's death, Basmanov for having trained his son Fyodor Basmanov to work alongside him in his murderous functions. The family that slays together stays together.

If Oprichniki alarmed Muscovites, they seemed to the citizens of Novgorod like horsemen of the Apocalypse. By 1570, an on-again-off-again war had raged for more than a decade between Ivan and Sigismund Augustus, the King of Poland (and, from 1569 onwards, of neighbouring Lithuania as well). Novgorod, with a long history of opposing rule from Moscow, tended to look favourably on the idea of an alliance with the Poles. Thus in January 1570, Ivan marched into the city at the head of his loyal Oprichniki, having conveniently been presented with a document said to contain proof of Novgorodians' willingness to serve Sigismund Augustus. The Oprichnina's resultant month-long terror left at least two thousand Novgorodians, and perhaps as many as sixty thousand, dead. It is comforting to learn that subsequently Ivan sent a spirited complaint to the French court about the St Bartholomew massacre.

Characteristically, within two years of the Oprichnina achieving its greatest heights, Ivan had turned against it. Living in constant panic at plots against himself – some real enough, most of them the fantasies of his own increasingly erratic brain – Ivan spent much of the early 1570s accusing principal Oprichniki of having gone over to his Polish, Swedish, and Tatar foes. With one such Oprichnik, Prince Viazemskii, Ivan conducted a seemingly cordial interview while his henchmen were busily murdering Viazemskii's servants; Viazemskii then went home, discovered the corpses strewn around his house, and soon afterwards found himself imprisoned for life. The Tsar forced Fyodor Basmanov to kill his own father, and then cast Fyodor into the wilderness: literally so, for Fyodor soon died of exposure. German-born Oprichnik Heinrich von Staden, who lived to tell the tale of his bosses' downfall, supplied posterity with a résumé of the purges that Tsar Ivan (or, as most Western Europeans called him, the 'Grand Prince') carried out:

> Malyuta Skuratov was shot near Weissenstein in Livonia. He was the pick of the bunch, and according to the Grand Prince's order, he was remembered in church. Prince Mikhail, the son of the Grand Prince's brother-in-law from the Circassian land, was chopped to death by the harquebusiers [musketeers] with axes or halberds. Prince Vasilii Temkin was drowned. Ivan Saburov was murdered. Peter Seisse was hanged from his own court gate opposite the bedroom. Prince Andrei Ovtsyn was hanged in the Arbatskaia street of the Oprichnina. A living sheep was hung next to him [in a play on Ovtsyn's name; *ovtsa*, in Russian, means 'sheep']. Marshal Bulat wanted to marry his sister to the Grand Prince. He was killed and his sister was raped by five hundred harquebusiers. The captain of

the harquebusiers, Kuraka Unkovsky, was killed and stuck under the ice. In the previous year [name unclear in Staden's original manuscript] was eaten by dogs at the Karinsky guard post of Aleksandrova Sloboda. Grigorii Griaznoi was killed and his son Nikita was burned alive. His brother Vasilii was captured by the Crimean Tatars. The scribe and clerk Posnik Suvorov was killed at the Land Chancellery. Osip Ilyin was shamefully executed in the Court Chancellery.

All the chief men of the Oprichnina … who were to be killed were first publicly whipped in the marketplace until they signed over all their money and property, if they had any, to the Treasury of the Grand Prince. Those who had no money and property were killed in front of churches, in the street, or in their homes, whether asleep or awake, and were thrown into the street. The cause of the death, and whether it was legal or not, was written on a note, which was then pinned to the clothes of the corpse. The body had to lie in the street day and night as a warning to the people.

With typical genius for anticipating modern totalitarianism, Ivan decreed in 1572 that simply mentioning the Oprichnina would henceforth be a capital crime (although he briefly resuscitated the institution in 1575, only to discard it again within a year). He died in 1584, having displayed heightened consciousness of the need for family values in government by smashing his son's skull with one mighty blow of an iron staff.

• • • • •

No subsequent Tsar organised as effective an internal surveillance system as Ivan's Oprichnina; before the nineteenth
century, few Tsars even tried. Boris Godunov, Russia's most
powerful individual during the two decades immediately after
Ivan's death – first as Regent for Ivan's slow-witted successor,
later as Tsar in his own right – put his cousin Semen Godunov
in charge of a secret police force. Yet this force entirely failed
to stamp out the Tsar's antagonists; within weeks of Boris'
demise in 1605, Semen himself had been strangled (along with
Boris' widow and only son) in a more than usually violent
palace revolution. After this coup Russia experienced years of
anarchy as complete as the history of any European state can
show: during which turmoil pretenders to the throne so
abounded that, we are told, 'no little local army or gang of
brigands felt complete without its portable autocrat'.

Only when the Romanov dynasty had attained some
security of tenure, under Tsar Alexis – who in 1645 became
the first Russian ruler for half a century to acquire power by
peaceful inheritance, rather than by conquest or by bribed
electoral colleges' acclamation – did significant internal policing resume. Four years after coming to the throne, Alexis
promulgated a law code which maintained, among much else,
that any failure to denounce intended treachery against the
monarch would be *itself* treachery against the monarch. To
make a denunciation, all a loyal subject needed to do was to
shout in a public place 'Sovereign's word and deed!', and then
to specify the charge against whomever he wanted to accuse.
This procedure, admirable in its simplicity, remained in force
till the 1760s. And if all other means of quashing unruly

subordinates failed, Alexis took to spiking their drinks. 'His Majesty,' wrote an Englishman at the Tsar's court, 'will laugh to see his subjects handsomely fuddled, and sometimes he will put mercury in their liquor.'

Alexis' son, Peter the Great, who became Tsar in 1682 when only ten years old, refined in adult life his father's policing methods. He did this via two mechanisms. First, he overhauled the Preobrazhensky Office, which earlier had been mainly the administrative arm of an eponymous Guards regiment, a role it combined with a profitable monopoly over Russia's tobacco trade. Whilst initially staffed (from 1697) by only two clerks and no more than eight assistants, the Preobrazhensky Office acted on several thousand denunciations, showing great skill at keeping order in a society where almost no-one could read at all. For extra intelligence-gathering, Peter set up the Secret Chancellery, a still more formidable institution. When Peter conceived his grand design of destroying his son and heir – another Alexis, who had openly promised that on his accession he would undo all Peter's westernising works – he entrusted the Secret Chancellery with the task of digging up dirt confirming Alexis' filial ingratitude. Confronted again and again with evidence of his son's hostility, Peter alternated between sessions of dragging him along the palace floors by his hair, and haranguing him by correspondence:

How often have I not scolded you for this, and not merely scolded you but beaten you ... but nothing has succeeded, nothing is any use, all is to no purpose, all is words spoken to the wind, and you want to do nothing but sit at home and enjoy yourself ... If [you

persist], understand that I shall deprive you of the succession and cast you off like a gangrened limb.

A terrified Alexis fled to Vienna – unavailingly begging
Austria's timid Emperor Karl VI for active help – then to
Naples. There Peter's Secret Chancellery agents arrested
Alexis, and held out assurances of a full pardon if he would
return home. Once in possession of him, the agents handed
him over to his father: who in July 1718 not only ordered his
recalcitrant heir tortured to death, but apparently killed him
(some say by the rack; in others' versions, by the knout) with
his own hands. Once Alexis had breathed his last, the exultant
Peter ordered a week of public rejoicing throughout Moscow,
and launched new warships to celebrate his son's departure
from this vale of tears.

• • • • •

The thirty-seven years following Peter the Great's death in
1725 witnessed a series of mostly brief and always mediocre
reigns by sovereigns who (as one writer delightfully says of
them) 'passed in and out of sight like the saints of a Cathedral
clock'. Nevertheless, covert operations maintained a certain
consistency throughout. In 1731, a year after ascending the
throne, Peter's niece, Anne, set up a Chancellery for Secret
Investigations to supersede the Preobrazhensky Office. A later
monarch, the lunatic Peter III – who reigned for less than a
year – abolished this organisation, only to set up a Secret
Bureau of his own (1762), with many of the same staff. These
included, in the bureau's higher echelons, a much-feared veteran of surveillance: Stephen Sheshkovsky. Through every

change of monarchical incumbent over four decades, he exhibited a Vicar of Bray-style cunning that kept him in office till his death in 1794. Sheshkovsky attained his greatest power during the reign of Peter III's widow (and probable killer), Catherine the Great. Of great piety, Sheshkovsky won substantial acclaim for decorating his favourite torture chamber with holy icons, and chanting prayers from the Orthodox liturgy while thrashing his victims. An initial blow by him to the suspect's jaw with a stick would usually elicit data from even the least fluent conversationalists.

Catherine's grandson, Alexander I, shortly after he took over as Tsar in March 1801, announced that forthwith the Secret Bureau would cease to exist. What he failed to announce was his foundation of not one, but two, similar organisations in the bureau's stead. Real or imagined sedition, at least when committed in a main Russian city, continued to find its way to the desks of surveillance officers. But punishments for it no longer included the slitting of offenders' nostrils, as they had done under Alexander's predecessors. Penalties during Alexander's rule tended to be altogether somewhat less severe than they had been in Catherine's day, or would be again once Alexander I's brother, Nicholas, had seized the imperial crown in December 1825.

This last transfer of power almost failed to occur in the first place; and the narrow margin for political error by which it eventually succeeded left Nicholas, as Tsar, with an eagerness to impose unrelenting discipline in place of Alexander's lack of resolve. When Alexander died, it had been generally assumed – above all by those rebels, ranging in spirit from cautious liberals to passionate republicans, who called themselves the Decembrists – that the next Tsar would be Alexander's brother, Constantine. Crowds formed outside Moscow's Winter Palace on 14 December,* repeatedly calling out 'For Constantine and the Constitution!': the more simple-minded protestors having apparently imagined (Russian's word for *constitution* being a feminine noun) that 'Constitution' was Constantine's wife. Entirely unknown to the Decembrists, and for reasons never adequately explained at the time or afterwards, Prince Constantine had renounced his hereditary rights: leaving them to Nicholas, who was many years Alexander's and Constantine's junior. Nicholas' troops dispersed the Decembrist rank and file – *mes amis du quatorze* ('my friends of the Fourteenth [of December]'), he called them in his sardonic way – with volleys of gunfire. Several months later five of the leaders were executed publicly and amateurishly; 'My God,' one of the condemned protested in his last moments, 'they can't even hang a man decently in Russia.' Hundreds of others prominent in the attempted rebellion underwent imprisonment or banishment to Siberia.

To spare himself and Russia a repetition of the Decembrist uprising, Nicholas – who took pride in his nickname, 'Gendarme of Europe' – revamped political police institutions. From 1826 the chief responsibility for secret surveillance rested with a newly established department, the Third Section of His Imperial Majesty's Own Chancellery: known, for short, as The Third Section or the Third Department. Like the

---

* That is, 14 December according to the Russian calendar: which then lagged eleven days behind the West's, and which in the early twentieth century came to lag a full thirteen days behind. Not till 1917 did Russia adopt the Gregorian calendar which had operated in Catholic territories since 1582, in Germanic Protestant territories since the late seventeenth century, and in Britain since 1752. All pre-1917 dates in this chapter are non-Gregorian ones.

Preobrazhensky Office in Peter the Great's time, the Third Section operated on what by later standards seems an extraordinarily limited personnel basis. As late as 1846 its headquarters had only forty full-time officials, and when founded it made do with a mere sixteen. Moreover, the Third Section's chief executive, a general named Andrei Benckendorff, wholly lacked the ruthlessness of predecessors like Sheshkovsky. Far from inspiring terror by his very presence, Benckendorff suffered from a bizarre tendency to forget his own name, at one juncture being obliged to remind himself of it by consulting a visiting-card on his person. And though his terms of reference from the Tsar included the right to investigate 'all matters whatever', those political victims confined to Siberia endured little of the physical and mental hardship that their counterparts in Soviet times considered normal. Several of them applied for – and received – permission from the authorities to transport to their Siberian prison private libraries, even grand pianos.

Such respect as Benckendorff (who remained in at least nominal charge of the Third Section till his death in 1844) managed to inspire from Nicholas' subjects lay in the contrast between the very idea of political surveillance, however ineffective, and the comparative freedom prevailing in contemporary Britain or France. A foreign visitor describing Nicholas' system noted that as far as he could tell, 'its very spies are spied on'. France's Marquis de Custine, another disenchanted observer of Nicholas' Russia, interpreted even Russians' proverbial hospitality as a chance for spying: 'They refuse you nothing, but they accompany you everywhere. Politeness is here a surveillance technique.'

Indubitably Nicholas' régime subjected most of Russia's

leading writers to censorship that British or (post-Napoleonic) French governments of the nineteenth century would have neither sought nor enforced. Since most historians consider it axiomatic that maltreating artists is far more heinous a sin than maltreating butchers, bakers or candlestick-makers, Nicholas owed much of his ill-repute to his hounding of authors, rather than his other misdeeds. Mikhail Lermontov and Alexander Herzen experienced exile at first hand, after they had angered officialdom by their respective styles of literary irreverence. Pushkin, despite or because of Nicholas himself having called him 'the cleverest man in Russia', spent much of his later life chafing under Tsarist interference with his output. More dramatic was the fate of young Dostoyevsky, who had joined a political discussion group which Nicholas considered subversive. Arrested in April 1849, Dostoyevsky and three of the group's other participants faced a firing squad the following December. Only when the marksmen had actually taken aim did a soldier arrive with the news that Nicholas had commuted the sentences to prison terms. Displaying life-long fondness for grim jocularity, Nicholas assigned the announcement of these tidings to a general afflicted with a famously severe stutter.

• • • • •

If in Nicholas' reign the Third Section usually harassed opponents of Tsarism rather than permanently silencing them, it became little more than an administrative joke under Nicholas' son and successor, Alexander II, Tsar from February 1855. How much of the blame for this decline resided with Alexander himself – devious and indecisive, where Nicholas had been direct and resolute – and how much with factors no single man could have controlled, historians for almost a century have argued against one another to determine. What matters to us is not such internecine scholarly conflict, but the unmistakable result to which the Tsar's and the Third Section's debility led: a culture where the very idea of effective central authority (an idea still extant at Nicholas' death) had, by the end of Alexander's life, become inconceivable. To read about Alexander's later years (1873–81), in particular, is to be reminded of W.B. Yeats' words:

The best lack all conviction, while the worst
Are full of passionate intensity.

The date 1873 is instructive, since in that year a loose federation of agitators, which had already operated for a decade (the name popularly given to its members, 'Nihilists', comes from Turgenev's 1862 novel *Fathers and Sons*), began missions to infiltrate the peasantry. These 'pilgrimages to the people', as the Nihilists sanctimoniously termed them, met limited success: the gap between the average Nihilist – an overeducated, unkempt, garrulous, newly atheised university or seminary drop-out – and his equally unkempt but illiterate, stolid, devout peasant audience being too great for even the most loquacious agitator to bridge. Far better results derived from systematic assassinations, which most Third Section staffers had too little foresight even to oppose, let alone prevent. Passport controls upon the movements of suspicious persons within Russia itself, controls stringent in principle, were in practice derisory. Such minor inconveniences for individual Nihilists as being in gaol never stopped the dissemination of letters designed to teach novices the subtle art of political murder. Whether through corruption or feeble-mindedness, the very prison guards employed to intercept these documents usually let them through unexamined.

Rare, though, was the Nihilist who did time behind bars at all. Frequently juries refused to convict him. Or, indeed, her: when Nihilist Vera Zasulich shot and crippled St Petersburg's police chief, she walked away from court a free woman, the jury realising her guilt but fearing the consequences to themselves and their families of announcing a guilty verdict. In the same year (1878), 193 Nihilists, during their public trial's later stages, turned the proceedings into 'a running seminar on revolutionary methods and aims': with the result that around eighty of the defendants were acquitted. The killer of General Mesentzov – the Third Section's own boss, who during August 1878 was stabbed to death in a St Petersburg street – received no worse a punishment than a blow on the shoulder from an umbrella wielded by Mesentzov's guard. In 1879 it was the turn of Kharkov's Governor, Dmitri Kropotkin (cousin of the anarchist philosopher Peter Kropotkin), whom a student shot dead. Shortly after Kropotkin's murder, a Nihilist sub-group calling itself The People's Will vowed to eliminate Tsar Alexander. After several attempts – including one which dynamited the Winter Palace, killing two dozen, but failing to finish off its intended target because he was late for dinner that evening – the would-be regicides succeeded in St Petersburg on 1 March 1881. Going to the aid of two of his guards, whom an earlier hand-grenade hurled from the anonymity of the crowd had cut down, Alexander fell victim to a second grenade.

He had outlived by less than a year the Third Section

ostensibly devoted to protecting him. The Section's uselessness having become obvious to Tsarist bureaucrats themselves,
however mulish, the institution was wound up. Its eventual
substitute, the network of Protective Sections (*Ochrannye Ode-
leniya*), soon became known throughout Europe by a
shortened version of its original name: the Ochrana.

• • • • •

With 20,000 staff, but too badly organised to achieve its long-
term goals (notwithstanding an annual budget of more than
fifteen million roubles, plus access in emergencies to the Tsar's
own slush fund), the Ochrana soon suffered from its combination of notoriety and clumsiness. Absurd legislation requiring
a new Ochrana executive director each time the relevant cabinet minister's post changed hands bred cynicism and defeatism
among the service's hierarchs. Finding 'a type of agent who
would not easily be recognised as an Ochrana member' created
problems from the start. When Ochrana employees shadowed
Tolstoy – fearing that he might either be murdered on his tour
or be treasonous in his utterances – they did so in a manner
overbearing enough and crass enough to inspire the celebrated
novelist's amusement. Admittedly, the widespread notion that
the Ochrana cobbled together the *Protocols of the Elders of Zion*
has now been refuted; but the document's sheer slatternliness
(it charges Jews with a desire to destroy underground railway
systems in cities which at the time did not even have underground railway systems to destroy) made such an attribution
plausible. At least the Ochrana, unlike the Third Section, could
boast the occasional director with a work ethic. One such
head, Sergei Zubatov, kept

the most minute anthropometric records of prisoners and suspects ... He also insisted that as soon as any agent's nickname or code-word became too well-known in the Ochrana hierarchy it was to be changed immediately.

Unfortunately for the Ochrana, Zubatov could not be everywhere at once. And though (thanks partly to the refusal of Alexander III, Tsar 1881–94, to be bullied into a liberalism alien to every Russian tradition) the nineteenth century's last two decades saw far fewer assassinations than did the years 1878–81, the twentieth century had not yet turned two months old before the political murders began again. The list of officials killed is a long one, numbering more than a thousand, of whom space allows only the most conspicuous to be mentioned here. In February 1901 the education minister, N.P. Bogolepov, was fatally shot. In April 1902 D.S. Sipyagin, who as minister for the interior had the final say concerning Ochrana activities, was also fatally shot: his murderer being from the nascent, but impressively homicidal, Socialist Revolutionary movement. In July 1904 a bomb thrown by terrorist Boris Savinkov blew to pieces Sipyagin's successor as interior minister, V.K. Plehve. Another bomb six months later slew Alexander III's brother Sergei, though the Ochrana had been given ample notice of the circumstances in which this killing would occur.

In murdering Plehve, Savinkov acted under orders from Yevno Azef, a Jew who particularly abhorred Plehve for his encouragement of pogroms the previous year. Azef had helped to found the Socialist Revolutionaries in 1901, and remained for the next seven years a leader of the party's political assassination wing, the Fighting Organisation. (The Socialist Revolutionaries' enthusiasm for political violence – preferably peasant violence, but really any old violence would do – made them the chief scourge of late Tsarist rule. By comparison, most of those few Ochrana officials who had heard about Bolsheviks considered *them* predominantly decent folk, who at least did not go around murdering every civil servant they could find. Russian translations of *Das Kapital* had circulated in Moscow and St Petersburg ever since 1872, with no interference from the censors.) Unbeknownst to his comrades, Azef had also been from the late 1890s on the Ochrana's payroll, dutifully reporting to Ochrana superiors details of the mayhem that he himself coordinated. Sipyagin and Plehve had made bitter foes within the Ochrana itself: and at the interior ministry, among fellow officials who, if not exactly pleased to see them slain, contrived to repress undue sorrow at their deaths. Azef maintained especially close contacts with the Ochrana's St Petersburg chief, Alexander Garasimov, an unusually adept and determined figure who infiltrated opposition parties – both legal and illegal – with no fewer than one hundred and fifty Ochrana operatives. One such operative, Roman Malinovsky, rose so high in Bolshevik ranks as to become the Communist Party's leader in the Duma (parliament), until Lenin discovered his Ochrana background and had him executed. An English commentator, noting the cordiality between the policeman Garasimov and the revolutionary stool-pigeon Azef, wrote thus:

> In a 'cloak-and-dagger' world full of bungling
> dilettantes it must have been a relief to each man
> to find himself dealing with a fellow professional.

Only in 1908 did a suspicious Socialist Revolutionary blow Azef's cover, and produce to his horrified fellow party members evidence of the activist's Ochrana collusion. Azef met an extraordinarily mild fate: he escaped to Berlin, where he conducted a profitable trade in women's corsets, and died in 1918 of natural causes.

For a more colourfully Russian instance of the human clay which the Ochrana had to work with, we need look no further than Father Georgi Gapon, chief secretary of a government-sponsored trade union that had received lavish subsidies from Zubatov and Plehve. Gapon achieved in January 1905 a fame greater than Azef could have imagined, when he led to the Winter Palace a vast delegation of peaceful protestors – many of whom belonged to his union – wishing to present Tsar Nicholas II with a petition for increased workers' rights. The Tsar's Cossack guards panicked, and fired on the crowd with such effect that Nicholas II became known to socialists throughout the world as 'a blood-stained creature' (Ramsay MacDonald's phrase), and the day of this disaster as 'Bloody Sunday'. Hundreds of protestors perished that morning, but Gapon was not among them. An Ochrana agent standing next to him pulled him to the ground when the bullets started flying; both priest and agent survived unhurt. International newspaper ballyhoo over his role in Bloody Sunday having rather gone to his head, Gapon quit his native soil, not before demanding 100,000 roubles – and obtaining at least 25,000 – from his Ochrana controllers. He spent most of the sum at Monte Carlo's gaming-tables and on the French Riviera's strumpets, meanwhile keeping his revolutionary hand in by issuing a widely published statement denouncing Tsar Nicholas as 'soul-murderer of the Russian empire'; but by now neither the Ochrana nor his Socialist Revolutionary contacts trusted him. Lured by Socialist Revolutionary pledges of support, Gapon headed in March 1906 for a villa in Finland, where the insurgents whom he had arranged to meet promptly hanged him from a rafter with a clothes line. A month elapsed before anyone found his corpse.

When the Tsar appointed Peter Stolypin as prime minister in the year of Gapon's death, having been compelled to do so by his promises of fully constitutional administration, it looked for five tantalising years as if terrorism might no longer be a paying prospect. Tactless and intelligent, 'a whirlwind of energy', Stolypin enforced the statute books' existing penalties against left-wing extremism – the hangman's noose came to be known as 'the Stolypin necktie' – while simultaneously carrying out agrarian reforms designed to improve the peasantry's wretched lot. This Indian summer of Tsarist expertise (sparing neither furtive radical nor slothful bureaucrat) ended in September 1911, during a performance of Rimsky-Korsakov's *Tale of Tsar Sultan* at the Kiev Opera Theatre. There a certain Dmitri Bogrov espied Stolypin in the audience, and gunned him down. Both an Ochrana agent and a well-attested figure in revolutionary circles, Bogrov is more likely to have been acting in the former capacity than in the latter. A sincere revolutionist would not have wasted gunpowder on Stolypin, since the Tsar was also present and would have made a much more spectacular revolutionary target than any prime minister – however powerful – could do. On the other hand, those Russian right-wingers with a vested interest in reinstating a gutless central government hated Stolypin's dynamism like poison. For Alexander Solzhenitsyn and many other mourners of Tsarism's death-agony, Stolypin constituted the last best hope of civilised Russian rule.

The rest of the Romanovs' tale – and by extension the Ochrana's tale – is all too familiar: the Great War; Rasputin's death at the hands of that very social class which had so resented Stolypin; Nicholas resigning the crown; that weird, dizzying limbo of the Provisional Republic (which in its earliest weeks abolished capital punishment, thereby guaranteeing its own collapse); the sealed railway carriage that transported back to Russia 'the plague bacillus' (Churchill's words), Lenin; finally the 'ten days that shook the world', the triumph of Bolshevism under Lenin and Trotsky ('Robespierre plus Napoleon', as one historian has called the duo), and Russia's metamorphosis from limbo to hell, including the carnage in Ekaterinburg's cellar.

From Lenin to Stalin: The Cheka, GPU and OGPU

Less than a year after Lenin had prevailed, the first truly major figure in Soviet surveillance, Felix Edmondovich Dzerzhinsky, delivered himself – in his capacity as pilot for the Ochrana's high-octane successor, the Cheka – of a statement remarkable for its frankness:

> We stand for organised terror ... Terror is an absolute necessity during times of revolution ... The Cheka is obliged to defend the revolution and conquer the enemy even if its sword does by chance sometimes fall on the heads of the innocent.

Truly 'the old order changeth, giving place to new'. These assertions – following as they did Lenin's signing, on

134

7 December 1917, of the statute that brought the Cheka into being – announced something altogether novel even for the Russian mind. It is impossible to conceive of Tsarist secret police leaders speaking thus about secret police work without at least attempting to sugar the pill. Yet Dzerzhinsky himself found total candour for Bolshevism's sake to be the most natural thing in the world. So dedicated that tradition credits him with a willingness to clean the Communist Party headquarters' lavatories – a chore which other Bolsheviks, preferring a more abstract lustration of Augean stables, all shirked – Dzerzhinsky blended with terrorist adroitness a fear-inducing virtue. In describing Dzerzhinsky's nature, at once magnetic and forbidding, his contemporaries (after seeking vainly to compare him with any more recent historical figures) resorted time and again to invoking archetypes long since defunct. As guiding spirit, and eventual director, of the Cheka – or, to give the department its full name, the All-Russian Extraordinary Commission for Combating Counter-Revolution and Sabotage (*Chrezvychai naia Komissiia po Borbe s Kontr-revolutsiei i Sabotazhem*) – Dzerzhinsky was usually likened to a mediæval monk, to Savonarola, or (most often) to Dostoyevsky's Grand Inquisitor.

This last analogy is all the more surprising in view of Dzerzhinsky's origins: not Russian at all, or even Eastern Orthodox, but Polish and Catholic. Born on 30 August 1877 of aristocratic Polish parents in what is now Belarus, he seems from the start of his adult life to have been thoroughly indigestible. Intended at first for holy orders, he maintained his belief in Catholicism with a youthful fervour entirely unlike the backslapping mockery with which the young Stalin regarded his late-adolescent status as an Orthodox seminarian.

It could be argued that, indeed, Dzerzhinsky never abandoned his religious zeal: that when forsaking his allegiance to Rome (as he did in 1895, upon becoming a Marxist agitator), he merely transferred his ardour from the supernatural sphere to the mundane. Having inherited his father's tubercular condition, he put extra strains upon his physique by the regularity with which he received sentences of banishment to Siberia: banishment to which (between 1897 and 1908) he was condemned five times, and from which five times he made spectacular escapes.

In September 1912 Polish policemen – almost always more professional and determined at this time than their counterparts in Tsarist Russia proper – tracked Dzerzhinsky down to a café, where they arrested him. Accustomed to dealing with recognisably human troublemakers, they had never met anyone like Dzerzhinsky before. A brief and hopeless love affair's violent ending had robbed him of what little mental balance he possessed. (Dzerzhinsky's grand passion, a Polish girl named Zosia Kaszprzak, bore him a son. Some years afterwards – in one of several episodes from his biography which read like the synopsis of a bad Russian novel – he tracked his adored Zosia down to a brothel in Tomsk. There she admitted to having drowned the boy because she could not hope to feed him. Dzerzhinsky responded to this confession by beating her to death in the brothel with a flat-iron.) Immured in Warsaw's Mokotovski Prison, where he remained for almost a year and a half before sentence was passed, he repeatedly 'shook the bars ... screamed imprecations, clambered up like an animal, bit at the iron till all his teeth were broken, dashed round his cell looking for something to throw'. A judge in April 1914 condemned him to two years' hard labour – 'the dreary routine of the treadmill, hemp-picking, road-building and bricklaying' – mainly because of his preceding breakouts. Thirteen months and countless hunger pangs later, the authorities transferred him to Moscow, where they announced that his term of confinement would be increased by a further six years. They proved unduly sanguine. The Tsar's downfall, so fatal to others' hopes of freedom, guaranteed Dzerzhinsky's own: as he joined other leading prisoners in carrying out a revolution in miniature against the 'imperialist' prison governorship.

Once at liberty, Dzerzhinsky laboured with all his strength in the Bolshevik cause. In April 1917 he declined membership of the Bolsheviks' Central Committee, citing ill-health as his reason; but his health proved robust enough to let him accept membership only four months later. During the Bolshevik Revolution itself he carried out the vitally important task of capturing Petrograd's telegraph offices, on behalf of his comrades' Military Revolutionary Committee. Yet he eschewed the chance of becoming the Cheka's first *de jure* boss.

That job went to a less formidable character than Dzerzhinsky: Moses Uritski, a comparative moderate by Bolshevik standards, who sometimes opposed the executions of 'counter-revolutionaries' that Lenin demanded. Not (Uritski hastened to point out) that this opposition sprang from soft-heartedness; rather, he was old-fashioned enough in his thinking to assume that state terror on a grand scale would lead to reprisals from anti-Bolshevik elements. Lenin knew better; and when twenty-one non-Bolshevik Socialists were arrested in July 1918 for having plotted to blow up the Smolny Institute (Bolshevism's Petrograd headquarters at the time), he persuaded Uritski to sign their death warrant. This document he ordered to be published in the newspapers, complete with Uritski's signature, just after the defendants had been put to death in August. One of the dead had a friend named L.A. Kanegisser; and this unstable youth exacted revenge by fatally shooting Uritski in Moscow on the morning of 30 August. That very afternoon, also in Moscow, Lenin himself was shot and wounded in a wholly separate incident by a Socialist Revolutionary, Fanny Kaplan. Arrested within minutes, Mlle Kaplan was over the following week flayed with knives and forced to drink molten wax before being shot in the head within the Kremlin walls: either by Kremlin Commissioner Pavel Maltov or, according to some accounts, by Dzerzhinsky himself.

Certainly nothing in Dzerzhinsky's post-1917 character precluded such 'revolutionary justice' carried out with his own hands. Female suspects inspired him with particular disgust. For him, 'all human feeling for women had gone: they could be the most insidious agents of the Class Enemy'. It is worth noting that the Cheka's most vicious assassins included numerous women. It is also worth noting that whereas usually a Burghley, a Walsingham, or a Fouché no more wanted to carry out their own tortures than an architect normally wants to lay his own building's bricks, Dzerzhinsky was among his own best thugs. When sleep evaded him (which it often did; he worked an average of sixteen hours a day, seven days a week), he would stride through the cells of the Lubianka – which in 1920 had become the Cheka's chief prison and chief Moscow office, occupying the whole of what later became known as Dzerzhinsky Street – and beat up inmates, male or female, himself.

If in his callousness towards women Dzerzhinsky

followed a long revolutionary tradition within Russia, another of his chief aversions was as un-Russian as possible: he could not abide drunkards. To one minor official charged by the central government with preventing alcohol abuse in his baili- wick, Dzerzhinsky barked: 'I want you to breathe in my face!' The official's respiration showed that he had himself been boozing; Dzerzhinsky therefore ordered him taken away and killed. On at least one occasion, though – New Year's Eve 1918 – Dzerzhinsky himself overindulged in drink. This led to a scene of orgiastic self-reproach in which he blubbered to Lenin: 'I have spilt so much blood that I no longer have any right to live. You must shoot me now.' Secret police work, Dzerzhinsky whined, can be done by 'only saints or scoundrels … but now the saints are running away from me and I am left with the scoundrels'.

The squeamishness Dzerzhinsky revealed on this occa- sion did not make him unique among Chekists. American journalist Eugene Lyons, visiting Russia in the 1930s, fell in with various former Chekist hoodlums who drank themselves stuporous to blot out the memories of their job. 'Remember?' one of the hoodlums asked his companion in Lyons' presence: 'I strangled them with these bare hands to save bullets! My fingers are like iron pincers.' By the time of which Lyons wrote, individual Communist functionaries had had two decades in which to get blasé about the deaths they dealt out. In Lenin's day, Communist strategies remained enough of an innovation to inspire a certain shock even among those implementing them.

This shock resulted in such statements as the following, by Latvian apparatchik Martin Latsis, one of Dzerzhinsky's chief lieutenants:

However honourable the [Chekist] man, and however crystal-pure his heart, [Cheka] work … conducted in conditions deeply affecting the nervous system, leaves its mark.

Cheka killers, admittedly, had the legal right to extra rations of vodka and – by an unwritten, but rigorously enforced, law – the right to uncontested ownership of their victims' gold teeth. Even these privileges could not always compensate Chekists for the unpleasantnesses of their jobs. Bolshevik Central Committee member Nikolai Bukharin shared Latsis' concern, and agreed with both Latsis and Dzerzhinsky on the Cheka's need to recruit its manager corps from the cream of revolutionary society:

Do not let us forget how many of them [Chekists] … are nervous wrecks, and sometimes hopelessly ill. For their work was such torture, demanding such enormous concentration, it was so hellish, that it called for a truly iron character.

For Bukharin, the solution to this problem was not (heaven – or, rather, Marx – forbid!) to cut back the Cheka's terror campaign, but to provide adequate accommodation and rest for frazzled Chekists to take time out. (Individual Chekists sometimes required more than mere rest. Leading Chekist and People's Deputy Military Commissar M.S. Kedrov had to be confined to a madhouse after his atrocities during the Civil War; and the Odessa Cheka's boss, M.A. Deich, required not only admission to an asylum but treatment for cocaine addiction.) To the end of his days Bukharin revered Dzerzhinsky for his 'justified cruelty to enemies, which guarded the state against any kind of counter-revolution'. Dzerzhinsky, for his part, inspired among his subordinates not only respect but profound affection. Many of them called him *Batushka* – 'Daddy' – and even the most improvident among his 'children' could rely on his tolerance for most forms of financial irresponsibility. Sometimes he even 'lent' sums to hard-up Chekists, knowing full well that he would never be repaid. Indifferent himself to what pleasures money could buy, Dzerzhinsky regarded extravagance as a weird but harmless quirk. Communist males imprisoned for non-political and non-erotic crimes also benefited from his tolerance:

> Belonging as they did to the salt of the earth, their lot
> was easier [than that of Dzerzhinsky's other captives].
> Of course, Communists, like those less favoured by
> grace, could sin … But they were permitted to
> converse with their fellows, could roam freely [within
> their gaols], and at certain seasons organised lectures
> and concerts. Moreover, they were allowed, as far as
> possible, to carry out their Party duties …

Not so the sexually immoral, who suffused Dzerzhinsky with white-hot loathing. On any bordello-keeper foolish enough to come to his attention, he would mete out special vengeance. Non-Cheka spies he inveigled into transferring to the strength that he alone could provide. Once Lenin hired a detective named Dmitrev to report on Dzerzhinsky's doings, only to be soon told that Dzerzhinsky had so charmed the detective – his charm, when he wanted to exercise it, could be still more formidable than his anger – as to have inducted him into the Cheka itself. Thereafter Lenin, who knew how to cut his losses, refrained from attempting to spy on his alarming comrade.

That some outright lunatics should have slipped through the net of recruitment, despite Dzerzhinsky's care for the highest ethical standards among his murderers, became inevitable in view of the Cheka's sheer size. As of January 1919, the Cheka had at least 37,000 members; by June 1921 this number had gone up to 261,000, though by the following December it had sunk to 143,000. Cheka administration consisted of five major departments: the Investigation Section; the Special Section (responsible for most of the Cheka's infiltration programmes); the Operation Section (the Cheka's military arm); the Commandant's Section (responsible for carrying out formal executions); and the Subsistence Section, which not only handled Cheka salaries, but oversaw what was obscurely described as Chekists' 'spiritual welfare'.

On 6 February 1922 Lenin ordered the Cheka to be renamed the GPU (short for *Gosurdarstvennoe Politicheskoe Upravlenie*, 'State Political Administration'), and in July 1923 the GPU became the OGPU. Almost all GPU and OGPU staff had worked as Cheka staff; but in accordance with its bland new name, the GPU – like the OGPU afterwards – showed itself to be an altogether more sanctimonious organisation than the Cheka had been. Cheka prisons were always called Cheka prisons; the later organisations renamed them 'houses of correction', 'houses of isolation', and 'houses of supervision'. Even before the title changes, the surveillance system after 1921 exhibited occasional mercy that before 1921 would have been unimaginable. One General Popov, when hauled into Dzerzhinsky's presence after a Cheka tip-off, berated his captor for making the Cheka an indiscriminate agent of hangings and shootings. The enraged Dzerzhinsky retorted: '*That sort of thing doesn't happen here!*'; but Popov lived to tell the tale of his encounter, as most other suspects did not, and as he himself would never have done in the Cheka's earlier days. Altogether more typical, though, of Dzerzhinsky's later years was the arrest and execution (August 1921) of sixty-one 'conspirators' in Petrograd, among whom only one enjoyed wide contemporary fame: Nikolai Gumilev, first husband of Anna Akhmatova, and himself a poet of stature. To pleas by the literary community for Gumilev's life, Dzerzhinsky answered, with a genuine bewilderment that the more cynical and publicity-hungry Stalin never allowed himself: 'Are we entitled to make an exception of a poet and still shoot the others?'

• • • • •

In his final years Dzerzhinsky combined his Cheka-GPU-OGPU leadership with less exciting but almost equally demanding functions. He served as Trade Commissar; he directed the national railway system; he chaired the Friends of the Soviet Cinema; and he headed the Extraordinary Commission for the Struggle Against Snowdrifts. As unconcerned with popularity in these more humdrum spheres as in his best known post, he quickly mastered the smallest official detail, and felt contempt for those among his fellow Bolsheviks – the majority – who preferred theoretical blathering to administrative competence. Besides, a new generation of party bosses was by this time emerging: men such as the aforementioned Bukharin, but also Grigori Zinoviev, Lev Kamenev, Genrikh

Yagoda, Nikolai Yezhov, and Vyacheslav Mikhailovich Molotov. Several of these younger figures were, in terms of
Bolshevik tradition, *arrivistes*. None had endured anything like
the physical suffering for Communism's sake that Dzerzhinsky
had undergone. Many of them fancied themselves as intellectuals, and thus as members of a caste that the autodidact
Dzerzhinsky himself had never cared for. Most were Jews, and
though Dzerzhinsky himself had cultivated Jews' society in the
Poland of his youth, he never forgot his original Polish
Catholic upbringing. All had been born to comfortable, if not
downright rich, bourgeois families liable to irk anyone of
Dzerzhinsky's noble blood (Molotov's real name had been
Scriabin, the eponymous composer being his cousin). They
represented a future force that Dzerzhinsky, on the whole,
hated and feared.

On 20 July 1926 Dzerzhinsky, increasingly troubled by
angina pectoris – and more enslaved than ever to a mood of
après moi le déluge – addressed the yearly Plenum of the Communist Party in terms calculated to scandalise his hearers. The
noisier the protests in the auditorium, the firmer Dzerzhinsky's rebukes grew.

You all know that whatever strength I have consists in
the fact that *I have never spared myself.* You respect and
believe me because I never mince matters, and if I see
anything amiss attack it relentlessly ... It has never
ceased to astonish me how persons in the posts occupied by the People's Commissars, their deputies and
responsible subordinates should reveal so abysmal an
ignorance of those very matters in which they claim to
be expert ... You have slandered me and those who

have worked with me. Look in your hearts. You will be forced to admit that the reproaches with which you have loaded us have no basis in fact but are designed to injure us and the protective, constructive benefit we have consistently and willingly rendered the State. This is a senseless, negative tactic unworthy of anyone who would call himself a Communist. It is most injurious to the best interests of the proletariat. I must say here that the well-being of the workers is to me what a child is to its mother, the one thing I hold supremely dear … [Shouts of 'Order!'] I can see that what I have said has gone home. No doubt such candour is unpalatable; but it is not within the power of anyone here to gag me. And if anyone thinks he can disown any of the fundamental principles of Bolshevism while I am here, let him take warning! For if he attempts any such iniquity I shall have him and his destroyed.

Pandemonium among his hearers ended only when Stalin, according to unconfirmed but intrinsically plausible accounts, ordered Dzerzhinsky to 'f__k off'. Overcome with emotion at this public chastisement by one whom he had always viewed as a supporter, Dzerzhinsky staggered away from the building, went to the office which served as his bedroom, and locked himself in. A few hours later, to the amazement of those who had been peeking through the keyhole of his door, he fell dead of a heart attack.

Those who had followed him in order to scoff remained, if not to do anything so counter-revolutionary as pray, at least to mourn one whose personal dedication they could never dispute. Newspapers surrounded their front pages with black borders. At Dzerzhinsky's funeral the pallbearers included two future presidents of the Soviet Union (Anastas Mikoyan and Marshal Kliment Voroshilov), a future prime minister (Molotov), and one general secretary (Stalin). 'In Dzerzhinsky,' Stalin proclaimed as part of his graveside encomium, 'the old guard of Lenin has lost yet another of his best directors and warriors.' Less predictable was a delirious tribute voiced, whether voluntarily or under compulsion, at the other end of the penal system:

> We, the occupants of the Odessa Isolation House, met together in the club to hear the heart-rending news of the death of Felix Edmondovich Dzerzhinsky. We therefore passed a resolution asking the administration to convey our profound regrets for this irreparable loss ... in the firm faith that this terrible loss is only physical and that the great Cause to which Felix Edmondovich gave his life will continue to grow and spread until that happy day when the universe is converted to Socialism.

As to Dzerzhinsky's true achievements, the official figure for the Cheka's victims was given by the Soviet régime itself, with suspicious fussiness, as 12,733. But this number fails to take into account the approximately 100,000 anti-Bolshevik captives during the Civil War, whom Cheka squads shot and sometimes (perhaps in deliberate homage to the French Revolution) drowned in barges, or a further 29,000 Ukrainians killed by the local Cheka after 1920. Robert Conquest has estimated, on these and other indications, the total deaths at Cheka, GPU or OGPU hands to have been 200,000 between

1917 and 1923. By contrast, the total deaths at Tsarist officials' hands during the last third of the nineteenth century amounted to only ninety-four.

Dzerzhinsky's machine succeeded in generating not only carnage, but also portents. In February 1919 Socialist Revolutionary leader Maria Spiridonova, arrested by the Cheka, became the first recorded victim of Communism to undergo compulsory psychiatric hospitalisation on political grounds. A month later, Cheka units in the province of Astrakhan killed between two thousand and four thousand anti-Communists within three days. Their handiwork inspired tributes from a particularly energetic young commissar, who congratulated the Cheka for having eliminated what he called 'White Guard lice'. This commissar, little-known outside Russia during his life, would become world-famous after his death. His name: Sergei Kirov.

Stalinism: The OGPU, NKVD and Other Security Forces

Two and a half years before Dzerzhinsky's fatal collapse, Lenin had been carried off (21 January 1924) by the last in a series of massive strokes. As for Stalin, he had not yet attained world notoriety, or even world fame. Between 1924 and 1927 he still (in Eugene Lyons' expressive words) 'moved vaguely in the haze around major planets like Lenin, Trotsky, Zinoviev and Dzerzhinsky'. The uncertainty of ultimate Central Committee control at this stage proved no barrier to OGPU surveillance. OGPU bosses especially concerned themselves with monitoring unacceptable 'peasant attitudes', held by 'those obviously under the influence of counter-revolutionary cells' and, more vaguely, by 'politically backward groups'. In its

annual report for 1924, the OGPU boasted of having intercepted exactly 5,078,174 letters. A new penal code that year
extended the legal definition of a 'socially dangerous person'
to include anybody 'whose past actions *might* [emphasis added]
be considered a danger to society'. Extra legislation in 1925
included, in its Article 58, no fewer than fourteen new defini-
tions of 'counter-revolutionary' behaviour.

Vyacheslav Menzhinsky, Dzerzhinsky's immediate successor as OGPU chief, owed his elevation more to having
shared Dzerzhinsky's Polish background than to overwhelming strength of will. OGPU staff found it bizarre, after years of
Dzerzhinsky ordering them around, to receive instructions
from Menzhinsky beginning 'I humbly request ...'. He could,
apparently, speak sixteen languages; yet from the start his personality counted for much less than that of his nominal
second-in-command (and junior by seventeen years), Genrikh
Yagoda, who possessed a comprehension of agitprop techniques far beyond anything Menzhinsky knew about. Devoid
of all compassion and of most emotion (though capable *in
extremis* of behaving like a cornered rat that can mete out
savage bites and scratches before being clubbed), Yagoda –
born in 1891, the son of a Jewish pharmacist in Lodz,
Poland – knew better than to push himself forward. After
Menzhinsky's near-fatal heart attack in 1929, Yagoda wielded
all the authority he craved, without needing to fight for it.
Meanwhile he dealt with the 'Trotskyites' and 'Zinovievites'
who, having first been used by Stalin against each other, eventually shared the same scrap heap. Trotsky himself fled the
USSR in 1929, having been confined for a year to Kazakhstan's capital, Alma-Ata. Between 1928 and 1931 Zinoviev,
Kamenev, fellow Old Bolshevik Karl Radek, and ex-Prime

Minister Alexei Rykov all suffered disgrace and expulsion from the Communist Party: but not, as yet, physical violence.

Simultaneously the OGPU led what Stalin called (1929) 'the elimination of kulaks as a class'. To Stalin's régime, with its collectivist mania, the very notion of peasants being allowed to continue owning small farms was an abomination. At this early point the average kulak was likelier to be deported by OGPU squads, and to have his property set on fire, than to be killed outright (although in the depths of a Russian winter the dividing line between homelessness and death became perilously thin). By June 1930 OGPU-run prison camps accounted for no fewer than 140,000 kulaks. In such surroundings the kulak might yet be turned into a loyal and useful slave of the Revolution. After all, Lenin's New Economic Policy of 1922 had permitted a modest reintroduction of private enterprise, without thereby weakening Bolshevik rule in the merest particular. Only sufficient thoroughness in redirecting the kulaks' efforts was needed. Sometimes this thoroughness' verbal expression took oddly pompous forms, as in the September 1929 case of kulaks found to have killed their pig 'with the intention of consuming it for themselves and thus keeping it from socialist appropriation'. Not till the OGPU faced, on its own admission, eight thousand kulak revolts between January and March 1930 alone did murder become Moscow's first resort against kulaks, rather than its third or fourth. Even then, Stalin initially attributed kulaks' uprisings to the undue vigour of a few overenthusiastic functionaries 'dizzy with success' (the title of a front-page newspaper feature by him, published on 2 March).

In 1932 the truly exterminationist, deliberately engineered famine began. It quickly became, and stayed, *the* great

Soviet unmentionable. Neither Khrushchev (who helped carry it out in Ukraine) nor Gorbachev (while in office) publicly admitted to it, though Stalin privately acknowledged its occurrence in an August 1942 conversation with Churchill. At the lowest possible estimate, it killed six million. This did not stop Stalin, during the famine's early stages, from writing the remarkable first sentence to the USSR's first official culinary guide, *The Book of Healthy and Tasty Food*: 'Life has become better, life has become merrier.'

The lies that the famine elicited from Stalin's Western apologists are fairly well known. Stalin's sycophants of intellectual distinction included France's former Prime Minister Édouard Herriot and an actual OGPU victim, Maxim Gorky. The gullible Herriot compared Ukrainian agriculture to 'a garden in full bloom'; Gorky's fawning was still more systematic.

During Lenin's early reign Gorky had given Bolshevism his full support; but when Lenin's campaigns against writers took lethal forms, Gorky left the Soviet Union in disgust and went to live on Capri. There he received a stream of begging letters and telegrams, all transmitted under Yagoda's supervision, all imploring him to return to his homeland. He had, the communications assured him, nothing to fear from Lenin's successors. To soften Gorky up still further, Yagoda made sure than Gorky's secretary in Capri was an OGPU agent. In 1930 the treatment worked: Gorky made Moscow his home again. A novelist with Gorky's talent outweighed dozens of vulgar party hacks in the eyes of Stalin, who entertained no illusions about the standards of typical Bolshevik art. Gorky acquired a splendid dacha, where on a 1932 visit Stalin coined the felicitous phrase 'engineers of human souls': meaning originally by these words the role in society of writers themselves, although the aphorism quickly permitted wider connotations. Gorky justified all Stalin's hopes in him. Not only did he deny the very existence of famine; his toadying went much further than Bernard Shaw's contemporaneous efforts, in that while Shaw freely conceded Stalin's dictatorial status, Gorky viewed Stalin as a genuine democrat. He occupied the place of honour in the Soviet Writers' Union, which in 1934 publicly eulogised the Baltic–White Sea Canal death camp's idyllic conditions, the resultant published account of this locale being described years aftewards as 'the most disgraceful book in the history of literature'. OGPU control of the camp system, babbled Gorky, 'clearly demonstrates the humanism of the proletariat'. Nothing ever publicly soured Gorky on Stalinism, although Yagoda eventually – and perhaps accurately – confessed to having ordered, in June 1936, Gorky's death.

• • • • •

As of July 1934, Stalin entrusted the OGPU's functions to the NKVD (*Narodni Komissariat Vnutrennykh Del*: 'People's Commissariat for Internal Affairs'), under the directorship of Yagoda, who had been confirmed as the OGPU's head when the long-ailing Menzhinsky died in May. Less than six months after this restructuring – which in practice amounted to little more than a letterhead change – occurred the event that Robert Conquest, notwithstanding such celebrated candidates for the title as Archduke Franz Ferdinand's assassination, called 'the crime of the century'.

On 1 December 1934 Commissar Sergei Kirov – whose eulogies to Cheka-organised slaughter have already been cited – was murdered as he entered his office in the Smolny Institute of what had once been Petrograd, but in 1925 had become Leningrad. No one disputed the identity of the man who pulled the trigger: Leonid Nikolayev, an erstwhile employee of the city's Worker–Peasant Inspectorate and of its Party History Institute. Tortured by NKVD operatives into a state of insanity over the next forty-eight hours (one NKVD witness reported: 'This was not a person in his right mind, but only a sack of bones and meat … He literally went into hysterics every five minutes'), Nikolayev then underwent a trial on the night of 28–29 December, along with thirteen alleged accomplices. The process remained a strictly *in camera* affair, nothing like the show trials of later fame; within hours of its conclusion Nikolayev and all the other defendants were shot dead. In preceding weeks *Pravda* had reported the executions of ninety other Kirov murder suspects, carried out in Leningrad, Moscow and Kiev.

Stalin's complicity in Kirov's death (first gingerly mooted by Khrushchev's 1956 address to the Party Congress) is now universally admitted. Still unclear, nonetheless, are Stalin's motives and his means for the killing. The optimistic – and once widespread – notion that Kirov represented a new, humane, libertarian form of Communism colliding with Stalin's ideology has no justification in Kirov's own utterances, which were pure Stalinist boilerplate, though delivered with far greater oratorical skill than anything other Stalinists could command. But simply through being a recognisably sane administrator, rather than an intellectually pretentious scribbler of the Bukharin–Radek sort, Kirov just might have offered effective resistance to Stalin. From the vast literature on Kirov's death it appears that Yagoda must have served as an accomplice, if not (as some historians have posited) *the* accomplice. The murder's timing in relation to international events warrants note. Earlier that same year, Hitler had launched the Night of the Long Knives, which struck down not only his National Socialist rivals, but his conservative foes. Discussing the news of this bloodbath, Stalin firmly disputed colleagues' views that Hitler had over-reached himself. Untrue, said Stalin; by the purge Hitler had strengthened, not weakened, his own authority. If, in disposing of Kirov, Stalin was deliberately imitating Hitler's method, then Kirov's demise marks a rare occasion when Nazism influenced Communism, rather than the other way around.

All that can be said for certain is this: first, that Kirov's murder provided the perfect excuse for Stalin to launch his most ferocious oppression yet; second, and much less famously, that Stalin expressed admiration for the career of none other than Fouché. 'He tricked them all; he made a fool of everyone,' Stalin approvingly noted of his French predecessor. Fouché became one of only three pre-1917 leaders (Ivan the Terrible and Peter the Great being the other two) whom Stalin regarded as deserving esteem by post-1917 criteria. Stefan Zweig's biography of Fouché became a Soviet bestseller during the 1930s – which could not have happened unless the book bore, so to speak, Stalin's imprimatur – and Yagoda eventually found himself accused of 'conducting a policy *à la* Fouché'.

On 1 February 1935 every Soviet Party member had to hand in his or her card; and those who received new cards did so only after the most rigorous checks. Three years earlier, party official Mikhail Ryutin had audaciously complained in a 160-page document that Stalin was abusing his powers and should be deposed. Ryutin lived to boast of his courage, partly because Kirov had persuaded most Politburo members to oppose the death penalty in Ryutin's case. By 1935 such forbearance was unimaginable. Now began the misleadingly titled Great Terror: misleadingly titled, because it differed little from the anti-Kulak, anti-White Russian and anti-Cossack great terrors prevailing since 1917. It acquired its main significance less through its body-count than through its concentration on killing Communists instead of killing anti-Communists. Nearly all its victims belonged to the Party, supported Bolshevism as their lifelong creed, and in all too many cases praised Stalin till the end.

Equally misleading is the standard Russian term for the disaster: *Yezhovshchina,* deriving from the name of Nikolai Yezhov, who succeeded Yagoda as NKVD chief in September 1936. Contrary to what this neologism implies, the terror raged long before Yezhov's ascendancy and continued to rage long after it, nor was Yezhov ever more than Stalin's stooge. Born in 1895, and a mere five feet tall, Yezhov had held the specific title of Purge Commissar ever since 1933 (unlike Yagoda, he came from an Army and Party rather than Cheka-OGPU-NKVD background). One NKVD operative said of Yezhov, 'In my whole life I have never seen such a villain.' Surviving photographs of him show a smirking face conveying schoolboyish, rather than mature, evil: as if he were being screen-tested, anachronistically, for a film version of *Lord of the Flies.*

Yezhov's staff brought to their tasks the same dispassionate, assembly-line approach that Stalin forced upon the USSR as a whole. Dzerzhinsky-type self-flagellation became, for the NKVD's professionals, a distant memory. 'Each morning,' we are told,

when they [the NKVD killers] collected their auto-matics from the guardroom, they were given a glass of vodka. Then they loaded the day's victims onto trucks, drove them to a pit dug by a team of criminal con-victs, lined them up and started shooting …
[Sometimes they] tried to see how many they could kill with a single bullet. Then the execution squads returned to camp, put their automatics back in the guardroom, were given as much free vodka as they could drink, and slept.

• • • • •

During August 1936 the first of Stalin's three grand Moscow show trials occurred (other show trials, far less publicised, were held in other cities): its victims being Zinoviev, Kamenev, and fourteen others. (Not long before, Zinoviev had protested: 'Does Comrade Stalin know the meaning of ordinary grati-tude?' Stalin retorted: 'I do, I know very well what it is, it's a dog's disease.')

Some indication of the NKVD's industry in stitching together 'evidence' emerges from the fact that in August 1935, the régime had extended capital punishment's scope to cover children over the age of twelve; and the crimes among such children punishable by death included failure to denounce their parents. The 'heroism' three years earlier of a twelve-year-old Ukrainian boy, Pavlik Morosov, had much impressed the authorities. Young Morosov had reported his own father to the police for sheltering kulaks during the Ukrainian famine, and though other kulaks had lynched the juvenile informant, he had been posthumously hailed as a Soviet hero.

Concerning the show trials themselves, and the NKVD's role in them, Ronald Hingley's description of their purpose cannot be improved on:

The entire spectacle of the show trials may best be understood as a theatrical performance ... for which the NKVD supplied script-writers, producers, scene-shifters, stage-managers and prompters. Not less dramatic was an element often overlooked – even as he struggled to extort the required co-operation, each NKVD inquisitor knew himself to be fighting for his own life, since failure or suspected lack of vigilance on his part might drag him down with his victim. This kept the torturers on their toes.

In January 1935 Zinoviev and Kamenev had been tried in closed session for 'moral responsibility' in Kirov's death, but (to Stalin's amazement) had been sentenced only to short prison terms. Yagoda's failure to torture both men into making inventive confessions disgusted Stalin: 'You're working badly, Genrikh Grigoryevich!' he roared, reducing Yagoda to tears by his threats. Accordingly, at the August 1936 show trial, the charge sheet for Zinoviev and Kamenev included actually organising – rather than just condoning – Kirov's murder. Andrei Vyshinsky, the chief prosecutor at this trial (as at the later two), browbeat the defendants with a convert's enthusiasm.

The seventeen defendants at the second show trial (January 1937) included Karl Radek and the Deputy Commissar for Heavy Industry, Yuri Pyatakov: charged with civil as well as military sabotage, not to mention with scheming alongside

Trotsky to install a pro-Hitler government in Moscow. Yagoda had been dismissed on the preceding 29 September, the day on which Stalin sent a telegram to the Politburo.

We deem it absolutely necessary and urgent that Comrade Yezhov be nominated to the post of People's Commissar of the NKVD. Yagoda has definitely proved himself to be incapable of unmasking the Trotskyite-Zinovievite bloc. The OGPU is four years behind in this matter [because it had failed to liquidate Ryutin after his 1932 reproofs of Stalin].

Characteristically, Stalin let Yagoda dangle for months, uncertain as to how much of Stalin's favour, if any, he retained. (Stalin had similarly allowed the chief and deputy chief of the Leningrad NKVD – whose combined failure to prevent Kirov's assassination might have been expected to disgrace them immediately – to keep their jobs until 1937, though later both men were shot.) From October 1936 Yagoda held the post of Communications Commissar; the following April he was arrested and imprisoned.

The sentence for Radek, Pyatakov, and nearly all the rest – death by NKVD bullets – surprised no one. Less predictable was the fate of Pyatakov's boss, Sergo Ordzhonikidze, at this stage the most powerful non-Russian in Moscow apart from Stalin himself. By Stalinist standards Ordzhonikidze seems to have been positively conscience-stricken, and thus a danger to himself and others. In February 1937, grieving over Pyatakov's fate, he suddenly died from a self-inflicted gunshot wound, according to Khrushchev's subsequent testimony; from NKVD-inflicted injuries, according to rumour; from a heart attack, according to the implausible verdict of Health Commissar Grigori Kaminsky (himself executed only months afterwards). At any rate, his death removed from the scene the one Georgian of Stalin's own generation whom Stalin himself considered a serious rival.

It needs emphasising that the show trials – which Joseph Davies, America's first Ambassador to the Soviet Union, solemnly described as having given 'proof … beyond reasonable doubt to justify the verdict of guilty' – accounted for but a tiny proportion of Stalin's NKVD-aided butcheries. Much less publicised, but at least as significant, were such *épurations* as the shooting (on fraudulent charges of spying for the Nazis) of eight Soviet commanding officers on 11 and 12 July 1937. These victims included Marshal Mikhail Tukhachevsky, among the few Soviet soldiers capable of serious and imaginative strategic thought. The loss in terms of defence manpower is best illustrated by statistics. During the years 1936–38 fifteen out of the USSR's sixteen army commanders were executed; sixty corps commanders out of sixty-seven; 136 out of 199 divisional commanders; all seventeen army commissars; 221 out of 397 brigade commanders; all four Admirals of the Fleet; all six admirals; and nine vice-admirals out of fifteen. Little wonder that Hitler gloated to his trusted Field-Marshal Wilhelm Keitel:

The very best staff among the highest Soviet military cadres have been destroyed by Stalin. This means that the generation that is coming up to replace them still lacks the necessary minds.

Unlike the first and second show trials' victims, who – Pyatakov occasionally excepted – had confessed to whatever ludicrous accusations Vyshinsky hurled at them in court, the victims at the third trial (January 1938) showed enough defiance to ensure that Stalin henceforward abandoned the whole show trial mechanism as unnecessarily hazardous. The three leading defendants on this occasion – Bukharin, Rykov, and the once-feared Yagoda – actually dared several times to dispute the whole proceedings' justice. They rejected officialdom's description of them as the 'Bloc of Rightists and Trotskyites'. Moreover, during Vyshinsky's cross-examination, Yagoda (having been charged with murdering Gorky, murdering Menzhinsky, and attempting to murder Yezhov by having poison sprayed over the walls of Yezhov's room, as well as the more conventional crime of Third Reich espionage) repeatedly uttered such hitherto unusual phrases from the dock as 'That is not so' and 'That is not quite true.' This problem was solved the following day, when renewed overnight torture sessions left him with a permanently dislocated shoulder, and less willing than before to question Vyshinsky's abuse. Bukharin, though, maintained to the last (he and Rykov were executed on 14 March, the day before Yagoda) his innocence of the allegations against him. Most of Yagoda's leading subordinates lasted little longer than Yagoda himself did: seventeen of Yagoda's top eighteen NKVD officials were put to death under Yezhov, and when Yezhov fell from power, 101 of *his* top 122 NKVD officials were likewise dispensed with.

After the third show trial Stalin, having had all his most obvious enemies or ostensible enemies within the USSR disposed of by bullets to the brain-stem (Trotsky, sentenced to death *in absentia* at the third show trial, continued to haunt

Mexico), saw no reason to continue protecting his friends. Yezhov therefore lost his NKVD post on 21 August 1938, having been arraigned for protecting 'Trotskyites' within the NKVD itself. His *amour-propre* soothed at first with the title of Commissar for Water Transport, he was last publicly seen in January 1939, and was probably executed in early 1940; a persistent rumour nevertheless maintained that the authorities committed him to a psychiatric hospital, where he hanged himself with his underclothes.

• • • • •

Only on 8 December 1938 did Stalin formally confirm Yezhov's successor, Lavrenti Pavlovich Beria, in the NKVD chief's role that he had been fulfilling since August. Like Stalin, Beria (born on 29 March 1899) came from Georgia; he spent most of his youth either in that country or in neighbouring Armenia and Azerbaijan. While at Azerbaijan's Baku Polytechnic in 1915, he joined an illegal Marxist study group. Once Baku surrendered to Bolshevik conquest, Beria entered the local political police – known as the AzCheka – and acquired a reputation for such violence and treachery that even M.S. Kedrov complained to Moscow about him, urging his demotion, but without success. Eventually transferring from AzCheka to its Georgian counterpart (at, it seems, Orzhonikidze's behest), Beria very effectively smashed a Georgian independence movement that early in 1924 had achieved considerable victories against Bolshevik rule. The following year his Georgian Cheka superior, S.G. Mogilevsky, conveniently died in a plane crash that Beria himself was widely suspected of arranging. By the late 1920s Beria had come to know well his fellow Georgian Stalin, who several times invited Beria to his dacha – a photograph survives of Beria dandling Stalin's aghast-looking daughter Svetlana on his knee – and who promoted him in 1931 to the position of Georgian Communist Party chief. In this capacity he is thought to have shot dead (July 1936) his opposite number in the Armenian party, A.G. Khandzhian, who 'suicided' during a stormy meeting of regional apparatchiks held at Georgia's capital, Tbilisi.

Thus far Beria differed from most of Stalin's hangers-on through exceptional relish for individual brutality, rather than through any more distinctive qualities. Still, with his increasing renown came ever more prominent indications that there was more to him – or possibly less – than mere thuggee. For one thing, he showed no mature interest in Marxist-Leninist doctrine. Had circumstances placed him in some old-fashioned South American military dictatorship, or in a New York gangster racket, rather than in the USSR, he would have done just as well. For another thing, his sexual tastes made the greatest imaginable contrast with those of the puritanical Stalin. Not all the resources of totalitarian mind-control could conceal from the public Beria's enthusiasm for raping women and girls, the younger the better. A guard named Vadoraya afterwards recollected pimping for Beria on Moscow streets; during World War II Beria would admit to undergoing treatment for syphilis. His erotic habits gave Stalin – whose wife, interestingly, regarded Beria with open contempt – the perfect weapon for keeping him in line: fear of captivity. No one appreciated better than Stalin the disgust which sex criminals, and child-molesting sex criminals above all, inspire in prison populations. Years later the poet Yevgeny Yevtushenko recalled, in his autobiography, seeing Beria's 'vulture face …

half hidden by a muffler, glued to the window of a limousine as he drove slowly by the kerb hunting down a woman for the night.

Under Beria, the NKVD continued the methods of terror in which Yagoda and Yezhov had so well trained it. The actual execution rate might have dropped slightly from its 1936–38 levels (although notable post-Yezhov victims included Béla Kun, the former Hungarian Communist dictator, slain in November 1939); but the basic procedures continued.

NKVD functionaries preferred arresting victims in the earliest hours of the morning, with the result that any black car became an object of dread. Readers familiar with Dmitri Shostakovich's life will recall the nights he spent sleeping in the hallway of his block of apartments, clutching a packed suitcase so that his family would not be disturbed when the NKVD came to call for him. Surprisingly, physical torture by NKVD staff was not formally permitted till 1937: though as the means of extracting confessions already included such non-physical means as sleep deprivation and slogan-baying loudspeakers over periods of days or weeks, this lacuna scarcely cramped the NKVD's style. From 1937 occur frequent accounts of beatings with chair-legs and, in particular, the slamming of fingers in a door; when these modes of enquiry failed, individual torturers sometimes resorted to urinating on their victim, or to shoving his head into an overflowing spittoon.

For those who survived these methods, there remained the gulag: its subdivisions including Kolyma in Siberia, originally founded with the aim of employing slave labour to work the local gold mines. Kolyma became an undisputed NKVD fiefdom in 1937, the year that an NKVD detachment overthrew the camp's local ruler, Reinhold Berzin, who had become too independent of mind for Stalin's liking. Persuaded to resign by being presented with a fake edition of *Izvestia* which proclaimed that he had been admitted to the Order of Lenin, Berzin went eagerly to the local airport, where the NKVD arrested him. Soon after the plane had arrived in Moscow, he was executed.

Nadezha Mandelstam, most eloquent of Stalinism's memoirists – and widow of the poet Osip Mandelstam, whose brief and tragic life ended in a camp near Vladivostok only weeks after Beria had become the NKVD's chief executive – found the chief torment of the 1930s to be the ubiquitous, enforced mendacity:

We were capable of coming to work with a smile on our faces after a night in which our home had been searched or a member of the family arrested. It was essential to smile – if you didn't, it meant you were afraid or discontented. This nobody could afford to admit – if you were afraid, then you must have a bad conscience. The mask was taken off only at home, and then not always – even from your children you had to conceal how horror-struck you were; otherwise, God save you, they might let something slip in school.

• • • • •

Beria found the requirements of war as congenial as the demands of peace. Under the Nazi–Soviet Pact, which gave Stalin a free hand against the Baltic States and Finland, while ensuring a gratifying number of captives from that longest established of Russian enemies – namely Poland – the NKVD flourished. Its handiwork included the April 1940 Katyn Forest massacre (not revealed to the world until a German radio broadcast of April 1943) of 4,433 Polish army officers who since September 1939 had been prisoners-of-war.* Another NKVD group eliminated Willi Münzenberg, the erstwhile agitprop genius of Bolshevism, who once Stalin and Hitler had joined forces had fled to France, and whose decomposing body was found in a forest near Grenoble in August 1940. Walter Krivitsky, an actual NKVD agent who had lost faith in Stalinism and had barely managed to escape the country with his life, died by gunshot in a hotel room in Washington, DC in February 1941.

Yet easily the most famous of the NKVD's murders on foreign soil – murders which the NKVD viewed, not as an aspect of external affairs, but as a mere extension of its home front obligations – was that of Trotsky. In April 1940 Trotsky had released his last political will and testament: *Letter to the Soviet Workers*. It was couched in such vehement terms that Stalin accused Beria to his face of insufficient willingness to

---

* This massacre occurred (it is worth noting) only after established NKVD methods of torturing suspects into fraudulent confessions of 'Trotskyite-Fascist' behaviour had been tried on the victims and proven ineffectual. Old Bolsheviks like Kamenev and Zinoviev might well, as Solzhenitsyn argued, have been too morally corrupted by their doctrine to have mounted the slightest useful defence against its Stalinist manifestations; anti-Communist Poles, however harsh the treatment they received, broke less easily.

eradicate the letter's author. An initial NKVD murder attempt on 24 May, by submachine-gunners wearing fake police uniforms and emptying three hundred rounds of ammunition into Trotsky's home, failed to kill or even to wound its intended target. Only when NKVD agent and Spanish Civil War veteran Ramon Mercader (alias 'Frank Jacson', alias 'Jacques Mornard', alias – more grandiloquently – Jaime Ramon Mercader del Rio Hernández) arrived in Mexico and wormed his way into Trotsky's confidence could the deed be properly done. On 20 August Mercader, posing as a heterodox Marxist journalist, requested Trotsky's opinion of an article that he had written. As Trotsky prepared to read the typescript, Mercader drew forth the ice-pick which he had concealed on his person – none of Trotsky's bodyguards had bothered to frisk him – and brought it down upon the skull of his victim, who died in hospital the following day. Amid the Battle of Britain headlines which at the time consumed most of the Western world's newsprint, Trotsky's end was scarcely noticed.

• • • • •

On 3 February 1941 Stalin, still refusing to believe (despite the admonitions of Churchill, among others) that Hitler intended to invade Russia, restructured the NKVD. From that day, it was subsumed into a larger organisation, the NKGB, under the command of a staunch Beria ally, V.N. Merkulov. Beria himself remained in official favour: as witnessed by Stalin's decision on 30 June to include him in a Defence Committee that had only four other members (Stalin, Molotov, Marshal Voroshilov, and a future prime minister, Georgi Malenkov). Henceforward, even as the Red Army suffered two million

165

casualties in the winter of 1941–42, the NKVD concentrated on less immediately hazardous tasks: on sabotage; on controlling the Special Branches of Eastern Europe's partisan forces, most notably Yugoslavia's; on hunting down individual German agents ('a pursuit', Ronald Hingley drily remarks, 'for which extensive peacetime experience in inventing imaginary German spies was not the ideal preparation'); and on deporting hundreds of thousands of 'objectively pro-Fascist' subject peoples – notably Chechens, Ingush, Kalmuks, Balkars and Karachays – in 1943–44.

Beria, though rewarded in July 1945 with the title of Marshal of the Soviet Union, appeared to be in danger the following January when a military rival, Colonel S.N. Kruglov, ousted him from his NKVD post. That Beria was less at risk than his demotion might have indicated emerges from the fact that notwithstanding this snub – and the renaming (March 1946) of the NKVD as the MVD, the NKGB becoming at the same time the MGB – Beria continued to enjoy the unofficial honorific of 'Atom Bomb Tsar': a tribute to his interest in nuclear science ever since the mid-1940s. When the first Soviet bomb was exploded at the Semipalatinsk testing ground (Kazakhstan) on 29 August 1949, those in the observation tower included Beria. And once his chief opponent within the Politburo, Culture Commissar Andrei Zhdanov, had died that same month – possibly helped to his grave by NKVD hirelings – Beria led the campaign against Zhdanov's surviving supporters, whom he accused of counter-revolutionary activism. These supporters, including such Leningrad bosses as N.A. Voznesenky (an Atom Bomb Commissariat member, who also headed the economic bureaucracy known as Gosplan), came under dire suspicion during late 1949 and early 1950 for ostensibly encouraging a breakaway Leningrad-based movement to weaken Moscow's hold. In the resultant 'Leningrad Affair' most of the accused, notably Voznesensky himself, were put to death; several whom the NKVD did not dispose of were forced, like Voznesensky's own brother, to take their own lives.

By this time friend and foe alike viewed Beria as the likeliest heir to Stalin: a role that became growingly tantalising, and growingly dangerous, as Stalin's own arteriosclerotic final years adumbrated an overt return to the intra-Party slaughter of 1936–39. A particular risk for Beria lay in his long-standing association with the Jewish Anti-Fascist Committee, which had enjoyed limitless favourable publicity in 1941–45 within the Soviet Union, but which Stalin regarded as eminently dispensable after Yalta. In November 1948 Stalin abolished the committee; four years later, several of its former leaders were shot on his orders, another prominent committee member having already died in a car 'accident'.

Distrust of the Jew had bubbled away for years in Stalin's private life. He especially resented Jews' disproportionate representation in pre-Stalinist leadership circles, as well as in most Soviet administrative departments; they had been particularly prominent in the Ukrainian Cheka. With Hitler's eclipse, Stalin's pretence of philo-Semitism – which in 1931 had led him to call anti-Jewish attitudes 'the most dangerous vestige of cannibalism' – no longer needed upholding. As early as 1944, Stalin had called and addressed a meeting of Politburo members, defence industry leaders, and regional party bosses. There he urged a 'more cautious' policy towards appointing Jews, while on the same occasion Malenkov demanded 'heightened alertness' concerning possible sabotage by Jewish cadres. A later memorandum, signed by Malenkov, specified which jobs Jews should never be given. Stalin might well have suspected Beria of being himself Jewish; others certainly did, though no clear evidence has survived to justify or to invalidate this belief. In 1951 and 1952 Stalin removed from office Beria's supporters within the Georgian Communist Party's Central Committee, while enforcing much more spectacular retribution upon Czech Communists thought to favour Beria. One of these Czechs, Rudolf Slánský, went on trial in Prague (November 1952) along with ten other Jews and three Gentiles. The charges, at once nebulous and capital, included not just those old faithfuls 'Trotskyism' and 'Fascism', but the comparative novelty 'Titoism' – deriving from Marshal Tito's anti-Stalinist histrionics in the Yugoslavia of 1948–49 – and a new emphasis upon most of the defendants' Jewishness. All except two of those in the dock were hanged the following month; and few would have given long odds on Beria's survival, though he surprised observers by retaining his Politburo position while the Prague trials did their worst.

Stalin's last months proved, in some respects, his strangest. On 13 January 1953 the front pages of both *Izvestia* and *Pravda* announced the discovery, and foiling, of a new plot to murder Stalin: the so-called 'Doctors' Plot'. This took the form of an accusation by Kremlin Hospital physician and MGB informer Lydia Timashuk against nine (including six Jewish) medical practitioners. According to Timashuk – who reported her allegations to Deputy MGB Chief M.D. Ryumin, and is also said to have notified Stalin in her own handwriting – the suspects not only had aimed to kill Stalin along with several Red Army marshals, but had already poisoned Zhdanov and former General Shcherbakov. In repeated articles over subsequent weeks, for the first time, the Soviet press openly criticised a security police boss for laxity: its three main targets being Beria, the Beria loyalist Merkulov, and Merkulov's successor, Viktor Abakumov. Amid the resultant hysteria a play about Pavlik Morozov, the pubescent stool-pigeon of 1932, was staged to packed houses; Timashuk meanwhile became a member of the Order of Lenin. Then, on 22 February, the media campaign stopped as suddenly as it had begun: perhaps halted by Stalin falling fatally ill on that day, although some historians credit him with being well enough to attend the Bolshoi Ballet's *Swan Lake* production less than a week later, and even with working at his desk as late as 2 March. However that may be, he breathed his last on 5 March, Beria having typically alternated between solicitous attendance at Uncle Joe's deathbed – where he frantically kissed the old man's hand – and spitting on the floor once Stalin had lost consciousness.

The Post-Stalin Interregnum

With Stalin gone, power theoretically devolved to a triumvirate comprising Beria, Molotov and Malenkov. In practice the hour belonged to Beria alone, and he knew it. He announced the release of all the surviving doctors whom Timashuk's testimony had convicted; he kept out of power Stalin's inordinately ambitious private secretary, A.S. Poskrebyshev; he reinstated the Georgian party officials whom Stalin had deprived of their jobs two years before; and he expelled Timashuk from the Order of Lenin's ranks. Indeed, he went so far that some, farcically in view of his background, have called him a born-again liberal.

How small a contrast this febrile activity made with

blatant old-style Stalinism became obvious in June 1953, when East German workers took at face value his vague chatter about increased autonomy for nations within the Soviet empire, and went on strike in protest against Moscow's demands for unrealistically high manufacturing quotas. To this unconscionable insubordination, the 'born-again liberal' Beria responded in exactly the way that every other Stalinist over succeeding decades would respond: he sent in the Red Army, which murdered two dozen protestors, wounded several hundred others, and incarcerated more than a thousand suspected sympathisers with the rebels. His government had, in Brecht's celebrated (if surreptitious) witticism, 'passed a vote of no confidence in the people, and appointed another'. But that a popular uprising should have been allowed to menace the East German régime at all, however dismally the uprising failed, constituted evidence to Beria's rivals that they could no longer trust him to keep order on Soviet-controlled soil. Most vocal of these rivals was Khrushchev. Already approaching sixty, he saw his own hopes of supreme rule (and quite possibly of staying alive) fading if Beria remained long in power. With varying swiftness, other Politburo leaders – Malenkov, Molotov, Mikoyan, and Defence Commissar Nikolai Bulganin – decided to support Khrushchev. Their resolve increased with their anger at Beria's personal crassness, revealed afresh in his withering scorn for East Germany's administration: 'It's only kept in being by Soviet troops,' Beria pointed out, 'even if we do call it the "German Democratic Republic".' This accurate yet discourteous assessment of the GDR's leadership scandalised Beria's colleagues. 'I strongly object to such an attitude to a friendly country,' snorted Molotov.

Beria's arrest occurred on 26 June, but became public

knowledge only with announcements in *Pravda's* 10 July edition that the police strongman had been charged with 'criminal anti-Party and anti-Soviet activities', with infringing 'Socialist legality' by displays of 'bourgeois nationalism', and with having been an anti-Bolshevik spy back in 1919–20. Thereafter no one is known to have seen him except those who killed him.

Officially Beria was, and is, said to have been tried in an emergency Supreme Court session of 18–23 December 1953, after which he met the fate to which he had condemned so many others. A transcript published in English in 1992 purports to detail the July Central Committee sessions that determined Beria's fate. (Beria's attackers place, in this transcript, exceptional emphasis upon their victim's sheer vulgarity: the clear implication being that if only he had minded his table manners and boned up on some serious Marxist-Leninist dialectic, his crimes would have been eminently forgivable.) Nonetheless, Beria's own son always insisted that his father – whose official death date is given in most sources as 23 December – had really been executed at the time of his arrest, or no more than a few days afterwards. Six months does seem an impossibly long time for the party chiefs to have delayed acting against him once they had toppled him. As Tbilisi journalist Georgii Bezirgani put it, so long as Beria was living,

> even under the heaviest guard in the brick army
> bunker, neither Malenkov, Khrushchev, Molotov,
> nor Mikoyan could sleep peacefully in their private
> dachas.

Khrushchev, for his part, developed an extraordinary fondness for giving different accounts of Beria's end, changing his story according to his audience's likely reaction. To Italian Communists in 1956 he boasted of having been present at a Party meeting when Beria was felled by a flying tackle from, and then choked to death by, Malenkov, Mikoyan and others. To a French Socialist delegation (also in 1956) he averred that at this same meeting Beria died, not by strangulation, but by gunfire. *The Great Soviet Encylopædia* took a blander approach to the problem of eliminating Beria. Unable to reveal the truth of how he had died, it simply pretended that he had never been born. Subscribers to the encylopædia's periodic updates were instructed in 1954

> to cut out with scissors or razor blade certain pages containing Beria's picture and the offending article. These were to be replaced by other pages specially supplied and including material on the German diarist Friedrich Berkholtz, together with photographs of the [no less alphabetically convenient] Bering Sea, showing a whaler towing two dead whales and several dead walruses on an ice floe.

After Beria

During the anti-Beria reaction from 1953 to 1982, two iron rules dominated Soviet political policing. First, it would always be subordinated (theoretically at least) to the Communist Party, rather than enjoying that direct access to the supreme Soviet ruler which had always characterised Dzerzhinsky and his successors; secondly, no political police chief could ever again lead the Soviet Union. Indeed, becoming such a chief, or even the likelihood of becoming such a chief, was widely considered the kiss of career death. From this it follows that political policing no longer attracted *en masse* the USSR's front-line ideologists or even its front-line administrators. By the lofty standards of a Beria or a Yagoda, let alone the non-pareil Dzerzhinsky, subsequent surveillance bosses tended to be grey figures indeed.

The first of these grey figures has appeared earlier in this tale: Kruglov, who from July 1953 ran the combined MGB-MVD department now known as the MVDLP. But this arrangement lasted less than nine months. On 13 March 1954 – as a sign of that almost spastic administrative reshuffling which would characterise the whole of Khrushchev's reign – the principal security organisation formally acquired the name that it would keep for the next thirty-seven years: in full, *Komitet Gosudarstvennoy Bezopasnosti* (Commissariat for State Security). In other words, the KGB. Consisting of seventeen sub-sections and able to call on 300,000 troops of its own – not to mention the news agency *TASS* and the trade-oriented front organisation Amtorg – the KGB had a legal obligation to notify local party secretaries before making arrests. This seldom presented undue difficulties, given the friendship between its first chief, Ivan Serov, and his next-door neighbour, the Supreme Soviet's chief legal authority, Procurator-General R.A. Rudenko. A subordinate of Serov's, double-agent Oleg Penkovsky (one of the CIA's most valuable plants), later describe the two men's dealings thus:

One would drop into the other's flat in the evening for a drink, and together they would decide who should be put in gaol and who should be shot. Very convenient.

Under such an arrangement Serov could not hope for the individual power that Dzerzhinsky and Yezhov once wielded; his lack of intellectual sophistication guaranteed his limits, at a time when Khrushchev had begun spouting the attitudes of what later came to be called 'socialism with a human face'. To quote Penkovsky again, Serov 'knows only how to interrogate people, imprison them and shoot them'. In the dawning television age, this *curriculum vitæ* was not quite enough. With the deposition from the prime ministry of Serov's – and Beria's – former ally Malenkov in February 1955, Serov's political significance suffered a further blow. December 1958 saw him transferred to the KGB's rival bureaucracy: GRU, centre of Red Army intelligence. Five years later, after Penkovsky's cover had been blown and Penkovsky himself executed, a guilt-stricken Serov blew his brains out.

Taking Serov's KGB place was the forty-year-old Alexander Shelepin, outwardly a more affable figure, for all his fundamental steeliness (Solzhenitsyn called him 'Iron Shurik'). Apt to use the word 'request' instead of his predecessor's 'demand' when issuing instructions to staff, he struck Khrushchev as gratifyingly docile on issues that mattered (despite his reformist gestures in dismissing various KGB Stalinists); and he lacked the overt aggression of his vociferating second-in-command V.Y. Semichastny. Born in 1924, Semichastny took over the directorship from Shelepin on 14 November 1961, when the latter joined the Central Committee. Three years beforehand he had achieved his first Western headlines when – in language not publicly heard from Moscow apparatchiks since Zhdanov's 'anti-formalism' crusade of 1948–49 – he frenziedly assailed Boris Pasternak

over the Western publication of *Dr Zhivago*, for which Pasternak had won (but had been compelled to reject) the 1958
Nobel Prize. 'Even a pig,' Semichastny complained, 'does not
shit where it eats.' The anti-*Zhivago* campaign became a KGB
obsession during the last few years of Pasternak's life, and
afterwards. Pasternak died in May 1960; within four months
agents arrested the novelist's mistress, Olga Ivinskaya, and
accused her of currency speculation, because Pasternak had
bequeathed to her and to her daughter – arrested in September – most of his Western royalties.

In an increasingly xenophobic KGB, Pasternak's evil
consisted partly of his Jewish blood, a feature he shared with
another celebrated author subjected to KGB harassment and
worse: Joseph Brodsky. During February 1964 in Leningrad,
Brodsky went on (show) trial under newly imposed laws
against 'parasitism'. As Hingley commented, the defendant
'was already a distinguished translator and poet, but these are
not disciplines in which norm-fulfilment can easily be meas-
ured'; and to the surprise of no one except those Western
fellow travellers taken in by loose Khrushchevite talk of an
artistic 'thaw', the judges condemned Brodsky to five years'
hard labour. Every feature of Khrushchev's régime suggesting
an inclination to mercy – for instance, the mid-1950s early
release programme for several categories of gulag prisoner –
acquired a counterbalancing feature of steadily maintained,
and in some areas increased, internal repression. Soldiers murdered at least seventy-six female inmates at the Kingir camp
on 17 May 1954; dozens of striking labourers in the city of
Novocherkask (the exact death toll remains unclear) were
mown down by KGB troops during August 1962. Nor did the
captivity which U2 pilot Francis Gary Powers experienced

after his arrest in Sverdlovsk (May 1960) suggest a basic ame-
lioration in political prisoners' conditions, though it is true
that the authorities commuted his original ten-year sentence
to two years once they had agreed to exchange him for a
KGB agent behind American bars. Making ribbons and lip-
stick without State permission became, under Khrushchev, a
capital offence, accounting for several of the approximately
three hundred executions for 'economic crimes' carried out
between 1961 and 1964. Jews, who made up less than 2 per
cent of the USSR's total population, made up 30 per cent of
those put to death.

None of this precipitated Khrushchev's downfall on
13 October 1964, an event as unexpected in the West as it was
widely prophesied within the USSR. Admittedly, the atro-
cious grain harvest of 1963 much weakened Khrushchev's
domestic position; the supply of ever-compliant journalists for
hiding details of famine from Western newspaper readers had
thinned out somewhat over the three decades since Ukraine's
agrarian genocide. (Most of those who in 1933 had barracked
for Soviet Russia now lusted after Third World revolutionary
doctrine, above all, after Mao's China, which in August 1960
had flounced out of its alliance with the Soviets, citing
Moscow's 'bourgeois deviationism'.) In Khrushchev's last year
of office, for the first time since World War II, the Soviet bloc
actually imported food. But that disgrace he could have survived. Even the Cuban missile crisis and its aftermath did not
doom him (for had not Lenin and Stalin turned foreign policy
disasters into foreign policy triumphs?). His main blunder lay
in antagonising Shelepin and Semichastny, who joined forces
with their fifty-year-old KGB colleague Yuri Vladimirovich
Andropov. Ambassador to Hungary during the 1956 uprising,

Andropov was haunted all his life by one particular image from that event: the spectacle, from his embassy window, of Hungarian security officers being hanged from lamp-posts. These lynchings confirmed him in his view that Khrushchev was insufficiently tough for the top job. Years afterwards the dictator's son, Sergei Khrushchev, wailed:

> I had always assumed that the KGB ... [was] there to help us. Suddenly it was no longer the great protector but the great shadower, knowing our every move.

To the question of what could be done should Khrushchev decide to fight against his challengers, Andropov responded by invoking Stalinism's zenith: 'If Khrushchev is stubborn, we shall show him documents which bear his signature about arrests which took place between 1935 and 1937.' In fact the great bear surprised his hunters by his willingness to go into hibernation. As a reward for departing quietly, he kept his freedom, and received without fail a pension of five hundred roubles each month until his death on 11 September 1971.

Andropov and His Successors

Just as a triumvirate had followed the end of Stalin's reign, so a triumvirate followed the end of Khrushchev's. The party secretaryship went to Leonid Brezhnev, who had misleadingly presented himself as an amiable lightweight, and who quickly saw off the leadership hopes of his colleagues Alexei Kosygin and Nikolai Podgorny. Meanwhile Semichastny remained in charge of KGB operations, with Central Committee member Shelepin to vouch for him. Neither Semichastny nor

Shelepin, though, achieved the protracted tenure which both were widely credited with having ensured for themselves. Shelepin fell so ill in May and June 1967 as to require extended hospitalisation; meanwhile, Semichastny lost most of his influence after allowing Stalin's daughter, Svetlana, to defect to America, and after botching the KGB's attempt to kidnap her from her New York sanctuary. These lapses failed to please Brezhnev, who continued to resent Semichastny's outright refusal in 1964 to kill Khrushchev with his own hands, a course of action that Brezhnev had then regarded as indispensable. (The most Semichastny agreed to do was to place a bugging device in Khrushchev's office telephone, which he did.) Both Semichastny and Shelepin lost their jobs in June 1967, though in the prevailing climate of comparative Soviet moderation, both avoided execution or even imprisonment. Semichastny faded from view, while Shelepin was obliged to accept a post thoroughly demeaning to anyone of his abilities: chairmanship of the USSR's trade union council. Once in this position, he found to his consternation that his predecessor had installed in the council's head office a private massage parlour. (A comeback attempt that Shelepin made in 1975, when Brezhnev suffered a stroke and looked likely to die, ended in ridicule when Brezhnev recovered.)

Andropov, by this time thoroughly disillusioned with Semichastny's bungling and fundamental lack of interest in surveillance, took his place as KGB chairman. Among post-Beria police chiefs in the Soviet Union, Andropov ranked as far and away the most capable and the most intelligent. He committed what amounted to heresy in Soviet ranks by giving frequent off-the-cuff speeches to TV reporters and party faithful: a mode of expression that Shelepin had occa-

the engineers of human souls

sionally tried, but one eschewed by all other leading 1960s
Soviet politicians, who retained their long-standing habit of
droning forth from prepared scripts. This intermittent evidence of human feeling inspired sanguine journalists in
Newsweek and *Time* to babble on about Andropov the 'closet
liberal', who, when not seeking 'friendly discussions with dissident protestors', would passionately collect recordings of
Glenn Miller and other American bandleaders. (Almost two
decades afterwards, *The New York Times'* 16 November 1982
issue saluted Andropov's splendid grasp of the English language and his discriminating taste in cognac.)

In one respect, despite themselves, the Fourth Estate's
useful idiots proved right. Andropov had a far more penetrat-
ing intellect than his colleagues, and (within the strict limits of
Marxist-Leninist philosophy) a genuine knack for original
strategic thought. With an alacrity that no other apparatchik
at the time could equal, Andropov perceived the changes
needed in the KGB's – and by extension the USSR's – entire
approach if Khrushchev's promise to the West, 'We will bury
you', were to become a reality. He appreciated, to an extent
that hacks like Brezhnev could not, the hopelessness of repeating the 1930s successes in winning the Western intelligentsia
over to supporting Soviet imperialism. What was needed
(Andropov saw) was not *positive* propaganda for anything, let
alone for anything as economically rachitic and ethically
objectionable as the Soviet Union, but a steady diet of negative propaganda against all Communism's main opponents: a
diet, that is, of disinformation. This diet Andropov perfected,
without inventing it. Henceforth every serious, consistent
anti-Communist Western leader or potential leader – particularly if he dared dispense with Queensberry Rules when

179

fighting the Left – would be subjected to The Treatment, whether bellowed directly from Moscow radio, or disseminated more subtly through Western broadsheets and United Nations fora. Spain's General Franco; Portugal's Dr Salazar; Rhodesia's Ian Smith; Germany's Defence Minister Franz-Josef Strauss (disgraced for daring to arrest journalists who had leaked confidential NATO information); later, and most spectacularly of all, Chile's General Pinochet: every significant shaper of Western opinion would be compelled to regard these figures as Princes of Darkness, or lose his job. Such comprehensive demonising had the merit, from Andropov's viewpoint, of leaving the average Westerner as ignorant of his historical ignorance as were most of Andropov's own countrymen.

The urgent need for disinformation increased after August 1968, when Soviet tanks ended the Prague Spring. Andropov feared that even the ludicrously compromised Czech leader Alexander Dubček – 'our Sasha', the KGB called him – might so far transcend his pro-Soviet background as to attract genuine and lasting Eastern bloc opposition to Moscow rule. On the home front, Andropov established the KGB's Fifth Directorate, the chief activities of which included locking up genuine or suspected anti-Soviet activists in mental hospitals. This useful mode of crushing opponents, one unaccountably neglected by Stalin, demonstrated its worth anew after the February 1966 show trial of writers Yuli Daniel and Andrei Sinyavsky (sentenced to, respectively, five and seven years in the gulag for daring to satirise the USSR in Western publications) had attracted much unfavourable comment abroad. When setting up and maintaining the USSR's psychotropic terror network, Andropov wisely relied upon such

notorious global phenomena as the medical profession's institutionalised moral cowardice, and psychiatry's clearly
incorrigible condition as – in the words of Viennese wit Karl
Kraus – 'the disease that it pretends to cure'. Soviet psychia-
trists' regular diagnoses for their victims included 'creeping
schizophrenia' and 'paranoid reformist delusions': conditions
caused, in the words of Andropov's eventual KGB successor,
Vitali Fedorchuk, by 'abnormal psyches' needing to be (what
else?) 're-educated'. As a 1979 *New York Review of Books* article on dissidents' autobiographies noted, those who survived
this demoralisation still needed to endure:

> sulfazine, haloperidol, and a murderous treatment
> which involves being wrapped up in a wet sheet that
> suffocates you as it dries. Prisoners who are driven
> crazy by these techniques automatically confirm the
> theory … that dissidence is caused by brain disease.

Never too proud to learn from fellow experts in oppression, Andropov maintained the most cordial relations with his
counterparts throughout the Warsaw Pact; above all, with the
leaders of East Germany's *Staatsicherheitsdienst,* better known
as the Stasi. Between 1950 and 1989 the Stasi not only
employed 274,000 full-time staffers to spy on their compatriots, but could call for the same purpose upon another 174,000
regular informers (*inoffizielle Mitarbeiter*), 10,000 of whom
were under the age of eighteen. All fifteen Stasi district offices
had KGB staff.

And while Cold War espionage *per se* lies outside this
volume's scope, the value that Andropov's own temperament
brought to his dealings with foreign Communists cannot be

denied. At every stage of his career – whether as party youth league hierarch in Soviet-controlled Finnish territory during World War II, in the USSR's Budapest embassy during the 1950s, or in his subsequent Moscow eminence – Andropov stayed free from the faintest hint of ideological vacillation, while he had only contempt for the very idea of personal enrichment. This incorruptibility enabled him to blackmail those comrades abroad whose probity had its limits. Andropov knew, for example, the danger posed to Italian Communist Party boss Enrico Berlinguer by the latter's long-standing involvement in his native Sardinia's real estate rackets. The brutish Georges Marchais, who ran France's Communist Party from 1972 to 1994 – he once condemned the USSR for not shedding *enough* Hungarian blood in 1956 – had a dark wartime secret: he had volunteered in 1942 for work in an air-craft factory on German soil, and stayed there for most of the next three years. Marchais concealed all proof of this war record from the West until his death in 1997, but could not conceal it from Andropov. Moreover, in 1977, when Spain's newly legalised Communist Party disturbed Andropov by its talk of possibly adopting an independent 'Eurocommunist' stance, he unleashed on it the eighty-two-year-old Spanish Civil War crone Dolores Ibarurri ('La Pasionaria'), who, after almost four decades of Moscow comfort, returned to Madrid and took up parliamentary office, still cackling her encomia to Stalinist rule. Such loyalty Andropov understood and appreci-ated. By contrast, the failure of Poland's government to stamp out rebellion in 1970 and 1980 disgusted him.

The limits of Soviet hi-tech manufacture in Andropov's day – limits which, as Clive James noted, compelled Moscow to import Western computers for printing the very *Pravda* issues that announced how hopeless Western computers were – impeded the KGB very little. One extremely simple, and most effective, device for assisting KGB work was the identity book (rather than a mere identity card) that every Soviet citizen was obliged to carry. This book – a *sine qua non* for acquiring accommodation, holding down a job, or carrying out any remotely complex financial transaction within the law – gave full details, not only of the bearer's name, date of birth, birthplace and address, but also of his previous addresses, his work history, his present employer, and whether or not he was Jewish.

Of Andropov's attitude towards those artists whom, like Solzhenitsyn, world fame protected from the Therapeutic State's worst hospital treatment, one instance will serve. In August 1971 a friend visited Solzhenitsyn's home – unaware that Solzhenitsyn had gone away – and there surprised two KGB agents who were rifling through the writer's belongings for incriminating manuscripts. Other KGB staff soon arrived and gave the friend a sound beating. Andropov issued orders to advise Solzhenitsyn 'that the participation of the KGB in this incident is a figment of his imagination'.

• • • • •

When Brezhnev died on 10 November 1982, not even the pretence of a succession crisis occurred: Andropov became Communist Party secretary the same day. To avoid accusations of Beria-style ambition, he had ceded the KGB chairmanship to Fedorchuk, who possessed neither the courage nor the intellectual gifts to make himself a serious rival. Yet Andropov's hopes of a long and peaceful term as Soviet dictator turned out to be illusory. After August 1983 he never showed himself in public. Illness, possibly liver cancer – American newspapers had reported in 1977 that liver trouble afflicted him – confined him almost entirely to his hospital bed, although in September he roused himself for long enough to dictate a tirade against the USA's alleged decision to disguise a spy plane of its own as a commercial passenger vehicle. (The vehicle in question was actually the Korean Air Lines jet that the Soviets had themselves shot down on 1 September over the Sea of Japan, killing all 269 on board.) On 9 February 1984 he died, aged sixty-nine.

• • • • •

Fedorchuk's successor as KGB chief, Viktor Chebrikov, survived not only Andropov's death but the still briefer rule of Party Secretary Konstantin Chernenko (February 1984 to March 1985) with his political power intact. Gorbachev's advent, far from diminishing Chebrikov's privileges, confirmed them. In September 1985 Chebrikov, with Gorbachev's permission, allowed Yelena Bonner – wife of the physician, dissident and Nobel laureate Andrei Sakharov – to leave the internal exile to which she and her husband had been separately sentenced. The announcement of such clemency occurred less for humanitarian reasons than because Chebrikov concluded that Sakharov on his own would be easier to browbeat. As it happened, neither Sakharov nor Bonner actually gained any freedom till December 1986; and when Sakharov used his new liberty to recommend in public that Gorbachev permit non-Communist political parties while reining in the KGB, Gorbachev dismissed such moonshine with open scorn. He

184

continued to dismiss it throughout 1989, as first Warsaw, then Budapest, then East Berlin, then Prague gave up the struggle to uphold Soviet rule by force. On 8 December 1989 Sakharov endeavoured to present Gorbachev with a pile of more than ten thousand telegrams, all imploring an end to one-party rule within the USSR. Gorbachev brushed him aside. Six days later Sakharov was dead, of 'a heart attack'.

• • • • •

Back in 1987 Chebrikov had signed a fresh pact with Stasi chief Erich Mielke, proclaiming – in language of Stalinist barbarity – the need for increased domestic action against 'military-political situations created by the adventurous policy of American imperialism'. Yet in September 1988, Chebrikov resigned from the KGB chairmanship in favour of erstwhile Andropov aide and overt hardliner Vladimir Kryuchkov. Little known in the West for most of his three years in office, Kryuchkov devoted much of his energy to improving the KGB's image domestically as well as outside the Soviet Union. The resultant public relations campaign included a beauty contest for the service's less obviously elephantine females, with the winner solemnly crowned 'Miss KGB'. Such novelties helped distract the public mind from new legislation of May 1991 that greatly increased KGB powers of arrest and wiretapping.

The following August, Kryuchkov led the coup attempt which resulted in Gorbachev being almost universally portrayed in the West as a courageous liberal hijacked by extremists. (In Russia itself, such Western gullibility inspired only the most hollow mirth.) Along with fellow conspirators including Boris Pugo – still smarting from his recent loss of Latvia's KGB chairmanship – and Defence Minister Dmitri Yazov, Kryuchkov kept Gorbachev under house arrest; broadcast announcements that Gorbachev had resigned through the ill-health that would undoubtedly be his if he did *not* resign; and vowed to arrest seven thousand KGB targets, not a single one of whom was brought into custody. Once Gorbachev had been released, Pugo and three other plotters died, ostensibly by suicide, while Yazov told his captors: 'I am such an old idiot. I've really f__ked up.' For fellow captive Kryuchkov a peculiarly personal humiliation lay ahead: on 21 August, when in the evening

a heavy crane arrived in front of the Lubianka and, before a cheering crowd, hoisted the giant statue of Felix Dzerzhinsky by a noose around his neck, toppled him from his pedestal and dragged him away.

The hurt to Kryuchkov's pride took little time to salve. Freed from gaol along with Yazov in early 1993, Kryuchkov received a formal pardon in December of that year.

• • • • •

After Kryuchkov's downfall the directorship passed to one Vadim Bakatin, who during his short tenure ostentatiously sacked his own son, even as he retained almost every other KGB staffer. Officially the KGB ended on 11 October 1991, when a decree of the Soviet State Council declared it abolished. On the following 26 November, Boris Yeltsin announced that domestic security would be monitored by a

186

new body, the FSA. Today the FSB (*Federal'naya Sluzhba Bezopasnosti*), as Russia's political police has called itself since April 1995, denies any resemblance to its Soviet forebears. Such denials become hard to sustain when, at the opening in April 2001 of a Moscow museum devoted to Soviet surveillance, tour guides sing to *Agence France-Presse* staff the praises of Dzerzhinsky, who gets the KGB Hall of Fame's pride of place:

> 'Dzerzhinsky knew a revolution could not succeed without repression and bloodshed', your guide tells you: 'Think of the French Revolution.'

The more obvious atrocities by Yagoda, Yezhov and Beria are acknowledged in the museum's displays. After about 1960 doublespeak resumes, such crimes as the hospitalisation of Brezhnev-era dissidents being ignored altogether.

As of March 2001, the veteran Semichastny remained very much alive. An issue during that month of *The Moscow Times* carried an interview with the old man, in which he reflected on his glory days under Khrushchev. Moreover, at the time this chapter is being written, neither Russia's President Putin nor its recently retired Prime Minister Yevgeny Primakov has expressed the slightest remorse over – or sustained the slightest career inconvenience from – his decades-long KGB employment. (Contrast this situation with the fate that would inevitably overtake any leader who had dared work for the Gestapo.) Perhaps the last words should go to the brilliant, iconoclastic Moscow journalist Yevgenia Albats, who wrote in 1994:

For the most part, the security people go on doing what they were doing before, albeit with decreasing enthusiasm as the atmosphere becomes more chaotic … In an interview with me, Bakatin explained: 'Everyone says, Bakatin destroyed the KGB system. For God's sake, that's not true – go to Kazakhstan and you'll see; not a single hair of a single officer's head has fallen. Or go to Kyrgyzstan – everything's stayed just the way it was. Same in the Moscow Directorate … All the structures remained the same.'

show me a no-man not six feet under:
SURVEILLANCE UNDER GERMAN NATIONAL SOCIALISM

> When we told Göring that the Western press all con-
> sidered the Nazis to be a group of yes-men, he said
> 'Well, that was certainly true, but show me a no-man
> who is not six feet under the ground.'
>
> *John K. Lattimer, American army surgeon, interviewing*
> *Göring at the Nuremberg trials, 1946*

Germanic Exceptionalism

ONE FACTOR UNITES all the societies dealt with in
previous chapters: a clearly defined, centuries-old,
uncontested seat of administration. The opponents of
Elizabeth I, of the Jacobins, of Napoleon, of Stalin, never disputed the primacy of their respective countries' capitals:
merely the right of that capital's current governing class to
command allegiance. With the history of German surveillance we have a wholly different case: a parvenu among
European countries, with (before the unification processes of

1871) no undisputed capital at all, and consisting of twenty-five major states as well as another two dozen minor realms.

That this loose federal arrangement worked as peacefully, on the whole, as it did was largely the result of a collective cultural tradition: the horrors, both genuine and mythical, of the Thirty Years' War (1618–48). In Germans' folk memory, this disaster filled a role similar to – though far stronger and more tenacious than – the Wars of the Roses in Elizabethans' outlook. Prevalent fear that an all-consuming civil conflagration would recur helped to ensure that the petty German kings, princes, margraves, landgraves and grand dukes usually carried out government not so much with the consent, as with the apathy, of the governed. The subject feared making undue demands for his own rights; the ruler feared taking undue measures to frustrate those rights. As British historian Sir Charles Petrie pointed out in 1952, Germany's pre-1871 dynasties

> naturally regarded their position in a different light from their contemporaries in London, Paris, and Madrid. They might ape the fashions of [Louis XIV's] Versailles, even to the extent of maintaining official mistresses for ornament rather than for use, but the broad national and popular basis upon which the Western monarchies rested was quite impossible for them to achieve.
>
> This fact drove them to rely upon military support to an extent unknown to the West of the Rhine, and military they remained. The memoirs of English and French visitors to Germany in the eighteenth and early nineteenth century are full of references to the great display of uniforms to be found there, and some

of the princelings, like the Landgrave of Hesse-Cassel, turned their dominions into establishments for the production and supply of mercenaries, which unpopular governments, like the Whig oligarchy in Great Britain, found extremely useful as police in times of crisis. A few of the German dynasties made themselves popular, either because they appealed to the particularist sentiment of those over whom they ruled, or because of the personal qualities of their members, but the principle which they represented aroused no great enthusiasm, and they were regarded as the countryman looks on the squire, not as the subject reverences his sovereign. On the other hand, there was equally no resentment against them, for they were not foreign, like the princes of contemporary Italy, and their shortcomings were those of their fellow-countrymen.

Such an administrative climate could hardly be conducive to engendering Walsinghams and Fouchés, let alone Ivan the Terribles. It is true that in Prussia, Frederick the Great's reign (1740–86) did see a substantial – by eighteenth-century standards – amount of political police work. Yet even at its best organised, this procedure always took second place to both Frederick's prowess on the battlefield, and his equally renowned legal codifying, which (at least in theory, and often in practice also) guaranteed his subjects' freedom of conscience. Even Frederick's incomparably harsher compatriot Bismarck, for all his eagerness during the 1860s to humiliate rival kingdoms such as Hanover, took great care after 1871 to observe the military, judicial and legislative prerogatives of most other German states.

the unsleeping eye

For something like proto-Fouchéan snooping we must
turn, not to the governments of Germany proper, but to the
Habsburgs, and above all to the eighteenth- and early nineteenth-century Austrian empire over which they ruled. By its
sheer ethnic, linguistic and religious heterogeneity – it then
comprised those lands now known as the Czech Republic, Slo-
vakia, Hungary, Slovenia, Croatia, northern Italy, and southern
Poland as well as modern Austria itself – this empire encouraged
centrifugal subversiveness. That encouragement, in turn,
induced a corresponding determination on the Viennese government's part to guard its own rights. Frederick the Great's
almost exact contemporary Maria Theresa, Austrian Empress
and Hungarian King from 1740 till 1780,* not only introduced
a comprehensive and effective censorship system but (as a corol-
lary of her hatred for all individualist excess) set up equally
enthusiastic overseeing of her subjects' morals. She it was who
conceived Austria's 'Chastity Commission', to whom she
entrusted the task of making certain that unmarried or widowed
women forsook fleshly delights. While this commission no
more stamped out all female licentiousness than today's drink-
driving police units stamp out all alcohol abuse, it managed to
become – like those units – a recognised nuisance factor. Her
reign also witnessed the founding of Vienna's *Geheime Kabinets-
Kanzlei*, which intercepted every item of correspondence that
the national post office handled, whether intended for a recipient within Austria itself, or for a foreign address.

* King, not Queen: since the laws governing Hungary's throne (which had
remained in the Habsburgs' gift for the preceding two hundred years) did not
permit female regnal succession, Maria Theresa observed the legal fiction of
her masculine status when on Hungarian soil.

Much more systematic internal security operations occurred under Maria Theresa's, son Joseph II, (reigned 1780–90), who considered his mother insufferably tractable, and who conducted his whole adult life according to the doctrine afterwards enunciated by English satirist A.P. Herbert: 'Let's stop somebody from doing something.' In 1782 Joseph appointed a trusted bureaucrat, Count Anton Pergen, as the head of his secret police network. Demanding that this network's very existence be concealed from the public, Joseph also ordered Pergen and his staff to maintain 'reliable information as to the true feelings of the subjects, so as to be able to take the proper measures … and to be able to uncover and destroy the hidden enemies who are dangerous to the public safety'. To this end, Pergen founded on Joseph's instructions a national identity system of registering the entire populace, as well as enforcing the Emperor's increasingly obsessive desire for legislative meddling. Joseph's six thousand-odd edicts covered such arcana as the citizenry's poltroonish reluctance to reuse coffins; householders' criminal failure to put clear street numbers on their properties; shameful extravagance in the purchase of candles; and peasants' deplorable habit of giving themselves stomach trouble by eating gingerbread. In Joseph's Austria, 'servants were to inform on their masters; clerks on their departmental chiefs; priests on their bishops … and coachmen on everyone', though mitigating such mischief was the longer standing Austrian habit of *Schlamperei,* an untranslatable term perhaps best rendered as 'slovenliness', albeit with frequent connotations of good nature that the English noun lacks.

For his peculiarly constipated brand of despotism, Joseph received only praise: since – like Frederick the Great and

Catherine the Great, but unlike most other Habsburgs – he took care to ingratiate himself with intellectuals, both genuine and bogus. By contrast Prince Metternich, the Austrian Empire's *de facto* prime minister from 1815 to 1848, acquired international odium for ostensibly spying on, and censoring, the populace to within an inch of its life. At times he enjoyed playing up to his reputation as the Continent's leading bogey-man. 'In me,' he remarked in 1817, 'you behold Europe's chief minister of police.' Nonetheless, with only seven hundred actual policemen at his disposal in all Austria, including only twenty-two agents in charge of monitoring the country's postal service, he had no resources (whatever his desire) for truly comprehensive snooping. More often he astonished individual prisoners by his compassion, providing reading matter for bookishly inclined captives such as the Italian revolutionist playwright Silvio Pellico, and resorting to capital punishment with a reluctance that British or French cabinet ministers would in their own respective lands have considered positively womanish.

Besides, Metternich's foreign opponents grossly exaggerated the extent of his domestic sway, even amid his prime. Publishers of books banned in Austria simply smuggled copies in from Germany or Belgium, with little official interference.

'There Is Nothing Sane to Report'

It is the winter of 1918–19. The German military juggernaut, which as recently as April had been still capable of inflicting upon British and French infantrymen some of their heaviest punishment in the whole Great War, lies in ruins. That great chain of being which has defined Germans, whatever their locality, from their birth – a theology, it might well be called; certainly a belief system imposing a certain attitudinal likeness upon every German official from the humblest village post-man to the Supreme War Lord himself, Kaiser Wilhelm II – has collapsed. In its place, Germany now has ... nothing.

To be sure, scattered remnants of administration survive. While almost all outward signs of ordered rule have gone, complete anarchy has not yet triumphed. Here and there committees' spokesmen on balconies are proclaiming a repub-lic, while rival committees' spokesmen from nearby balconies proclaim a rival republic. Of greater significance, bureaucrats' salaries continue to be paid, letters to be delivered; telephon-ists can still put through calls (the bands of marauding Marxists usually fail to seize a particular city's telephone exchange); in Berlin, a secret telephone line connects Germany's caretaker Chancellor with the Army's Chief of Staff. Lenin's jibe at German socialists, that they would never storm a railway sta-tion without first queuing for platform tickets, remains generally justifiable. But though the machine of government – after a creaking, spluttering, jerky fashion – still runs, it runs on empty.

Threatening to drown out its engine noise are the aftershocks of German monarchism's prompt and utter destruction. As late as October, every German state (save a handful of 'free cities') retained its own monarch. Now, in a republican purgation without historical parallel, every last one of these dynasties has gone. Few succumbed to, or were even confronted with, violence. Most simply fled. Bavaria's Prince Rupprecht learned of his father's deposition only when leading his troops home from the battlefield. The other royal families took the line of *sauve qui peut*, and escaped for fear that staying put would consign them to the Romanovs' fate. The impossible-sounding titles of yore – the Kingdoms of Württemburg and Saxony; the Grand Duchy of Saxe-Meiningen; the Duchies of Brunswick-Wolfenbüttel and Mecklenberg-Strelitz – all these resounding names, and many others, will henceforth be known only to historians, so shallow was the soil in which the monarchies themselves had been planted. Among most of the rulers' erstwhile subjects, there is not even an apocalyptic sense of a new republican millennium. As well expect such a sense from people caught up in a cyclone, and then suddenly dumped onto open farmland suffering only cuts and bruises.

Kaiser Wilhelm's reign, conversely, has died hard. He has blamed his downfall on Bolshevik agitation: which in fact is merely filling a vacuum that Wilhelm's own generals, by forcing him out, have left. No avenging pursuers have followed him. He has ended up in neutral Holland, as tedious as ever, but at least alive. (To the German High Command's pleas that he charge to his death in battle, he had replied with some asperity that as temporal head of the Lutheran Church he could never contemplate suicide.) A makeshift republican cabinet issues edicts from Berlin's Chancellery, until the Spartacists move in. The Brandenburg Gate, during December, is draped in red flags. Only on 11 January will the volunteer army (*Freikorps*) loyal to the moderate Social Democrat Chancellor Friedrich Ebert bloodily terminate the commissars' rule of Karl Liebknecht, Rosa Luxemburg and their comrades. Within twenty-four hours of their overthrow, both Liebkneckt and Luxemburg are hunted down and assassinated by the *Freikorps'* sharp-shooter division. One *Freikorps* general voices his disgust at the middle classes' reluctance to defend themselves, and their willingness to let the military shoulder the burden and risks of suppressing revolution:

> Would our intervention have been necessary if every-one had been at his post? ... I have acquired in five months of activity little respect for the constructive ability of the German bourgeoisie, but a high opinion of the organised workers.

Meanwhile Bavaria has been blessed with not one Soviet Republic, but three: each lasting only weeks, each wilder than the last. In some respects the outcomes are nearer to Groucho Marx than to Karl: not so near, however, that the Bavarian Bolsheviks overlook collecting their subsidies from Lenin. Luminaries of the consecutive workers' paradises include Franz Lipp, an ex-madhouse patient appointed foreign affairs commissar because he alone possesses a sufficiently diplomatic-looking grey frock coat. Lipp's other achievements include declaring war on Switzerland, and accusing Bavaria's new president of filching the keys to the foreign ministry's lavatory. Dramatist and journalist Ben Hecht, covering Central European affairs for Chicago's *Daily News,* cables home: GERMANY IS HAVING A NERVOUS BREAKDOWN. THERE IS NOTHING SANE TO REPORT.

Still, Bavaria's Soviets (for all their preposterousness) form a mere amateurish prelude to the Marxist-Leninist terror dominating Austria's fraternal twin, Hungary, from March to August 1919. Strongman of the Hungarian Soviet Republic is Béla Kun, whose régime mows down, without the faintest pretence of legality, at least five hundred opponents – most of them peasants peacefully protesting against the State's appropriation of their farms – within the 133 days that elapse before anti-Communist troops (Romanian as well as Hungarian) restore order.

· · · · ·

The Hungarian bloodbath's effect on the Western psyche defies full retrospective comprehension. Few Westerners in 1919 knew of Soviet Russia's murder rate, or had reason to believe that Russia could ever improve significantly on any other Oriental despotism. Hungary was different. The granary of Europe; the home of Haydn, the birthplace of Liszt; the land of Victorian England's swashbuckling pin-up idol, Lajos Kossuth ('the Magyar Garibaldi'); altogether a cradle of civilisation. In Hungary these things must not, could not, happen. And they had indeed happened, at precisely the time that peace on the Wilson plan should have been breaking out all over Europe.

As for Bavaria, its Marxist experiments quickly sank into oblivion, once Lenin – in a typical triumph of *post facto* casuistry – had deduced from their failure that they had represented 'infantile leftism'. They never faded, however, from the consciousness of one Corporal Hitler, Iron Cross Second Class, Iron Cross First Class, survivor of four years on the Western Front, who in November 1918 was lying crippled and temporarily sightless (through mustard-gassing's effects) in hospital. While in his bed he heard, from a Protestant chaplain, the news of Germany's surrender. It crushed and terrified him, as did the discovery that Jews dominated the

Prussian, Bavarian and Hungarian revolutions. Luxemburg and Liebknecht were Jewish; so were Bavarian Soviet leaders Kurt Eisner, Ernst Toller, Eugen Leviné and Gustav Landauer; so was Kun; so were twenty-five out of Kun's thirty-two commissars. Later, not very convincingly, Hitler attempted to retroject his loathing of Jewry onto his years of struggle in Vienna before 1914. The facts (notably his dealings with individual prewar Jews, and his failure to stand out in prewar Vienna from the Jew-denouncing commonalty represented by demagogic Mayor Karl Lueger), speak otherwise. Moreover, *Mein Kampf* cites the 'stab in the back' of 1918–19 as the crucial determinant for Hitler's world view. The Great War, one of his most prophetic passages maintains, would have ended in total German victory if only 'twelve to fifteen thousand of these Hebrew corrupters of the people had been held under poison gas'.

Gleichschaltung, 1933–38: The Gestapo and SD

Like Mussolini, Hitler felt compelled to conceal through retrospective propaganda the humdrum method of his accession to office. Mussolini's October 1922 train trip to receive his nation's highest elective post acquired the legendary status of a 'March on Rome'. Similarly, the compromises, threats, and horse-trading sessions by which the National Socialist (NS) Party entered Germany's government in January 1933 – sessions in what would have been smoked-filled rooms but for Hitler's detestation of tobacco – became subsequently invested with the grand appellation 'seizure of power' (*Machtergreifung*). Hitler's first cabinet contained only three NS members: Hitler himself (as Chancellor); Hermann Göring (who combined

199

Prussia's premiership with the title of Hitler's minister without portfolio); and Wilhelm Frick (minister for the interior). The rest of Hitler's team consisted of Catholic Centre Party members like ex-Chancellor Franz von Papen (now Vice-Chancellor); businessmen like the newspaper tycoon Alfred Hugenberg (leader of the neo-Bismarckian Nationalist Party); generals like Werner von Blomberg (representing the Prussian *Junker* class); and, from 1934, internationally respected banker Hjalmar Schacht (the only German official who in the 1920s had shown enough courage and expertise to overcome hyper-inflation). At the apex of this improvised administrative structure still stood Paul von Hindenburg, president since Ebert's death in 1925. A monarchist at heart, Hindenburg (aged eighty-six in 1933) continued hoping against hope that Hitler would invite the Hohenzollern family back as a line of future constitutional sovereigns, meanwhile both fearing and despising Hitler himself.

From this *ad hoc* arrangement no drastic, Dzerzhinsky-style political police force stood much chance of being conjured forth; nor was it. Hitler owed his subsequent posses-sion of such a force to three individuals above all: Göring, Heinrich Himmler, and Reinhard Heydrich. Even after all three men had risen to power of life and death, the force remained by Soviet standards fractured and inconsistent. The much-uttered abstract noun of early Hitlerism, *Gleichschaltung* ('coordination'), had more to do with conviction than with reality.

Of the three, the originally Bavarian, though Prussian-domiciled, Göring – born on 12 January 1893, the son of a prominent colonial administrator in Namibia – was the oldest, the most flamboyant, the most capable in pre-NS life, and by far the most intelligent. Unlike the other two, he could boast a combat record of great distinction: his heroism in leading the air squadron founded by Manfred ('the Red Baron') von Richthofen won him, in the war's closing stages, a *Pour le Mérite* award. While Hitler put Göring in charge of the SA (*Sturmabteilung*, or 'Storm Troopers') as early as 1922, chap-fallen fanaticism never held great appeal to this most obviously clownish of the NS leaders, who conceived for his SA successor, Ernst Röhm, an unbounded and eventually mortal abhorrence. To Röhm's demands for ever-increased class warfare, Göring responded with a heterosexual sybarite's contempt for a homosexual ideologue. His creature comforts included a pet lioness and a Swedish countess. With the former – which enjoyed a daily diet of fresh meat during even the most severe national food shortages – he had himself photographed, never appearing fully convinced by his own assurances that proximity to this beast was entirely safe. With the latter (Karin von Kantzow, who became his wife in 1922; they fled to Austria after the 1923 Beer Hall Putsch's failure, and two years afterwards went to Sweden) he led a rather more uniformly alarming existence, not least because she forced him to break his morphine habit. Once back on German soil following a 1926 amnesty, Göring entered national politics, and within three years had charmed and cajoled his way into one of the Reichstag's Prussian seats, acquiring the Reichstag's presidency (a job approximately corresponding to the Westminster system's post of Speaker) in 1932.

With such a career background, including *entrée* to aristocratic circles that Hitler as an individual had no likelihood of gatecrashing, Göring needed the NS movement less than it needed him. In this respect his fellow Bavarian Himmler constituted Göring's antithesis. His whole adult life had been devoted to hero-worshipping Hitler: first from afar, then close-up. The more one studies Himmler, the less comprehensible he becomes. Perhaps any of us, accorded governmental power of Himmlerian proportions, could organise murder and torture on a genocidal scale. But could we, while doing so, construct (as Himmler did) elaborate philological theories to 'prove' that Japanese were authentic Aryans? Or bring about military disaster by spurning (as Himmler, in 1941–42, spurned) an alliance with several hundred thousand impeccably anti-Communist Ukrainians, on the grounds that 'subhuman' Slavs deserved only to be enslaved or killed? Himmler constitutes one of the best arguments for the theory that evil comes, not from an overabundant imagination, but from the complete absence of imagination.

Born on 7 October 1900, Himmler – whose father was a schoolmaster – underwent military service, of sorts, during the Great War. There he distinguished himself by a litany of tireless complaints against the poor quality of the food served, the discomfort of sleeping conditions, and other inconveniences of infantry life that his fellow conscripts managed to endure in stoic silence. After demobilisation, he took to poultry-farming (in which he attained a modest success) and joined a paramilitary organisation then under Röhm's command, although he never shared Röhm's sexual tastes. A comrade of Göring in the putsch attempt of 1923, Himmler escaped the imprisonment to which the Bavarian judiciary condemned Hitler, and seven years afterwards joined Göring as a Reichstag member. Already he had founded and headed the organisation with which his name would be indelibly associated: Hitler's own bodyguard, the *Schutzstaffel* (roughly translatable as 'Protective Echelon'), shortened by popular usage to SS. By 1931 the SS had 10,000 members; within two years its numbers had quintupled.

One future SS leader, Walter Schellenberg (who testified in 1946 at the trials of Göring and others), explained how glamorous the SS appeared to so many German youths like himself. Schellenberg felt no such overwhelming enthusiasm for the NS's civilian organisation. He became an NS card-holder at the age of twenty-two in 1932, partly through 'my financial difficulties … though I cannot truthfully say that I took the decision reluctantly'. But the SS meant much more to him than mere party affiliation. A definite snobbery attached to it, aided by its striking uniform, so much more agreeable to wear than the SA's proletarian brown shirts. 'In the SS,' Schellenberg explained, 'were to be found people "of the best kind" and to belong to it gave you considerable prestige', a prestige completely denied to 'the rowdies of the SA in the beer-halls'.

Yet although by 1931 Himmler had already given the SS much of its basic character, it lacked a proper security apparatus, such as Himmler's constantly bubbling paranoia judged essential. On a colleague's recommendation Himmler interviewed a young man whose nature, unlike his own, was tormented but recognisably normal. Reinhard Heydrich, born on 7 March 1904 (to a Catholic opera singer in the largely Lutheran town of Halle, Saxony), had been too young for war service. To compensate for this handicap he joined the navy after leaving school, only to be forced out of it upon the discovery that he had acquired two fiancées at once. Numerous women found Heydrich wildly attractive in spite, or because, of a squeaky voice that had subjected him (as his Catholic upbringing had done) to imaginative school playground tortures. He evaded instructions to marry the fiancée he had been sleeping with, by arguing that a lieutenant like himself could not possibly jeopardise his promising career through wedding a harlot. The fiancée he had refused to sleep with stood by him, and he married her instead, but the navy dismissed him in any case.

With nothing to live on except his meagre severance pay, Heydrich needed work, and fast. The moment he walked into Himmler's office – having pretended that completing one short naval course on intelligence activities qualified him as an intelligence expert – Himmler found himself much impressed. Blond and six-and-a-half feet tall, with a jutting chin (and, Himmler approvingly noted, 'real wolf's eyes'), Heydrich looked like the pure Aryan hero that moon-faced, bespectacled Himmler could only dream of resembling. To the newcomer Himmler explained his requirements:

> I want to create a Security and Information Service within the SS. I need a specialist … explain to me on paper how you propose to set about it. I will give you twenty minutes.

Whatever Heydrich wrote (nobody knows), it satisfied Himmler, who promptly put Heydrich in charge of a new SS division: the *Sicherheitsdienst,* or SD.

• • • • •

However greatly Hitler craved a new bureaucratic beginning, his circumstances initially forced caution on him. The Weimar Republic's police had won a remarkable repute among progressive criminologists, especially in America, for their punctilious respect of individual rights: a respect that often took the form of making no arrests at all, and that invariably hindered the short-lived Weimar administrations to which they notionally answered, since this hands-off approach's main beneficiaries consisted of the Communists and National Socialists whose street-battles against each other continued till late 1932. What the police recoiled from doing, its Weimar masters recoiled from demanding that it do. As in other European countries that produced right-wing dictatorships of various sorts between 1919 and 1939, so in Germany: a needful, and indeed sufficient, precondition for the dictatorships' emergence was the sheer impotence of mainstream conservatism. Alas for Hitler, mainstream conservative individuals abounded in the police (even after the Wall Street crash): especially in Prussia's police, now responsible to Göring.

From one unit in this organisation, Berlin's Department 1A, Göring drew most staff for what came to be known as the *Geheime Staatspolizeiamt*, or, in brief, Gestapo. (At first the abbreviation Gestapa gained currency, but it soon faded from general use, especially among non-Germans. The authorities actively discouraged another early abbreviation, GPA, because of its resemblance to the Soviets' GPU and OGPU.) Göring soon realised the aid that an outwardly – and in many respects inwardly – independent, non-politicised unit could give the régime. Thus, while refusing to inflate it overmuch (by January 1934 its head office still had only 645 employees, including 179 detectives, although the staff of the organisation's thirty-four regional offices brought the total to 1,329), he at first kept it out of ideologues' hands.

In April 1933, Göring appointed as the Gestapo's first director a career official: the thirty-three-year-old Rudolf Diels. Devoid of firm convictions, Diels mollified by his very presence not just nationalists outside Hitler's support base, but tensions within Hitler's party. Most leading NS figures at this stage belonged to one of three factions. Frick led the comparatively cautious rightist faction (as National minister of the interior, he in practice remained subordinate within Prussia to Göring, the *State* interior minister). The centre answered to Göring himself, playing the extremes off against each other. Then there were the hard-left revolutionaries, dominated by Röhm's SA. These last claimed Hitler as one of their own, and often appealed to him over Göring's and Frick's heads. Göring's best weapons against them included Diels, who back in 1932 had obtained the Prussian State Police's secret archives concerning politicians of all persuasions, and who had separately bought on the black market certain explicitly homosexual letters which Röhm had been incautious enough to write.

• • • • •

Meanwhile the SA, its protests against Göring's wealth and capitalist friends having grown ever more raucous, threatened to engulf the Party and the land. This threat compelled Göring and Himmler to form an alliance in April 1934. But Himmler extracted from Göring a punitively high price for his support: he insisted that Diels, the blackmailer, must resign. And resign from the Gestapo Diels did, still on civil terms with Göring (who gave him the consolation prize of Cologne's governorship), yet never again to play a surveillance role.*

Himmler and Heydrich now had no serious challengers left within the Party, save for Röhm's bloc. (Nor did they ever quarrel with each other, although rumours – apparently baseless – of a Jewish strain in Heydrich's ancestry came to his boss's notice. Moreover, at times Heydrich resented Himmler's intellectual limitations, and took to imagining the spectacle of his master clad only in underpants, so as to fear Himmler less.) The way had been cleared to smash Röhm's gang.

Even at this late moment National Socialism's course had nothing inevitable about it. Hitler, to Göring's and Himmler's indignation, very nearly spared Röhm's life. He admitted that nothing less than mass murder would be required in order to eliminate the SA as a whole; but ties of long-standing personal allegiance to Röhm made him wish to pardon the SA leader. Only Göring's and Himmler's insistence that death alone would ever stop Röhm from menacing the nation changed Hitler's mind. So Röhm and eighty-four others were slain on the night of 30 June-1 July 1934, which proved a perfect opportunity to wipe out not only SA members but also conservative adversaries. SS troops did most of the killing, though Gestapo agents shot dead former Chancellor Kurt von Schleicher (who had made no secret of his contempt for Hitler) and Schleicher's wife. Against Bavaria's

---

* Imprisoned after the 1944 conspiracy against Hitler's life, but saved from execution at Göring's behest, Diels went on to become a star witness for the prosecution at Nuremberg. He wrote an instructive memoir of his Third Reich days, *Lucifer Ante Portas* (Lucifer at the Gates), and died in 1957.

ex-Premier Gustav von Kahr, Hitler harboured an older grievance. Kahr had at first seemed to smile on the Beer Hall Putsch eleven years beforehand, yet had afterwards helped to suppress it. That night he too paid with his life, assailed with pick-axes by SS men. Music critic Willi Schmid perished through having been mistaken for SA officer Wilhelm Schmid. Papen, despite his outspoken complaints about Hitler's tyranny, survived; but his press secretary Herbert von Bose died from ten bullet wounds.

Instead of convulsing the German population in disgust, the purge left – as foreign correspondents noted – a dominant sense of relief, simply because the SA had become so hated. Such official complaints as came to Hitler's ears derived from other National Socialists: for example Frick, who sharply denounced the SS's bloodshed, as did Justice Minister Hans Frank. Heydrich, on the other hand, thought that thanks to Gestapo underachievement, the bloodshed had been too little; he urged Göring to get rid of Gestapo field officers deficient in the needed ferocity. Against such pressure, neither Frick nor Frank pressed their own points overmuch.

One factor that told against voices of circumspection was a demographic one: in Edward Crankshaw's words, 'the extreme youth of the men who first frightened the German people into abject submission'. In 1934 Himmler was only thirty-four, Heydrich thirty, Schellenberg a mere twenty-four; while even Göring had reached forty-one, and the increasingly sidelined Frick already approached sixty. Such statistics themselves indicated NS impatience with (in Crankshaw's words again) 'the proud Army tradition – embodied in grey-haired military leaders of proved courage and distinction'. A telegram purporting to be from Hindenburg, congratulating

Hitler on the purge's outcome, probably originated in – and certainly consisted, in its final form, of – a NS-written text. Hindenburg's death on 2 August marked not just one leader's passing, but the end of a whole military heritage which, while it lasted, blocked Hitler's road to supreme office.

• • • • •

During the Gestapo's first years of existence, its main victims – and the likeliest people to end up behind barbed-wire fences – were Communists (those who had not fled the country in 1933), male homosexuals (especially after Röhm's murder), vivisectionists (Göring boasted in a 1933 radio talk that the NS leadership would 'commit to concentration camps those who still think that they can continue to treat animals as inanimate property'), Pentecostals, Jehovah's Witnesses, Seventh-Day Adventists, and dissident Lutherans. (Over the issue of allegiance to the Third Reich, German Lutheranism split into two camps: the German Christian Church, which remained loyal to the régime; and the Confessional Church, which defied it. Hitler's June 1933 concordat with the Vatican had ensured short-term protection for most Catholics.)

National Socialist leaders repeatedly emphasised that they had not invented the concentration camp: that the British had done so, more than thirty years beforehand, locking up Boer women and children in South Africa as an emergency wartime measure. Ernst Thälmann, leader of the German Communist Party, became the best known early inmate of the NS concentration camp – or, as Germans quickly learned to call it, *KZ* – system. Thälmann, who had been the Communists' candidate for Germany's presidency in

1925 and again in 1932, fell into the Gestapo's hands in 1934. Campaigns in Britain (involving, among others, Orwell) and France for his release proved fruitless, and he remained a captive in Buchenwald until his execution ten years later. Having always refused to accept any variants on hard-line Marxist-Leninist dogma (variants like the 'Popular Front' strategy which dominated the later 1930s), Thälmann and his nomenklatura tirelessly derided Germany's Social Democrats as 'social fascists'. With his Old Bolshevik stubbornness, he probably lived longer in NS hands than he would have done in Stalin's purge-infested Moscow.

Three years after Thälmann's downfall, the fate of Confessional Church leader Martin Niemöller attracted still greater international controversy. A submarine captain during the Great War, Niemöller had inspired high initial hopes among the NS leadership that he would faithfully follow the German Christians' line. After all, on his own public admission he had voted for the NS ticket at the Reichstag elections of 1924 and 1933, objecting solely to undue NS interference in Lutheran policies. Arrested in July 1937 by Berlin Gestapo personnel, Niemöller at first made light of his troubles: having been imprisoned on five separate occasions within the preceding four years, each time for no more than a few days. This time, the régime immured him for eight years. Protests around the world from Norman Vincent Peale, Eleanor Roosevelt, the Anglican Bishop of Chichester, and other public figures failed to shorten his sentence. Only after World War II had ended did Niemöller, who spent almost half of his prison term in solitary confinement, know freedom again.

Eight- and ten-year sentences formed, however, the exception rather than the rule. More often KZ imprisonment before 1939 lasted weeks or months, Germany's rulers having concluded that simply releasing KZ inmates back into the community with some promptitude would provide an incentive for the public to take KZ conditions with due seriousness. In Bavaria, the average fortnight between 1935 and 1939 inclusive saw 504 persons sent to camps and 417 freed. One comedian, famous for his cabaret monologues, even treated his audience to a witticism about his recent incarceration:

> I'm sorry I'm late. I've just come back from a little excursion to – Dachau! Well, you ought to see that place! Barbed-wire fence, electrified, machine-guns; another barbed-wire fence, more machine-guns – but I can tell you, I managed to get in all the same!

Until the mid-1930s jokesmiths continued to ridicule Göring (notably for his greed), Goebbels (notably for his ugliness), and Hitler (notably for his alleged carpet-chewing rage – one anti-Hitler joke has the *Führer* buying a carpet, whereupon the saleswoman asks, 'Shall I have it sent straight to the Chancellery, or would you like a little snack of it right now?'). Clearly the Gestapo could not crack down on all such subversion, despite the government's March 1933 legislation prohibiting 'malicious gossip', by which it included any sharp criticism of itself, whether oral or written. ('Malicious gossipers' accounted for more than half of those whom the prewar Gestapo arrested in Düsseldorf; in Prussia, Diels had established an efficient system for monitoring the postal service.) But even the author of an encyclopædic 1995 guide to *Underground Humour in Nazi Germany* discovered no jokes concerning either Himmler or Heydrich.

This lacuna partly reflects administrative overhauling. As of June 1936, internal police activity in the Third Reich underwent so drastic a reorganisation that Himmler and Heydrich obtained almost unlimited control over it. (The preceding February, Prussia's legislature had passed a statute banning any appeals against a Gestapo-approved sentence.)

At first the post-1936 Gestapo continued to accord suspects certain rights which the SS forbade. True, specific Gestapo offices became notorious: Hamburg's Gestapo chief exhibited a penchant for smashing victims' kidneys with knuckledusters, after which obliging local coroners would return a verdict of suicide. Yet many and probably most pre-war Gestapo interrogations, though comprehensive and ruthlessly professional, did not of themselves involve greater physical maltreatment than other police forces of the time (anywhere in Europe or America) employed. Often the Gestapo would actually intervene to take into custody – and thus afford temporary protection towards – Jews who were being attacked by SS thugs. Over half its arrests derived from individuals' denunciations, rather than from SS strong-arm tactics. One survey of late-1930s Bavarian police figures shows that even after the 1935 Nuremberg Laws had greatly worsened Jews' conditions, the Gestapo made 62 per cent of its arrests on the basis of denunciations by members of the public, instead of acting on its own initiative or at the insistence of the SS. At this stage the Bavarian Gestapo freed no fewer than 41 per cent of its suspects, for lack of hard evidence against them.

Notwithstanding all the June 1936 changes, Göring retained the exclusive rights over one surveillance procedure that he refused to allow Heydrich or Himmler: authorising taps on telephones. The Göring-controlled *Forschungsamt* (Investigation Office), a subdivision not of the interior ministry but of Göring's own air ministry, prohibited any taps without Göring's express authorisation. On each warrant for a tap that he approved of, Göring wrote the letter 'G'. Heydrich, we are told,

> hated having to submit every wiretap [request] to Göring – 'But without that "G" on it [the warrant], I wasn't allowed to order the tap.'

As to how the authorities fitted out private citizens' phones with bugging devices, 'an engineer offering to replace a malfunctioning apparatus was the usual method'.

Pamphleteers and magazine publishers, obviously, ran greater risks and made more satisfying Gestapo-SD targets than those who confined their opposition to mere oral rebukes of NS rule. In August 1935 the Gestapo closed down *Blick in die Zeit* ('Look at the Times'), a scrupulous periodical which since its inception in June 1933 had specialised in soberly reprinting foreign newspapers' reports of German events, reports that the NS' tame journal *Völkischer Beobachter* either ignored or furiously denounced.

· · · · ·

The difficulty in determining how many staff Gestapo-SD units employed is compounded by two factors: first, Anglophone writers' habit of indiscriminately using the term 'Gestapo' to cover all surveillance activities; second, and more important, the essential role that unpaid informers played, after the mid-1930s especially. Crankshaw – writing in 1956, when primary source material for the Third Reich was by modern standards extremely sparse and inaccessible – put the total number of full-time bureaucrats at an improbably high 40,000. Later, better researched, estimates give a prewar number of approximately 7,000 in the Gestapo, and 5,000 in the SD. Clearly the government had a vested interest in making the surveillance bureaux seem impossibly large, impossibly tentacular, and infallible. Against such wishful thinking, departmental records from the time frequently point to specific Gestapo-SD offices being understaffed, overburdened with paperwork, and in no way capable of snooping on Hitler's preferred scale.

Himmler, with that grotesque optimism which never left him (optimism which in other circumstances caused him to view himself as the literal incarnation of early tenth-century German Emperor Henry I), told Gestapo members shortly after subsuming their organisation into the SD:

> The *Volk* must hold the conviction that the most just authority, which works the most exactly in the new state, is the dreaded Gestapo. The *Volk* must come to the view that, if someone has been seized, he has been seized with right; it must have the view that, in all things that are not to the detriment of the state, the members of the Gestapo are men with human kindness, with human hearts and absolute rightness. We must not forget – beginning from the highest to the last official and employee – that we exist for the *Volk* and not the *Volk* for us.
>
> I also wish that everyone who comes to you will

be handled courteously and sensibly. I wish that you will use on the phone a courteous and proper tone. I wish further that no man will growl in any way. Please, see yourself as helpers and not as dictators.

Götterdämmerung, 1938–45: the RSHA

For security policing, as for many other aspects of the Third Reich, 1938 was the year that dashed the hopes of the luke-warm and saw largely untrammelled power handed over to the fanatic. Some of this transformation's outward signs are blatant, most notably the *Anschluss* in March and *Kristallnacht* in November. Less often remembered than either of these events is the process by which, in January and February 1938, the Gestapo-SD machine first humiliated and then crushed the army establishment.

Werner von Blomberg, defence minister since 1933, inspired extremely diverse reactions. Opponents of the régime dubbed him, because of his willingness to collude with Hitler, 'the Rubber Lion'; to Hitler, he was not rubbery enough. In January 1938 the fifty-nine-year-old Blomberg wed an attractive blonde thirty-five years his junior. NS authorities – usually eager to make a grand theatrical production out of even the least significant governmental wedding – allowed only the sketchiest press coverage of Blomberg's nuptials. The reason for their media blackout soon emerged: Frau Blomberg's whoring had been known to police since 1931. A file on her background that ended up in Berlin's police department included photographs of group sex activities at a notorious brothel run by her mother, an already convicted madam. It seems that Heydrich himself assembled much, though not necessarily all, of this dossier. At any rate,

215

the revelations it included achieved the desired effect: Blomberg quickly resigned from the cabinet, and never again held office.

Blomberg's downfall having been gratifyingly easy to bring about, Heydrich collaborated with Göring and Himmler in his next move against the *Junker* élite: the destruction of Werner von Fritsch, Commander-in-Chief from 1934. Despite his eagerness to rearm Germany, and his vocal distaste for Catholics and Jews, Fritsch remained a danger in the NS leadership's eyes because of his well-advertised reluctance to abet a future European war. Göring unearthed a blackmailing male prostitute, who in January 1938 accused Fritsch of having had repeated carnal relations with him. When summoned to Hitler's presence, Fritsch furiously denied engaging in homosexual activity of any sort; but Hitler roundly called him, to his face as well as behind his back, 'pervert' and 'liar'. In February the *Führer*, who continued to take pride in how much political mileage he had obtained from Röhm's erotic predilections almost four years before, announced Fritsch's resignation 'for health reasons'. A subsequent court case totally exonerated Fritsch (the German judiciary retained a modicum of independence in 1938), but he remained in disgrace, scarcely eased by Himmler's scornful rejection of Fritsch's challenge to a duel. In the opening weeks of World War II, as his Twelfth Artillery Regiment approached Warsaw, Fritsch was shot down by a Polish machine-gunner.

· · · · ·

Hitler offered, as his immediate excuse for the Polish campaign, the so-called Gleiwitz incident in which (so he asserted)

Polish saboteurs had attempted to capture a German radio station. No such incident occurred; Heydrich dreamed it up, and SD officers carried it out. Heydrich selected a dozen concentration camp prisoners in late August, made them don Polish military uniforms, ordered lethal injections administered to them, and then had their corpses dumped near the radio tower so as to suggest a Warsaw-inspired military manœuvre.

The war itself started on 1 September; twenty-six days later began another reorganisation of the internal police, one still more dramatic than the 1936 changes. Completed in 1940, the new arrangements – given the overall name of *Reichssicherheitshauptamt* ('Reich Security Main Office'), or RSHA for short – were as follows:

- Office I: devoted to personnel selection.
- Office II: the legal and administrative headquarters.
- Office III: this division took over the SD's functions.
- Office IV: this remained the Gestapo, headed from 1939 by a career bureaucrat, Heinrich Müller. Publicity-shy, and never a household name even among his compatriots, Müller (born on 18 April 1900) earned the Iron Cross First Class during World War I. With the advent of peace he joined Bavaria's political police, where he meted out justice against Communist and National Socialist law-breakers with equal rigour. Of Fouchéan disposition, sceptical and coldly polite for the most part, he served the Third Reich with unobtrusive expertise – Heydrich, who feared that Müller would be more dangerous outside the Gestapo than in it, helped his career along greatly – but he disdained to join the NS Party till 1938. Celebrated among colleagues for

his interrogative skills, which scorned the cruder methods of assault and battery by which lesser men obtained results, Müller boasted an encylopædic memory. He suffered from few illusions about his fellows, going so far as to call (for example) SS general Odilo Globocnik 'a giant turd with a military hat on top', and responding to some erudite fantasist with the words 'One should herd the entire intelligentsia into a mine, and then blow it sky-high.' Müller's post-1945 career, of which more later, was probably the most bizarre of any leading Third Reich official.

• Office V: the so-called *Kripo* (short for Kriminal Polizei), headed by Arthur Nebe. A mysterious figure whose true motives have provoked anguished historiographical speculation ever since, Nebe was born in 1894 and spent much of his career as an SS officer, although his opposition to Hitler had become celebrated in military circles as early as 1938. During the 1940s – increasingly shamed by the carnage that he had seen and permitted, as commander of SS *Einsatzgruppen* death-squads in Poland, the Baltic States, and European Russia – Nebe found himself caught up in anti-Hitler efforts, for which (after eluding the Gestapo for six months) he paid on the gallows in 1945. His courage under torture in refusing to give information concerning other conspirators remains impressive.

• Office VI: the foreign intelligence service, a rival to – and much more reliably pro-Hitler than – the *Abwehr* military intelligence service.

• Office VII: the ideological and research division.

Readers confused by this array of diverse functions may draw some comfort from the fact that ordinary Germans found them equally confusing at the time. This confusion they shared with subsequent British and American prosecutors at Nuremberg, who, expecting a clearly linear chain of command on Soviet lines, found themselves confronted with the ruins of a system that had been specifically devised to prevent anyone taking decisive juridical responsibility for anything. Such a system enforced, *inter alia*, relentlessly conspiratorial habits of mind. Its upholders showed the greatest reluctance to accept a simple explanation for events, even – or especially – when the simple explanation happened to be the correct one. The Elser case illustrates this.

On 9 November Johann Georg Elser, a cabinet-maker, planted a time bomb of his own construction in Munich's Bürgerbräu cellar, where Hitler was scheduled to speak. Had the *Führer* kept to his normal schedule, he would certainly have been blown to bits. Yet on that night of all nights he left seven minutes before the bomb went off, since bad weather obliged him to catch a train instead of his usual plane. In the resultant blast, more than sixty were injured, and eight were killed; but none of the eight was Hitler. Himmler, once he had Elser in his grasp, simply assumed that the would-be assassin had been a foreign spy. In addition to employing such cutting-edge criminological techniques as organising a séance, Himmler subjected Elser to repeated SD interrogations (sometimes, it is said, sharing with his own boots the burden of kicking the suspect). All this failed to extract from his victim the confessions of Vatican, Masonic, or British secret service involvement that he and Hitler craved. Over and over again, with the obduracy of the born *naïf*, Elser insisted that he had acted alone.

Surprisingly, Elser stayed alive for almost the whole war: partly because Himmler planned a show trial for the culprit once hostilities had ended, but partly because the sheer freakishness of Hitler's escape engendered in Hitler himself a strange occult belief in Elser's magical powers, which made him fear 'to cut this earthly tie [with Elser] prematurely'. Himmler, meanwhile, sent Elser to the Sachsenhausen concentration camp – where his fellow captives included deposed Austrian Chancellor Kurt von Schuschnigg, deposed French Prime Minister Paul Reynaud, and Reynaud's fellow ex-PMs Léon Blum and Édouard Herriot – before transferring him to Dachau. There, on 5 April 1945 (by which time even Himmler had ceased hoping for a German military triumph), two SS men shot Elser on Himmler's instructions.

If Elser came closer than anyone else before July 1944 to eliminating Hitler, he was by no means the only German to attempt this task. At any given moment during the years 1938 and 1944 there existed at least one plot against Hitler, and sometimes several simultaneously. In September 1938, a planned anti-Hitler coup involved no fewer than eight army generals (as well as Admiral Wilhelm Canaris of the *Abwehr*, Canaris' deputy Hans Oster, former Prussian Gestapo officer Hans-Bernd Gisevius, and former cabinet minister Hjalmar Schacht), thwarted only by Hitler's Munich agreement with Mussolini, Neville Chamberlain and Édouard Daladier. This miscarried scheme presaged no fewer than seventeen subsequent attempts to overthrow the *Führer*. The contrast between these activities in National Socialist Germany, and on the other hand the sullen, brutish acquiescence of most Soviet Russians in Stalinism's nightmare – an acquiescence eloquently bemoaned by Solzhenitsyn in *The Gulag Archipelago* – signifies the difference between a nation which has lost its independent civic institutions, and a nation which never had independent civic institutions to lose.

• • • • •

Not all Hitler's domestic opponents wanted primarily to overthrow him. Some merely wanted him to cease breathing down their necks. In this category fell Helmut Hübener, a victim of legislation – imposed within days of World War II's outbreak – which forbade listening to any foreign radio broadcasts, however innocuous. Cases involving this 'crime' came under the jurisdiction of the Third Reich's so-called Special Courts, of which there were seventy-four by 1942; these institutions had the power to override the rest of the legal system. Heydrich announced to Gestapo leaders on 3 September that they must 'ruthlessly suppress' all efforts, civilian as well as military, 'to destroy the determination and fighting spirit of the German people'. Such wreckers would, Heydrich vowed, 'be brutally liquidated on instructions from above'.

Seventeen years old, scholarly and quiet, Hübener made an unlikely saboteur. A Mormon, and thus belonging to a religious movement regarded by the Third Reich with open repugnance, he did nothing more than listen to BBC broadcasts, transcribe their contents, and distribute these transcriptions among friends. Unfortunately one of these typescripts fell into an informer's hands, and the informer promptly apprised the Gestapo. Hauled before a Special Court, Hübener was sentenced to death. Even in the Third

Reich of 1942 seventeen-year-olds were not judicially murdered every day of the week, and his fate therefore attracted
public attention that the fates of other convicted listeners to
foreign broadcasts did not. But his youth failed to save him: on
27 October 1942 official notices of his execution – coloured
red, like all such notices in the Reich – were plastered over
Berlin's walls. That morning he had been guillotined in the
city's Plötzensee prison, which for the remainder of the war
would be notorious for the number of heroes slain in its death
cell.

• • • • •

Within two months of Hübener becoming an improbable
martyr, several very different personalities had sacrificed their
lives for a cause that, unlike Hübener's, lacked all moral justification. The *Rote Kapelle*, or 'Red Orchestra' (to use the name
that the Gestapo gave this subversive organisation), had been
founded in 1938 by a Polish Communist, Leopold Trepper,
who kept it going under cover of his Belgian leather-goods
business. Its leading members included journalist Harro
Schulze-Boysen and his wife Libertas Schulze-Boysen; Arvid
Harnack and his American-born wife Mildred Harnack (*née*
Fish), both – unlike the left-liberal Schulze-Boysens – convinced Communists; and a network of sympathetic radio
operators known as 'pianists'. The *Rote Kapelle* aimed to make
available for Stalin's use details of German military plans, convinced that its spying would somehow end the Third Reich.
Since most of its activities occurred while Stalin and Hitler
were still allies, it is hard in retrospect to know whether its

leaders were frauds or simply self-deluded; and recent English-language literature on the topic fails to clarify their actual motives.

At any rate, Stalin ignored every piece of information that the *Rote Kapelle* supplied for him, and the group's leaders were arrested in November 1942. Between that date and February 1943 the Harnacks and the Schulze-Boysens all went, on different days, to the scaffold; Trepper escaped to Moscow, where after a decade's imprisonment (partly on account of his Jewish blood) he moved to Poland, and finally to Israel.

•••••

Hans and Sophie Scholl were the children of a former mayor of Forchtenberg, near Heilbronn. Originally they took part in certain NS youth activities — Hitler Youth in Hans' case, the League of German Girls in Sophie's — but soon grew disillusioned, especially after attending their first Nuremberg rally. Sophie, in addition, shocked her fellow League members by praising Heinrich Heine, who as a Jew had been expelled from the officially approved literary canon. ('The person who doesn't know Heine,' an unrepentant Sophie announced, 'doesn't know German literature.') Increasingly Hans, Sophie and their friends took to reading banned authors: not only Heine, but Bernard Shaw — whom the National Socialists curiously supposed to be Jewish because of his red hair — and the novelist and librettist Stefan Zweig. Their activities came in 1938 to the Gestapo's attention, but not yet with a disastrous outcome: the authorities could prove nothing against them, and dropped the case. By late 1941 Hans and Sophie, who had begun studying at the University of Munich, firmly and defiantly opposed the war. Even the resources of NS censorship had been unable to keep from their ears the reports of *Einsatzgruppen* wiping out entire towns without the smallest military purpose: most notoriously Babi Yar, Ukraine, where more than 33,000 Jews died at *Einsatzgruppen* hands within three days of September 1941. The Scholls scandalised most of their fellows by refusing to donate warm clothes to the German war effort. Sophie explained: 'We must lose the war. If we contribute warm clothes, we'll be extending it.' Along with Kurt Huber, philosophy professor and musicologist at the university, they formed a clandestine organisation known as the White Rose.

From June 1942 the White Rose produced (on a battered typewriter) anti-government leaflets of the most outspoken and sarcastic kind. It might have been able to achieve still more had not a suspicious university caretaker, in February 1943, spotted Sophie delivering leaflets and reported her to the Gestapo. On 22 February Hans, Sophie and a fellow student, Christoph Pröbst, all went on trial. The judge was Roland Freisler, an ex-Bolshevik commissar who had joined the NS Party in 1925. In the intervening period Freisler had obtained successive posts in the Kassel municipal government, the Prussian legislature, and the Reichstag; invariably he left behind him a trail of financial scandals and libel suits. By 1943 he controlled the People's Court system (the very name being an oblique tribute to Freisler's Bolshevik origins); and there, unconstrained by the niceties of conventional legal practice, he screamed and jeered at defendants with such histrionic malice that Hitler admiringly called him 'our Vyshinsky'. Within hours of the trial's beginning, Hans and Sophie had been beheaded after a last harrowing interview with their parents. Hans was twenty-five years old, Sophie twenty-one. Pröbst, aged twenty-three, died with them; Huber met the same end in July.

• • • • •

By the time the Scholls and Huber began issuing the leaflets which would cost them their lives, Heydrich had joined his victims. On 27 May 1942 Heydrich – usually known as 'The Hangman', a fact acknowledged by *Time*'s 23 February issue, the cover of which consisted of his likeness surrounded by nooses – had been fatally wounded near Prague by Czech partisans. Seeming capable at first of surviving his injuries, he soon weakened, and died on 4 June in his Prague hospital bed. To suppress further Czech resistance activity, the SS moved into the village of Lidice (chosen at random) five days later, corralled its inhabitants, and slew 172 men and seven women in cold blood. For weeks afterwards this crime dominated the Allied countries' newspapers, and inspired a disgust that far greater atrocities further east – such as Babi Yar – had failed to provoke.

Until the following January Himmler carried out Heydrich's policing functions himself; on 3 January he appointed, in Heydrich's stead, SS leader Ernst Kaltenbrunner. An Austrian, born on 4 October 1903, Kaltenbrunner distinguished himself by sheer dullness of intellect (though, thanks in part to pressure from his father, the University of Vienna issued him a law degree of sorts) and by an exceptional disregard for the truth. The scars on his face he owed to a car accident, but he liked to encourage the belief that he acquired them in a glorious career of student duelling. Two years after joining the Austrian National Socialist Party – outlawed at the time – he played a key part in the July 1934 coup attempt that killed Chancellor Engelbert Dollfuss, for which activity he spent a year in prison. Once the *Anschluss* had reduced Austria to complete vassalage, he re-emerged as State security minister in the cabinet of Governor (and fellow-Austrian) Arthur Seyss-Inquart. Thus, between 1938 and the end of 1942 – by which time Seyss-Inquart had been transferred to an equivalent post in the Netherlands – Kaltenbrunner acquired ample training in the absolutist surveillance function that from January 1943 would be his for the entire Third Reich. In January 1942 Heydrich had chaired the secret Wannsee Conference which planned the Final Solution for exterminating Jews; Kaltenbrunner, who had attended the conference, ordered these plans' continuation once he had taken over Heydrich's role.

Among Kaltenbrunner's non-Jewish 1943 victims were the *Abwehr* figures around, and including, Admiral Canaris. During the late 1930s, the Spanish-speaking Canaris had maintained contacts with General Franco, whose distrust of Hitler he intensified, and whose refusal to sign a formal alliance with the Axis powers derived partly from Canaris' own exertions. (After the war, Franco honoured Canaris' memory by providing free accommodation in a Spanish castle to the latter's widow and daughter.) The role Canaris played in the abortive anti-Hitler army measures of 1938 has already been mentioned. By March 1943 Canaris, revolted by the *Einsatzgruppen's* slaughter and convinced that only Hitler's death could save Germany, had travelled to Smolensk. There he sought to do away with the *Führer* (who had planned to visit that captured city on 13 March) in alliance with dissident army officers. Yet this effort came to nothing: the bomb built for the enterprise simply failed to detonate.

A Gestapo raid on 5 April ended hopes that the *Abwehr's* 'Operation U7' (begun in late 1941) could continue to save Jews from death camps while remaining a secret from Kaltenbrunner. It led not only to Canaris' own dismissal but to the arrest of his chief subordinates: his second-in-command Hans Oster; brilliant jurist and fellow *Abwehr* agent Hans von Dohnányi (son of the Hungarian composer Ernö Dohnányi); and Dohnányi's brother-in-law, the Lutheran pastor Dietrich Bonhoeffer. Another Canaris loyalist – Gisevius, by this time *Abwehr* attaché to the German Consulate in Zürich – managed to elude the Gestapo's grasp. In his postwar memoirs, Gisevius paid Canaris this tribute:

Canaris hated not only Hitler and Himmler, but the entire Nazi system as a political phenomenon ... He was everywhere and nowhere at once. Everywhere he travelled, at home and abroad and to the front, he always left a whirl of confusion behind him ... In reality this small, frail, and somewhat timid man was a vibrating bundle of nerves. Extremely well read, oversensitive, Canaris was an outsider in every respect. In bearing and manner of work he was the most unmilitary of persons ...

Canaris had a natural bent for leading his opponents astray. He could recite the Nazi verses so convincingly that even the greatest sceptics temporarily no longer dared to question the genuineness of his claims. As one leading Gestapo official angrily exclaimed ... 'That Canaris fooled everyone, Heydrich, Himmler, Keitel, Ribbentrop, and even the *Führer.*'

Dohnányi, who had attracted official surveillance by accident – Swiss contacts' dubious currency transactions had brought him to the authorities' attention – outraged his tormentors still further when it emerged that from 1934 onwards he had been methodically collecting psychiatric evidence of Hitler's unfitness to rule. By the time of his capture, all differences between the Gestapo's approach to interrogations and that of the SS had vanished. His gaolers thrashed him so badly that he could not even summon the strength to turn over in his makeshift bed. Nothing, whether physical torture or the courtroom derision that spewed from Roland Freisler's lips, lessened his courage or that of his comrades. Until the Reich's end there always seemed to be some excuse to postpone putting him out of his misery. Finally, on 8 April 1945, on a makeshift gallows in Sachsenhausen, Dohnányi's sufferings ended. The next day Canaris, Oster and Bonhoeffer were all hanged at the Flossenbürg concentration camp.

• • • • •

The Kreisau Circle maintained contacts with Canaris' group, but never strictly became a part of it. Its principles prevented it from doing so. Canaris, Bonhoeffer and their fellows had accepted the need to kill Hitler; the Kreisau Circle's leader, Count Helmut James von Moltke (the great-grand-nephew of the Franco-Prussian War's military genius Field-Marshal von Moltke), opposed tyrannicide as incompatible with Christian ethics. Moreover, the Kreisau Circle – named after Moltke's estate, where, unsuspected by the régime, it held four major meetings between 1940 and 1943 – advocated a labour-oriented Christian socialism, placing them at odds with the *Abwehr's* military imperatives, and indeed with the Lutheran national-conservatism of anti-NS leader Carl Goerdeler. (As early as 1935 Goerdeler had resigned from the mayoralty of Leipzig, in protest against the removal of that city's monument to the Jewish Felix Mendelssohn.)

Moltke's allies at Kreisau included fellow Anglophile Adam von Trott zu Solz, the circle's adviser on foreign affairs. Trott had studied at Oxford in the early 1930s, there forming passionate (though probably platonic) friendships with fellow Oxonians A.L. Rowse and Christopher Sykes, both of whom wrote prolifically and movingly about him years afterwards. A regrettable tendency, severe even by Teutonic standards, to cram his correspondence with quotations from Hegel did nothing to lessen the affection in which most of Britain's establishment held Trott. Affection, though, seldom translated into respect. His repeated visits to London in 1939 – urging British support for the army's anti-Hitler schemes – all failed: to a certain extent because of Chamberlain's appeasement, but in part through the diametrically un-Chamberlain-like intransigence of the Foreign Office's Permanent Under-Secretary Lord Vansittart, a noisy and obsessive racialist who regarded all Germans much as Hitler regarded all Jews. Trott's subsequent voyage to Washington in October 1939 proved similarly ineffectual, succeeding only in convincing the suspicious J. Edgar Hoover that he was Hitler's puppet. It is true that Trott, through whatever combination of naïveté and panic, had during the 1930s spoken of Hitler with a deference that afterwards he bitterly regretted.

In January 1944 Kaltenbrunner decapitated the Kreisau movement by ordering Moltke's arrest. As with Dohnányi, so with Moltke, the false belief that his tormentors could wring endless quantities of subversive information from him kept him alive long after he might have been expected to die.

• • • • •

Moltke's doom came in the wake of the July Conspiracy and its grand collapse. Colonel Claus von Stauffenberg – the man whose name is forever associated with this conspiracy – shared the aristocratic background of Moltke and Trott, though in his case Bavarian-Catholic rather than Prussian-Lutheran. The greatest influence on his outlook was one of Germany's leading modern poets: the mystic Stefan George, whom Stauffenberg regarded as a spiritual father, and who died only months after Hitler gained the chancellorship. (He seems never to have been interested in George's homosexual propensities.) At first Stauffenberg looked on National Socialism kindly, believing that it at least genuinely opposed Communists. Later his youthful enthusiasm waned, partly through anger at *Kristallnacht*, partly because the George doctrines of patrician spiritual refinement inoculated him against the NS régime's yelping vulgarity and orgiastic communitarianism.

Between 1938 and 1943 Stauffenberg kept his doubts about Hitler's morality to himself. He served in Poland, France, Russia, and finally (under Field-Marshal Erwin Rommel) North Africa. There, on a single day's fighting in April 1943, he lost his left eye, his right hand, and the use of two fingers on his left hand (which both had to be amputated afterwards). His convalescence allowed him the leisure to reflect on precisely what he had been fighting for: in particular, on how inflicting torture and death upon anti-Communist Slavs could be reconciled with Hitler's unblushing boasts of anti-Communist fervour. Having been convinced by these reflections that Germany could only live if Hitler died, he threw himself into anti-Hitler plots with alarming boldness.

In June 1944 he obtained the coveted post of chief of staff to General Friedrich Fromm, supreme army commander on the home front. This position gave Stauffenberg access to the very nerve centre of Hitler's war strategy. It also convinced him that he himself should assassinate Hitler, and that Fromm would look on this assassination with approval. By this stage his fellow conspirators included Field-Marshal Erwin von Witzleben, General Ludwig Beck, General Erich Fellgiebel, General Erich Hoepner, General Friedrich Olbricht, General Karl von Stülpnagel, General Albrecht von Mertz von Quiernheim, Lieutenant Werner von Häften, and Werner's diplomat brother, Hans-Bernd von Häften. Goerdeler and Rommel were also kept informed of, and remained sympathetic to, the scheme. Even *Reichsmarschall* Göring (disgraced by his *Luftwaffe's* failure to finish off Britain in 1940) underwent brief consideration as a possible ally of the conspirators. Yet he no longer had the bodily or mental strength to offer useful service, thanks to what presumably ranks as the most important narcotic habit in world history. His morphine consumption, abandoned in the 1920s under his wife's ministrations, had begun again under the pressures of war. Berlin police chief Wolf von Helldorf firmly opposed recruiting the *Reichsmarschall*. As Helldorf's son remarked, 'there was no evidence that he [Göring] would be sympathetic to the plotters and … in any event his physical condition – the consequence of addiction to drugs – would make him a doubtful asset'.

On the morning of 20 July Stauffenberg had his chance. At the Wolf's Lair where the increasingly paranoid Hitler dwelt, Stauffenberg deposited the briefcase containing the bomb, and commandeered a plane to Berlin, confident that neither Hitler nor any of the *Führer's* entourage could have survived the blast. Only that evening did he learn that Hitler had been only slightly injured in the explosion, that the Third Reich remained intact, that everything to which he and his followers had devoted themselves for months had ended in ghastly defeat. Fromm turned from sympathetic-seeming confidant into Hitler's instrument of revenge. General Beck shot, but failed to kill, himself; one of Fromm's officers had to give him the *coup de grâce*. Fromm lived in terror that his own knowledge of the plot would come to Hitler's notice if Stauffenberg stayed alive. Shortly after midnight on the 21st, Stauffenberg faced a firing squad that also killed Mertz, Olbricht and Lieutenant Häften. His last, defiant words were: 'Long live Germany!'

· · · · ·

Stauffenberg's confederates underwent far grosser tortures. Hitler raved, shrieked, howled, insisted that even Freisler's abuse would for the defendants be an inadequate castigation. The *Führer* demanded that all those even tangentially involved in Stauffenberg's intrigue, or in any earlier intrigues, be brought before Kaltenbrunner and – in Hitler's own words – 'hung up like meat-carcasses'. And so, after their respective show trials, many of them were: in the same Plötzensee cell where the brief lives of Helmut Hübener and the Scholls had been snuffed out. One by one, these champions of the old, civilised Germany trod, with firm and steady step, their *via crucis*: Moltke; Trott; Witzleben; Hoepner; Goerdeler; Fellgiebel; Stülpnagel; Hans-Bernd von Häften ...

Some victims were allowed the comparative dignity of beheading. The others died slowly, from nooses of piano wire cutting into their necks.

Rommel, given a choice between suicide and execution, swallowed a cyanide capsule on 14 October 1944. For doing so, Hitler rewarded him with full military honours at his state funeral.

• • • • •

The last moments of Plötzensee's victims were captured on celluloid. Historians disagree as to whether Hitler ever watched, watched once, or watched repeatedly, the resultant film footage.

• • • • •

Meanwhile A.J.P. Taylor, whose entire war service fell substantially short of firing a water-pistol, gave it as his considered opinion that 'the German resistance ... did not in fact resist'. (From the page immediately preceding this singular verdict, Taylor's true complaint against the German opposition emerges: its failure to emulate his own idol, that freedom-loving democrat Josip Broz Tito.) The equally memorable view of historian Sir John Wheeler-Bennett also warrants noting. Britain, this erstwhile admirer of Goerdeler and Trott averred, was 'better off [with Hitler staying alive] than if the plot of July 20th had succeeded and Hitler had been assassinated'.

• • • • •

The tale of Third Reich surveillance is quickly concluded. Both Himmler and Göring, as is well known, took their own lives: the former on 23 May 1945, in British captivity; the latter on 15 October 1946, after a virtuoso performance of taunting self-exoneration at Nuremberg.

Freisler lived for his courtroom demagogy and died for it. On 3 February 1945, amid one of his beloved show trials, air-raid sirens sounded. Everyone evacuated the building before the bomb fell, but Freisler slunk back soon afterwards, because he had left behind him the file on the defendant. A massive stone column, its foundations dislodged by the bomb's impact, fell on top of him and crushed him to death. He was found with the file still in his hand.

Kaltenbrunner's obstinacy at Nuremberg astonished not only the prosecutors, but the others in the dock. American army surgeon John K. Lattimer reported the response when Kaltenbrunner over and over again denied all knowledge of security police crimes (authorised by documents bearing his signature), as well as of the Final Solution:

Other prisoners frequently muttered 'You devil, you swine' … The other prisoners treated Kaltenbrunner coldly and contemptuously, talking over or around him as if he were not there … His role in murdering

234

so many of their friends after the Hitler bomb plot was
very much in their minds.

He died by the hangman's rope on 16 October 1946.

Officially Gestapo chief Heinrich Müller was last seen
alive on 29 April 1945, amid Berlin's Armageddon. It now
seems certain that he fled subsequently to Switzerland, carrying as much SS-obtained loot as he dared, and was
interviewed by America's Office of Strategic Services (the
CIA's precursor) in 1948: not with a view to putting him on
trial, but to offer him a job. He subsequently laboured for the
CIA as a dedicated, extraordinarily knowledgeable anti-Communist, and apparently ended his days – at, of all places,
Honolulu – in 1973.

you don't fire god:
J. EDGAR HOOVER'S
EYE ON AMERICA

You don't fire God.

*John F. Kennedy, explaining his refusal
to dismiss J. Edgar Hoover from office*

Washington, DC: 2 May 1972

ACK ANDERSON, *The Washington Post's* gossip columnist, could not believe his ears. While he was conducting
an otherwise uneventful interview with a minor federal
bureaucrat, a secretary had interrupted: 'I thought you should
know – J. Edgar Hoover is dead.'

It seemed impossible. As well imagine that Mt Rush-
more had lost a presidential face overnight. But a few
telephone calls later, Anderson had to admit to himself that
the news was true.

Anderson had had precious little regard for the
deceased's sensibilities. The previous year, he had thought it
entertaining to include in his column a list of personal items
that he had strenuously acquired from Hoover's garbage bins.
But this was not the time to be reminding readers of *that* little

prank. He had to produce some sort of obituary for his old foe, and not to sound too smug at his foe's demise. Eventually Anderson came up with the following statement:

> J. Edgar Hoover transformed the FBI from a collection of hacks, misfits and courthouse hangers-on into one of the world's most effective and formidable law enforcement organisations. Under his reign, not a single FBI man ever tried to fix a case, defraud the taxpayers or sell out his country.
>
> Hoover was also scrupulous at first not to step beyond the bounds of a policeman. But I would be hypocritical not to point out that in his fading years he sometimes stepped across those bounds.
>
> I have been critical of the FBI for going beyond its jurisdiction to investigate the business dealings, sex habits and personal affairs of prominent Americans.
>
> It is my hope for the country that Mr Hoover's successor will run the FBI as Hoover did in the beginning.

When, later that same morning, the news of Hoover's death reached Capitol Hill, both houses of Congress observed a minute's silence. Then senators and representatives competed with one another to praise the departed. Congress also voted to grant permission for Hoover to lie in state within the Capitol Rotunda, an honour previously accorded to hardly any other civilians, and to no civilian whatever who had not been president.

The major East Coast newspapers rushed their death

notices of Hoover into print (except for *The Washington Star,* where staff found to their wonderment that no death notice existed: as one *Star* reporter put it, 'We didn't think that old bastard was mortal'). Alistair Cooke, writing for the *Manchester Guardian,* was characteristically even-handed:

> He [Hoover] was generally regarded by the liberal press and by some conservatives as a monster Big Brother. He was regarded in a recent poll by eighty per cent of Americans as a national asset … eight Presidents of every political stripe trusted him, depended on him, and looked on him as a permanent fixture of the Republic like the Washington Monument. That has never been explained. One day it will have to be.

A few discordant notes sounded forth in the media. Gus Hall, General Secretary of the Communist Party of the USA, bemoaned in *The New York Times* Hoover's failure to meet Communism's strict standards of loving kindness. Hoover had been, Hall said, '[a] political pervert whose masochistic passion drove him to savage assaults on the principles of the Bill of Rights'. Yet the Soviet news agency *TASS,* far from gloating over Hoover's end, contented itself with publishing one neutral sentence: 'J. Edgar Hoover, who headed the United States' Federal Bureau of Investigation since 1924, died in Washington at the age of seventy-seven.'

Richard Nixon delivered the eulogy at Hoover's funeral. 'J. Edgar Hoover,' the President intoned, in words chosen for him by White House speechwriter Pat Buchanan, was one of the giants. His long life brimmed over with magnificent achievement and dedicated service to this country.

Nixon's private reaction to the news of Hoover's death had been somewhat different. He had gasped: 'Jesus Christ! That old cocksucker!'

Young Man in a Hurry: 1895–1924

Businesslike as ever, and not one to let public holidays stand as an excuse for sloth, John Edgar Hoover came into the world on New Year's Day 1895. His birthplace was, with equal appropriateness, Washington, DC.

On each side of his family tree Hoover was descended from that improbable phenomenon in a country devoted to mythologising 'rugged individualism': a civil service dynasty. From the early nineteenth century on, Hoover's ancestors lived and worked on Washington's government payrolls. Dickerson Naylor Hoover, John Edgar's father, ran a printing shop under the Commerce Department's ægis. Hoover's mother Annie, *née* Scheitlin, was of predominantly German-speaking Swiss stock; her family had produced two Swiss consuls to New York in as many generations, and she retained a good deal of the Teutonic *Hausfrau* in her temperament. On her child's domestic habits she left her permanent mark. Unlike most small boys, Edgar – the 'John' soon fell into abeyance – took great pride in keeping himself and his belongings as tidy as possible.

Though neither Dickerson (raised a Lutheran) nor Annie (raised a Catholic) went often to Sunday services after their son's birth, Edgar's own religion quickly grew as fervent as his parents' had grown lax. He began going to Washington's Old First Presbyterian Church, which he continued attending – regularly though by no means invariably – for the rest of his life, and where he became a respected Sunday school teacher. That Edgar's students should have made a joyful noise in 'Onward Christian Soldiers' might not be surprising; that he elicited from them equally enthusiastic renditions of 'Jesus Wants Me for a Sunbeam' is less predictable.

Drilling the boys and girls under his tutelage, Edgar made the agreeable discovery of three talents that later served him well: how to orate, how to persuade, and how to command. In 1948 he went so far as to call his Sunday school, and by implication Sunday schools in general, a 'crime prevention laboratory'. No one can understand Hoover without understanding his spiritual convictions. He continued throughout his public life to think of himself as a lay preacher.

Over and over again after he had become famous, Hoover denounced Communism primarily because of its atheism. (Communist rule's economic horrors, military menace, and juridical travesties interested him far less.) In a speech at a 1947 symposium of Methodist clergy held in Evanston, Illinois, Hoover said that 'Secularism … is the basic cause of crime, and crime is a manifestation of secularism.' Denominational distinctions held no interest for the Protestant Hoover, who was as scandalised as any Catholic or Orthodox believer by irreverent treatment of religious objects. The 1958 book *Masters of Deceit*, which he painstakingly vetted and which bore his name on the cover (though newspaperman Don Whitehead, twice a Pulitzer laureate, did part of the actual writing), upheld for particular horror Lenin's blasphemous conduct:

At the age of sixteen, as he later said, Lenin ceased to believe in God. It is reported that he tore the cross from his neck, threw this sacred relic to the ground, and spat on it.

In 1959, during a speech in Austin, Texas, Hoover returned to the theme of impious behaviour:

As a youth I was taught basic beliefs. Cynics, perhaps, may regard them with derision. For instance, I was taught that no book was ever to be placed above the Bible …

Hoover's ability to speak on a platform at all surprised all who knew him in his childhood. As a boy in grade school he suffered from a stammer, not so severe as to make all conversation impossible, but quite severe enough to be made the subject of cruel playground japes. Gradually young Edgar overcame its worst effects, through compelling himself to join a debating society at Washington's Central High School. He succeeded so well as to win several debating prizes. For him, Saul Bellow's aphorism 'Words are the poor boy's arsenal' held a particular and deep significance. Eventually he cultivated a mode of speech so fast that friends called him 'Speed' Hoover. This machine-gun enunciation afterwards acquired considerable usefulness for him when bawling out subordinates, haranguing hostile Senate committees, or defying obstreperous reporters.

One element in young Edgar's make-up still needs mention: his obsessive interest, which proved lifelong, in journalism. Not blessed with a natural literary endowment, he

242

acquired authorial skill through force of habit and untiring curiosity. In 1908 his concern for the Fourth Estate had manifested itself in a two-page bulletin that he issued regularly for months: *Weekly Review, Editor J.E. Hoover*. Copies cost one cent each, and he sold them to family and neighbours himself. Never one to overlook the pedagogic opportunities a captive audience offered, Edgar made room for characteristic exhorting: 'Eat Potatoes. Eat Apples. Eat Puffed Rice.'

With his reliable scholastic record, Edgar easily entered the law school at George Washington University. Lacking an Ivy League campus' social lustre, GWU nevertheless had two overriding recommendations: it specialised in training future civil servants; and it scheduled most lectures for early mornings and late evenings, enabling most students to hold day-jobs. On 13 October 1913 Edgar began work at the Library of Congress, as Junior Messenger. In his limited leisure time he could be surprisingly effervescent, as crime writer Ovid Demaris found in 1974 when interviewing Hoover's surviving cousins for *Esquire*. Even the boyish ruthlessness of Edgar's practical joking could not quench the affection in which these cousins held him.

In April 1917 his stable, predominantly uneventful, environment fell to pieces. His father had to resign from his bureaucratic job for health reasons. Crushing melancholia made it impossible to continue working. He received a pension, but that did not go far. Edgar still had his duties at the Library of Congress, where by punctuality and diligence he had proved his value to superiors. But his income remained all too small, and he had to find some other position quickly, preferably one within the civil service.

Hopes that Dickerson's condition might improve faded

fast. For the first four years after his collapse the invalid func-
tioned, in a limited way, around the house. In 1921, though,
he had to be committed for several months to a Maryland
sanatorium; when released, he who had once been so meek
frightened his loved ones by his snarling temper. The following year, aged sixty-five, he died of pneumonia. Annie was left
with the family home and with little else, except whatever
Edgar could afford from his own wages.

Much has been made of Edgar's refusal to marry, and the
assumption of uncontrolled homoerotic lusts that his lifelong
bachelorhood inspired. Precious few of those who gossiped
over Hoover's single status knew about his father's psychiatric
illness, and about the fears of hereditary transmission that such
an illness inspires in even the most euphoric and mature of a
sufferer's children. Edgar, mature beyond his years but never
euphoric, concealed the nature of Dickerson's collapse from
even his few intimates. During his old age Hoover freely
talked with devoted aides, including a gentleman with the
improbable (even for America) name of Cartha DeLoach,
about his rejection of marriage. Prying interviewers he would
fob off with a quip: 'I became attached to the Bureau. What
wife would have put up with me then?' But to DeLoach he
furnished a more elaborate reason, confirming that he viewed
divorce as unthinkable:

> I've often been asked why I never married. The truth
> is that if I had – and gotten the wrong woman – my
> life and career would have been ruined forever.

He probably meant every word he said; yet he concealed
much more than he divulged. Very rarely the Hoover mask

slipped. Like all men and women in American public life Hoover found himself the target for more, and louder, cranks than any busy individual should be forced to endure. If the mental aberration that brought them to his office took a harmless form, he would listen in silence to their muttering, their incoherent conspiracy theorising, their sobs of anguish, then lead them away, until they reached the street. He no more derided them than Cordelia derided King Lear.

•••••

On 6 April 1917, 'the American century' (as *Time's* founding publisher Henry Luce subsequently called it) began in earnest, when Woodrow Wilson declared that America was entering the Great War on the Allied side. Wilson's administration signed into law the Selective Service Bill, which permitted all able-bodied men between the ages of twenty-one and thirty to be drafted. In practice, drafting tended to be capricious within the federal bureaucracy. Some departments encouraged their young men to enlist; others simply tolerated enlistment; still others were draft-exempt. Those in the latter category included the Justice Department, where Edgar began working on 26 July 1917, twenty-nine days after the first US troops had landed on French soil.

John Lord O'Brian, Edgar's supervisor, quickly noticed the young man's exceptional enthusiasm for working back late in the evenings and, when circumstances required, on Sundays. Such diligence appeared to augur a new spirit of vigour within a department that otherwise displayed a gentlemanly reluctance to acknowledge that the twentieth century had even begun. In the year Edgar joined, the department's total transport expenditure consisted of $2,486.44 spent on upkeep of horse-drawn carriages and the horses themselves, plus a further $1.80 to cover the cost of repairing a bicycle. Edgar impressed O'Brian so much that, as early as 14 December 1917, a document written by O'Brian describes the ambitious twenty-two-year-old as a 'special agent'. Precisely what Edgar's duties in this capacity then involved is not clear. What remains beyond doubt is that Edgar's main work involved the newly founded War Emergency Division, whose job it was to round up spies in the pay of Wilhelmine Germany and, from 7 December, the other Central Powers.

In theory the Justice Department remained subordinate to Wilson's attorney-general, who since 1914 had been Thomas Gregory. The languid Texan Gregory proved the exact sort of attorney-general whom Edgar, then as in later years, found most meritorious: a readily by-passable yes-man, with a taste for signing arrest warrants and with a distinct lack of enthusiasm for inspecting paperwork. The administrative result of Edgar's assiduity was the Alien Enemy Bureau, where he put to efficient use the appetite for statistics which stayed with him for another half-century. His principal initiative, as distinct from his performance of specific duties set out by others, was ensuring that all German women in the United States (as well as men) had to be registered as enemy aliens. Was this specific call to register females an early example of Hooverian prurience? Possibly; but one should not underrate the element of conspiratorial hysteria that the entire Allied war effort involved.

The war had entered its final stages when, on 15 August 1918, the Wilson Administration cut off all diplomatic links with Bolshevik Russia. Less than a month beforehand, on

16 July, the Romanovs had met their end in Ekaterinburg. To Hoover (as it now seems appropriate to resume calling him), the Justice Department showed both its gratitude for his conscientiousness and its realisation of America's immediate future peril, by formally inducting him into one of its subdivisions, the Bureau of Investigation. It did more. As of 19 April 1918, it had placed him in charge of an entire section, the General Intelligence Division. From 16 October it had a new legal weapon at its disposal: the Immigration Act, which made association with anarchist or Communist organisations illegal. The Act stated:

> Aliens who believe in or advocate or teach the overthrow by force or violence of the Government of the United States ... [or] who are members of or affiliated with any organisation that entertains a belief in, teaches, or advocates the overthrow by force or violence of the Government of the United States shall be deported.

Those who hoped to justify their opposition to this law by invoking the US Constitution's First Amendment (which states that 'Congress shall make no law ... abridging the freedom of speech, or of the press') received a sharp rebuff early in 1919, when Judge Oliver Wendell Holmes of the Supreme Court ruled:

> The most stringent protection of free speech would not protect a man falsely shouting 'Fire' in a crowded theatre and causing panic ...

Less immediately welcome to Hoover than such eloquent assertions, but ultimately acceptable to him, was Gregory's departure from political life. Taking Gregory's place was Mitchell Palmer of Pennsylvania, who in March 1919 became the first Quaker ever to occupy the attorney-generalship.

Whereas for Gregory, Hoover had been little more than a cog – an admirable and expedient cog, admittedly – in the machine of government, Palmer maintained a more personal relationship with the young man. Cabinet official and department administrator had little in common by temperament, but this fact alone made them initially indispensable to one another. Despite his sanctimonious air, Palmer had nothing of the reformer about him. Not all the waters of religious rhetoric could sweeten his hands, which reeked of the pork barrel. Hence Hoover's value. That which Palmer could not promise to do himself without eliciting hoots of laughter, he could claim the credit for getting done if, and only if, the cleanskin Hoover did it.

Hoover's chance soon came. In April 1919 a series of parcels arrived at the homes and offices of leading Americans: including Palmer himself; Ole Hanson, Mayor of Seattle, who had quelled a waterfront strike in his city earlier in the year; the country's two most celebrated plutocrats, John D. Rockefeller and J. Pierpont Morgan; and Albert Burleson, the postmaster-general. No injuries resulted from most of these packages, but all turned out to have explosives inside. Palmer maintained that 'Reds' must have sent all the parcels. Others assumed at the time, and have continued to assume since, that they were actually the work of *agents provocateurs*: a conjecture lent plausibility by the fact that those who sent them were never arrested. At any rate, the news of the bombs resulted in the Justice Department's great anti-Red campaign of 1919–20.

Historians usually refer to this campaign as 'the Red scare', a disingenuous appellation implying that the very desire to punish Reds denotes mass paranoia. This was not how it appeared to Hoover and to other serious observers of Europe in 1919. They feared – given events in Prussia, Bavaria, Finland, Spain, Hungary, and Italy – that the Communist virus would sweep the civilised world as quickly and ruthlessly as the misnamed 'Spanish flu' was doing. For Communists everywhere, 1919 was their hopes' *annus mirabilis*. The revolution looked to be weeks away at most, rather than the months or years that they had previously imagined.

Hoover, who previously had read little except law books, bureaucratic files, and the Bible, now undertook to acquaint himself with Communist dogma at its sources. Therefore he began, as Ovid Demaris put it, 'desperately trying to digest the voluminous writings of Marx, Engels, Lenin and Trotsky, a spicy broth for the young debater from Central High'. 'Know your enemy' was, at this stage and for decades to come, the motto by which he lived. Country-club Republicans, willing enough to grumble about Reds, lacked the ideological application to study the Reds themselves. This dire mistake Hoover avoided. Although never an intellectual in either the strict or the vulgarly pejorative use of that term, he had too much acumen to gainsay the power of ideas over others.

Between the Great War's close and Palmer's sanctioning of increased anti-Red activity, Hoover found the time to assemble a card-index file on no fewer than 450,000 individuals considered enemies of the State. On 7 November, in

249

New York City, his bureau carried out the first of what Americans soon learned to describe as 'the Red Raids', which produced a rich haul of alien troublemakers. In no way was the bureau's brief limited to the Communist Party. It also pursued the (separate and comparatively weak) Communist Labor Party, as well as the so-called 'Wobblies': in other words, the Industrial Workers of the World (IWW), the industrial movement which entertained dreams of One Big Union around the globe that would blow apart capitalism forever. The three best known individuals arrested were Emma Goldman, Alexander Berkman and Ludwig Martens. Goldman had been apprehended, not just for championing free love and contraception, but for an activity almost two decades in the past: publicly advocating in 1901 the assassination of President William McKinley, a proposal acted on within months by a deranged member of her audience. Berkman was celebrated primarily for having shot and wounded steel magnate Henry Clay Frick. Martens had yet to be officially recognised as Soviet ambassador to America – since the ban on US–USSR diplomatic relations continued – but had accorded himself the privileges of ambassadorial life anyhow. On 22 December, two hundred and fifty aliens found themselves expelled from the country. It was a promising prelude, but a prelude it remained.

In January 1920 Palmer and his loyal henchman increased the heat on radicalism. Palmer issued arrest warrants by the thousand, and bureau officials in thirty-three cities carried out raids that put almost six thousand suspects behind bars. Some were seized in offices, some in shops, and some from their beds. Protests went up, primarily over the unsanitary conditions prevailing in the most overcrowded police depots; but the overall public reaction to these raids varied

you don't fire god

from reserved acquiescence to passionate enthusiasm. One headline in a pro-Hoover newspaper jeered: 'All aboard for the next Soviet ark.' What Berlin's *Freikorps* had needed bullets to achieve, the General Intelligence Division had carried out severely but with full legal sanction. Towards the end of his life Hoover tended not to dwell with any great pride on the raids. At the time – and fortified by his laboriously acquired scholarship in Marxist doctrine – he regarded them as the only solution to the Red menace; and the majority of his countrymen agreed with him.

In an early manifestation of his lifelong desire for improving colleagues' morale, Hoover turned his journalistic aptitude to producing a regular (eventually weekly) newsletter for top civil servants only. Called *Bulletin of Radical Activities*, the publication – lasting from 1920 to 1921 – praised such patriotic groups as the Knights of Columbus, while reprimanding the liberal columnist Walter Lippmann and the American Civil Liberties Union as well as prominent socialists. Simultaneously it insisted on the need for American patriots to stay within the law: an indication that Hoover's aims went beyond his immediately obvious targets.

By striking as hard as he did, Hoover wanted not only to crush America's Communist and anarchist left, but also to deter vigilantism on the part of America's violent right. The years during and immediately after World War I marked a veritable orgy of civil strife, by no means wholly or even mainly in the Deep South: race riots in East St Louis (1917) and Chicago (1919) which left scores dead; Boston's police strike (also 1919); and, two months after the last-named event, the Armistice Day (of all days) shoot-out at Centralia, Washington State, between American Legion officers and IWW members, which ended when an IWW official who had killed three Legionnaires was then himself captured, castrated, and hanged from a nearby bridge. Worst of all disturbances of the peace during this period was the massacre – so little reported at the time as to have been largely forgotten even within America – over six days in 1921 at Tulsa, Oklahoma. Rumours that a black man had made sexual advances to a white female elevator attendant led to supporters of the accused fighting against whites bent on vengeance. Both sides went berserk, and although the official death toll stood at thirty-five (later increased to seventy-nine), the actual body count might well have been more than three hundred.

All this Hoover knew about in detail, which is more than his critics at the time – or, for the most part, later on – usually did. So when a similar collapse of civil society afflicted America during the late 1960s and early 1970s, Hoover witnessed it with a much keener sense of history than most Americans possessed. Of all those individuals who helped govern America during the anti-Vietnam protests, only Hoover was old enough to have been helping govern America during the Wilson presidency.

Even before Tulsa, however, the 'Red scare' ran out of steam. The raids' sheer success had frightened American leftists themselves, most of whom concluded that the revolution – so tantalisingly imminent the previous year – might have to be postponed after all. A law of diminishing returns would operate with future government initiatives in this area, since so much had been effected the first time around. American Communist Party membership plunged, from more than 60,000 in September 1919 to only 5,700 by the end of 1920. Further disheartening news for American Communists came from Europe, where anti-Communists were recovering much of the power that they had supinely forfeited in 1918–19.

In these circumstances, renewed anti-Red actions of a spectacular type suggested overkill. Palmer himself was becoming somewhat of a liability to colleagues. Of a blustery nature, which success rendered ecstatic, but which temporary frustration cast down, Palmer took to covert drinking and suffered increasingly from nervous exhaustion. The latter took unpredictable forms. On one occasion a distraught Palmer astonished Franklin Roosevelt, then assistant secretary of the Navy, by reverting, in his anguish, to the 'thee' and 'thou' speech patterns of his Quaker childhood. Especially hostile to Palmer was Louis Post, assistant secretary of Labor, who itched to strike back at Palmer's draconian attitudes. Of more than five thousand individuals arrested via Justice Department warrants, Post agreed to fewer than one thousand being deported.

There remained one course, and only one, for Hoover to adopt. Whatever the cost, he must distance himself from Palmer. When the Democrats held their presidential primaries in June 1920, Palmer – who had assumed beforehand that he had only to stay alive in order to get the party's nod – found himself easily defeated. The Republicans' mediocre candidate, Senator Warren Harding, won a crushing Electoral College victory in November. Yet the disgrace into which Palmer had fallen did not lastingly touch his confederate. Hoover's survival on this occasion marked the first instance of a talent that he afterwards showed many times: his gift for remaining loyal to a humiliated politician until that all-important second before the trapdoor opened under the latter's feet.

As Palmer's tenure dragged towards its close, a New York City bomb blast on 16 September 1920 killed thirty-three people. The bureau arrested more than two thousand aliens in connection with this outrage, and ensured that 446 of them (all Communist Party members) were deported. Meanwhile in Dedham, Massachusetts, an armed robbery of a payroll van – during which two security guards were shot dead – propelled to world fame the Italian anarchists charged with the killings: Nicola Sacco and Bartolomeo Vanzetti. Hoover could recognise an incipient public relations disaster when he saw one (though he never predicted the sheer scale of the international brouhaha the case proceeded to attract); and while the Bureau made plans to deport the two defendants if a court let them go free, it otherwise left the affair to the Massachusetts authorities. Despite thunderous condemnations of the guilty verdict from public intellectuals around the world who demanded a retrial, the two Italians lost their appeals and died in the electric chair. (Subsequently it emerged that Sacco, at least, was entirely guilty; a 1961 ballistics re-examination showed that Sacco's gun had discharged the fatal bullets.)

• • • • •

Nobody had a keener consciousness of Warren Harding's defects in high office than Warren Harding. One of his first acts as president was to appoint as attorney-general his campaign manager, Harry M. Daugherty, who ran the 'Ohio Gang' that surrounded Harding, and whose main formal qualification for the attorney-generalship consisted of an insatiable appetite for playing poker. (Let it not, however, be thought that Daugherty lacked eloquence; the English language owes to him, it seems, the useful phrase 'smoke-filled room'.)

Fortunately for Hoover, Daugherty bore no party-polit-ical malice towards servants of the previous régime. Thus Hoover found himself on 22 August 1921, when the Harding administration was only five months old, chosen as the Bureau of Investigation's assistant director. As such, Hoover earned $4,000 a year, and theoretically answered to the bureau's new director (also a Daugherty appointment), William J. Burns. In practical terms, the relationship between director and directee was precisely the other way about. Burns – a worldly goon, convenient for frightening Daugherty's newspaper critics, if need be by beating them up, but innately unimaginative – could never overawe the puritanical, visionary Hoover. Recollecting, long afterwards, the Burns directorship's cor-ruption, Hoover lamented: 'Those of us [bureau staff] who were honest kept quiet about where we worked.'

Hoover's conspicuous successes during this period included the downfall of Marcus Garvey, who at the height of his fame and political strength was America's most feared black demagogue. The Jamaican-born Garvey, undistinguished in appearance but with a voice that could galvanise crowds, had devoted his life to founding and maintaining the Universal Negro Improvement Association (UNIA). This movement took as its slogan 'Back to Africa', and sought to establish one vast Negro republic controlling most of the African con-tinent, where the earth's tired, poor, and huddled Negro masses could breathe free. Liberia's government made sympa-thetic noises concerning Garvey's scheme, and for a while it seemed about to become a reality. Hoover grumbled in a memo on 11 October 1919 that Garvey 'had not yet violated any Federal law'.

That soon changed. Garvey, though he stopped short of acquiring a Communist Party membership card, announced in his own magazine, *Negro World*, that the black man's best hope of salvation lay in Moscow. Hoover took due note of this development, and patiently waited for Garvey's ambitions to unravel. In 1922, Garvey found himself indicted for mail fraud. How much Garvey was a swindler and how much a bungler has been debated ever since; at any rate, his business activities sufficed to ruin him. Sentenced in 1923 to five years' imprisonment in Atlanta, Garvey served only two years and nine months of his term before being deported to Jamaica. Had the mail fraud accusation not stuck, Hoover planned to get Garvey charged with the same crime that undid Al Capone years later: tax evasion.

While Garvey self-destructed, Hoover continued to fight left-wing activity in its more conventional forms. A national railroad dispute that paralysed trains from July 1922 ended the following September, when bureau agents acted as strike-breakers. More dramatically, on 22 August 1922 top officials in the (still illegal) Communist Party of the USA, who were running a convention in Bridgman, Michigan, found themselves under arrest. One of their number turned out to be in bureau pay. Yet Hoover, though he might prevail temporarily against the CPUSA itself, could not prevail against juries. All of the Bridgman victims escaped prison, an outcome that confirmed Hoover in his lifelong resentment of the jury system more generally.

True to his earlier practice of hitting out at the radical right and the radical left simultaneously, Hoover combined the above bureau procedures with action (beginning in September 1922) against the renascent Ku Klux Klan. The original

Klan – 'Ku Klux' derived from *kuklos,* a Greek word for 'circle' – had arisen after the Civil War. Former Confederate general Nathan Bedford Forrest founded it in 1867 as primarily a Confederate veterans' league, and had declared himself its first Grand Wizard. Alarmed by its members' murderous propensities (exclusively, in those days, towards blacks; Forrest's Klan allowed Jews and Catholics to join it, though how many Jews and Catholics availed themselves of this offer is not certain), Forrest resigned from his own movement in 1869. By 1880 the movement itself had subsided. Then one day in 1915 a Georgian named William Simmons, who falsely boasted of military distinction – asked why he styled himself 'Colonel', he replied, 'People call me "colonel" out of respect' – interpreted a pattern he saw in the clouds as somehow constituting a divine command to save the white race's honour and set up a new Klan. Simmons obeyed his allegedly providential edict so well that by 1922 the revivified Klan boasted of having a million members.

Unlike the old Klan, the new Klan transcended the poor white South. It chose state governors in Oregon, Ohio, Indiana, and even California as cynically as if it were buying loaves of bread over the counter. National Klan boss during the early 1920s was a dentist, Hiram Evans, whose portrait graced the cover of *Time*'s 23 June 1924 issue, and who in the cover article over-modestly called himself 'the most average man in America'. One Alabama Klan Wizard, Hugo Black, became a Supreme Court judge, his background inspiring remarkably little public odium through a long, taxpayer-subsidised judicial career that ended only with his death in 1971. In Missouri, a politically ambitious haberdasher named Harry S. Truman paid the local Klan's $10 membership fee, though he demanded his money back on discovering that if he stayed with the Klan he would need to cut dead – if necessary in a literal rather than a purely social sense – his Catholic friends. And in Louisiana (with its unusually large Catholic population), the Klan concentrated on hounding anti-Prohibitionist Governor John M. Parker. In September 1922 Parker, doubting his own state troops' fundamental loyalty amid any shoot-out with the KKK, sent a journalist from New Orleans' *Times-Picayune* newspaper to ask Hoover for aid.

By the time of Parker's appeal things in Louisiana's capital, Baton Rouge, had become almost hopeless. Klansmen, with total impunity, were intercepting Parker's mail and monitoring his telephone calls. Finally the bureau hit pay-dirt: not in the case *sub judice,* but in the interesting private life of the Louisiana Klan's Imperial Kleagle, Edward Young Clarke. Like too many Klan protagonists, Clarke combined orations about the purity of white Southern womanhood with a surreptitious taste for violating same while on his frequent travels. Worse still, he had no objection to the objects of his desire being under the age of consent. So the bureau arrested Clarke for breaching the Mann Act, which Congress had passed in 1910 at the bureau's own insistence, and which prohibited the transportation of minors across state borders 'for immoral purposes'. Baton Rouge jurors who – whether eagerly or fearfully – acquiesced in Klan murder refused to stomach Klan rape. To Hoover's great satisfaction, Clarke landed in gaol (April 1924) and, unlike certain other incarcerated Klansmen, never regained political influence.

Hoover's victory against Clarke, while not the end of the Klan, was at least the end of the beginning. He had shown Clarke, and the Klan overall, the folly of underestimating federal pressure. By 1926 the Indiana Klan's Grand Dragon, David Stephenson, had been put on trial for indecently assaulting a woman who died only days after identifying her attacker. Confident that he could charm or scare jurymen into giving a 'not guilty' verdict ('I am the law here in Indiana,' he once said), Stephenson nevertheless went to prison, where he stayed for twenty-six years. From its heights of 1922–23, KKK membership crashed to a 1930 level of approximately five thousand. Most strikingly, the Klan forfeited – and never won back – its following among the educated classes. In 1944 it was formally dissolved.

The landslide victory in the 1924 presidential contest of Harding's successor, Calvin Coolidge, meant that Hoover stayed safe in his office. By the time it occurred, Daugherty had been disgraced, in the 'Teapot Dome' controversy that overtook him and the rest of the Ohio Gang after Harding suddenly died on 2 August 1923. Meanwhile Coolidge surrounded himself with sturdy, scrupulous patricians. Of immediate relevance to the Bureau of Investigation, New York lawyer Harlan Stone took over as attorney-general.

Stone had been among Palmer's harshest public critics during the anti-Red raids. The first meeting between the new attorney-general and the man partly responsible for organising those raids threatened fireworks of mutual recrimination. No such recrimination occurred. An assistant to Commerce Secretary Herbert Hoover (no relation) expressed amazement that the bureau could look around for a boss from outside 'when they have the man they need right over there now – a young, well-educated lawyer named Hoover'. Thus impressed, Herbert Hoover recommended his namesake to Stone's attention. Stone, having discovered how unsatisfactorily William

Burns had filled the role of Hoover's nominal superior, offered Hoover the bureau directorship. Hoover, we are told,

> did not immediately leap at the opportunity … 'I'll take the job, Mr Stone,' he said, 'under certain conditions.' Asked to explain, Hoover told Stone that he would not tolerate any political meddling, and that he wanted sole control over merit promotions. This response delighted Stone. 'I wouldn't give it to you under any other conditions,' he replied. 'That's all. Good-day.'

Hoover took one, entirely typical, precaution before formally becoming director. His researches had revealed to him the existence in Washington of *another* John E. Hoover, no kin to himself, who owed $900 to a local store. Before this discovery, the bureaucrat had signed his name 'John E. Hoover' ever since leaving college; but after it, he invariably used the signature J. Edgar Hoover, 'not wanting to be confused with a deadbeat'.

To Hoover's advancement Burns offered no opposition. Burns' career, like Daugherty's, had in effect died along with Harding. Daugherty accused Burns of lying under oath about a Bureau raid in Montana that Daugherty had first ordered in secret, and had then found it expedient to deny. What limited moral courage Burns possessed melted away under this, quite possibly unjust, charge; and on 9 May 1924, obliging to the last, he resigned. The next day Hoover, still in his twenties, had the job. For the next forty-seven years and 357 days, he continued to hold it.

you don't fire god

The G-Man's Rise, or,
Hollywood Anti-Babylon: 1924–36

Even by the most basic physical criteria, Hoover in 1924 was almost identical to his nationally televised self during the 1950s and 1960s. The young Hoover differed from the old Hoover not in any ideological convictions, but mainly in possessing a full head of hair, which at least minimised the reptilian physiognomy that gave him such a menacing look in his sixties and seventies. He had already lost the battle against excess fat, and while he later imposed weight limits on bureau personnel, everyone understood that he never meant such limits to apply to himself. Also in evidence were the protuberant eyes, which suggested goitre, and which might have had other origins. Rumours have persisted since the 1970s that Hoover had African ancestry,* and certainly his mother's visage in a family photo from Hoover's childhood adds credence to the idea. Interestingly, although not conclusively, the portrait of Hoover that most impressed Cartha DeLoach by its fidelity to the sitter was not an official photograph, but a drawing that could almost be of a black man. Hoover so disliked this drawing that, rather than be confronted with it again, he told DeLoach to keep it. Like most high public officials in 1920s America, Hoover had seen for himself how much damage Harding had suffered by repetitive imputations (baseless though they seem to have been) of black ancestry. The last thing that Hoover wanted, in his position at the top

---

* In Woody Allen's film *Bananas* – released in 1971, within Hoover's lifetime – a large black woman, when asked her name in court, replies 'J. Edgar Hoover.' The judge responds, 'You're very well disguised, Mr Hoover.' The woman says: 'I have many enemies.'

of the bureau's greasy pole, was to be knocked back to the bottom of it by a similar campaign from politically motivated malcontents.

That such malcontents would abound became inevitable once Hoover set to work as director: partly because the bureau had so ambiguous a legal standing from its very start. To read the tortuous jurisdictional narrative of the bureau's pre-Hoover period is to understand afresh how America's most celebrated national industry came to be the overproduction of lawyers.

In spite of Hoover's understandable fondness for implying that he not only cleaned up but invented his workplace, the bureau had actually come into being on 1 July 1908. The civil service reformer responsible for founding it gloried in the name of Charles Joseph Bonaparte, and was in fact a nephew of Napoleon III. Yet nothing could have been less Bonapartist, less redolent of the *Code Napoléon's* grand legalistic design, than this Bonaparte's improvisation once Theodore Roosevelt appointed him attorney-general. What could the bureau legally do, and what could it not legally do? Nowhere did Bonaparte or anyone else definitively answer this question. Its ostensible purpose was to fight 'crimes against the United States', a description so vague as to be nonsensical. What did 'crimes against the United States' consist of? Surely they included assassinating a president? No, they did not, a fact dramatically demonstrated by the chaos around JFK's hospital bed on 22 November 1963. Oswald's crime violated Texan law, rather than federal law: so that as Alistair Cooke commented, 'the first responsibility rested with the Dallas police'. In truth, 'crimes against the United States' meant pretty much what the executive, from day to day, wanted them to mean. Unable to get the bureau (not that it was *called* the bureau until March 1909) scrapped outright, Congress decided to limit its powers. Most notably, it forbade bureau agents to bear arms, thereby making them useless in serious crime-fighting, and also stymieing Roosevelt's idea of using them as secret service reinforcements.

During the reign of Roosevelt's successor, William Howard Taft (1909–13), the bureau confined itself largely to what would now be called 'feel-good' tasks: above all, to fighting the White Slave Trade, which state police lacked the resources, the coordination, and – most important – the desire to combat. It enjoyed its main victory in persuading Congress to pass the aforementioned 1910 Mann Act, which proved so popular that the Justice Department actually hived off certain bureau staffers to form a separate White Slave Bureau, though this organisation ceased in 1914.

In the freewheeling manner already entrenched, the bureau took most of its leaders from private enterprise, with nary a thought concerning possible conflicts of interest. William Burns had come to the government's notice through his success at running his own detective agency; he continued to run it on the side while employed first by the secret service, then as the bureau's chief. Within the pre-Hoover bureau, anything resembling *esprit de corps* (let alone an impersonal bureaucratic mandarinate on Whitehall, *Junker* or *École Polytechnique* lines) was unheard of. In this respect the ascetic Hoover – paradoxically for such a super-patriot – came much closer to British, German and French conceptions of well-educated incorruptibles serving the State, than to his own predecessors' roistering venality. However much it served

Hoover's purposes to cry up his precursors' vice (as opposed to his own virtue), the vice was there in cartloads. One close observer of it, Ugo Carusi – special assistant to six consecutive attorneys-general – flatly called William Burns 'a guy ... [with] no agency that was worth talking about.'

Once Hoover took control, he achieved a possibly unique feat among bureaucratic empire-builders, in that he made an already small department still smaller. In 1924 the bureau had 441 agents; by 1925 Hoover had reduced the number to 402; and by 1929 a mere 339 remained. He announced – and maintained all his life – a rule that any agent who drank alcohol while on duty would be dismissed 'with prejudice' (in other words, could never again obtain work on a Federal payroll). Agents who used bureau cars for their own purposes, or who tried to cheat the taxman, would meet the same fate. Those time-wasters whom Hoover could not actually dismiss, he made so uncomfortable by the demands he placed on their inadequate talents that they quit with relief.

The accomplishment of this period in which Hoover perhaps took the most pride was his ability to keep Gaston B. Means, a confidence trickster of homicidal intent, out of the bureau. To Hoover, Gaston B. Means was everything a bureau employee should not be; and while Hoover's accounts of Means' villainies no doubt improved in the repeated telling, the villainies themselves were abundantly ingenious. Means' early successes included inheriting a fortune from his wife (whose death he ascribed to an inadvertent gunshot wound in the head); winning damages from the Pullman railway company, for injuries incurred in an 'accident' that he had himself faked; and spying simultaneously for both the British and the German governments during the Great War. A suitably respectful

William Burns described Means as 'the most wonderful operator [he] ever met', and soon gave him a bureau office. When
Prohibition became law, Means made extra money from boot-
leggers by selling them their own bureau files. He also offered
to save Attorney-General Daugherty's flagging career by
arranging another Red Scare. To get the scare onto a proper
footing, Means offered to blow up Daugherty's own home,
'while your family's away, of course'. Even the latitudinarian
Burns drew the line at this, and Means duly resigned; but he
threatened to send Hoover insane by his skill in keeping himself – and the bureau – in the public eye. Burdened by the debts
he had accumulated while maintaining three live-in servants
and a chauffeur-driven Cadillac on a modest bureau pay-
packet, Means burst into print with a lubricious fantasy entitled
The Strange Death of President Harding, which alleged that the
late chief executive had been murdered by his jealous wife.
Afterwards he acknowledged the book to have been pure fiction. Eventually he swindled $100,000 out of a socialite by
promising that the sum would go towards solving the Lindbergh kidnapping. This entrepreneurship landed Means in a
federal penitentiary from which (to Hoover's profound relief)
he never emerged, except to provide invariably entertaining,
predominantly mendacious testimony at criminal trials.

Not content with purging the bureau of Means' presence and attitudes, Hoover acquired further kudos when
compelled to appear before the congressional committee
responsible for allocating the bureau's funds. He actually asked
that the bureau subsidy be reduced. This initiative so astonished the committee members that, once they had recovered
from the shock, they decided to give the bureau enough
money to ensure that it would never again suffer want.

Herein lies another of the numerous Hoover paradoxes: that Hoover, who hated revolutionists, could carry out a revolution of sorts himself. Through instituting a meritocratic ideal (one that in his best years he actually upheld), he was serving notice that one man in his own little bailiwick could defy the spoils system which has cursed American politics as a whole ever since President Andrew Jackson initiated it during the 1830s. Might the whole of American administration have undergone a similar overhaul? Perhaps not. Perhaps the bureau's sheer compactness made possible what in larger departments it would have been unavailing even to try. Besides, no president since Franklin Roosevelt has tolerated the encroachment on his own power that widespread civil service restructuring would demand. As an urbane and amusing political scientist, Godfrey Hodgson, once remarked:

> There was always an *ad hoc*, not to say an *ad hominem* flavour about the New Deal … he [Roosevelt] did nothing to strengthen the status, or the morale, or the training of the bureaucrats who were to run it. …
> The result, which was by no means accidental, was that the White House would retain day-to-day control of a machine which, if it had been more logically constructed, must have developed a momentum of its own.

And yet, and yet. Contrasting the bureau with the original CIA – or, as it was first called, the Office of Strategic Services – is instructive. Under the direction of that bizarre figure 'Wild Bill' Donovan (whom Hoover despised), America's foreign espionage corps was not much bigger than Hoover's bureau; but it entirely failed to implement Hoover's quality controls, and instead has for more than half a century given the distinct impression of raiding the world's mental homes and park benches to recruit fantasists, cowboys, traitors and dope-fiends. Had the Hoover rather than the Donovan attitude triumphed, how much anti-American sentiment mankind might have been spared during the Cold War.

· · · · ·

When Herbert Hoover took over the presidency from Coolidge in March 1929, any fears on J. Edgar's part that he might be expendable soon dissolved. In January 1932, looking back on the previous eight years, Harlan Stone – still very much a power in the land, despite his departure from the cabinet – wrote to J. Edgar in words that warmed their recipient's heart. Thanks to J. Edgar's efforts, Stone asserted, 'the Government can now take pride in the bureau instead of feeling obliged to apologise for it'. Still, it does not detract from Hoover's achievements to point out that, as well as being exceptionally industrious and ingenious, he was exceptionally lucky. Had Hoover's bureau been required by law to enforce Prohibition, not even he could have avoided being covered in the moral slime that (by its very nature) Prohibition spread. Until 1930, Prohibition remained a Treasury Department responsibility.

Instead, J. Edgar enabled the bureau to concentrate on crime-fighting and investigation that had bipartisan support. It kept close surveillance on a committee formed in the hope of freeing from prison two hard-left labour union leaders; on the

American Civil Liberties Union's banking transactions; on the Friends of the Lictor, an obscure fascistic group; and on the Navy League of the United States (a coalition of shipbuilders and armour-plate manufacturers irate at Herbert Hoover's naval cutbacks). The bureau also thwarted, in 1926, plans by Major-General Enrique Estrada to launch an invasion of Mexico from American soil.

Another benefit to J. Edgar from domestic events during the 1920s and early 1930s lay in Middle America's growing enthusiasm for – or rather, Middle America's declining hostility towards – a coordinated central policy against crime. Whereas until the mid-1920s such a policy would have been howled down by Democrats and Republicans alike as an intolerable affront to state governments' prerogatives, the bootleg years made it seem increasingly justified.

To this good fortune for Hoover, must be added a stroke of entirely personal luck. One of the bureau's chief tormentors ever since the Harding years had been Democratic Senator Thomas Walsh of Montana. As the Great Depression wore on, Herbert Hoover's chances of being re-elected sank to nothing. This raised for J. Edgar the chilling vision of Walsh being included in an imminent Democratic administration, to give the bureau yet more trouble. Certainly FDR, after lambasting the incumbent in the presidential election of November 1932, announced that on taking office he would appoint Walsh attorney-general. Then, on 2 March 1933, two days before FDR's inauguration, Walsh dropped dead after an overly strenuous honeymoon. Once more J. Edgar could breathe easily, even if the hapless Walsh could not.

• • • • •

At first glance it seems impossible that Hoover and FDR should have even shown civility towards one another, let alone become friends. Hoover was anti-Communist till his dying day, and of firm (if not always observed) principles in his private life. Fifty years' glutinous hagiography has failed to detect in FDR any principle whatsoever, other than the need to look after number one. In his first major foreign policy initiative, he established diplomatic relations with the USSR; and during the Spanish Civil War he permitted American Communists to recruit for Republican Spain's Abraham Lincoln Brigade. As late as 1940, amid the Stalin–Hitler love feast, FDR upbraided the firmly anti-Soviet Congressman Martin Dies: 'There is nothing wrong with the Communists in this country. Several of the best friends I have are Communists.' Yet Communism had no more intrinsic appeal to him than Albigensianism or Anabaptism; it was simply a gangster ethic that – despite its disappointing shortage of fireside chats and other populist touches – demonstrably worked. Had it not worked, had Stalin ended up like Al Capone, Roosevelt would have shed few tears. Where, in so cynical a being, could either fondness for or esteem from Hoover be found? There were in fact three places.

First, Hoover and Roosevelt had for one another the respect which any PR genius has for another PR genius. That Hoover's gifts in PR derived from burning conviction, whereas Roosevelt's were as much a smoke-and-mirrors display as everything else about him, became in the circumstances irrelevant.

Secondly, Hoover's sheer conventionality as a middleclass American ensured that he would, until old age, revere the *office* of president, whatever he thought of the office's holder.

It took the Kennedy tribe's sheer pubescent irresponsibility to degrade the presidential function in Hoover's eyes. For such irresponsibility Roosevelt, to his credit, had no enthusiasm. If only because of his paraplegia and his monarchical pretensions, Roosevelt retained a Bagehot-like determination not to let daylight in upon presidential magic.

Thirdly, FDR had the power-maniac's saving grace: a disinterested esteem for competence *qua* competence, wherever it might show itself. In his inner circle competence did not exactly abound. Most of his New Deal loyalists were ciphers and bunglers, when not Soviet stooges. FDR resembled a Diaghilev trying to extract serviceable performances from peevish road-company hoofers. Therefore he relished virtuosos, however otherwise uncongenial. Like Mr Salteena in *The Young Visiters,* Hoover was 'not quite a gentleman but that can't be helped'. Where gentlemen would fear to tread, Hoover would rush in. Hence his usefulness.

Hoover was fortunate in that simultaneously with his increased access to presidential power, his private life grew somewhat richer. Not at first; he continued to live with his mother until cancer killed her in 1938. Cartha DeLoach was adamant that J. Edgar loved his mother

> more than anyone in the world … He kept reminders of her in his office – including pieces of her china – but discarded or packed away most of the awards and letters of commendation he got from Presidents and other famous people.

From the late 1920s, Clyde Tolson became the dominating male figure in Hoover's world. Unlike the city-bred

Hoover, Tolson was very obviously a country boy, born in 1900 on a Missouri farm, and raised in Iowa. Once close to Hoover, he soon acquired a reputation as the kinder, gentler face of Hooverism. Those who dreaded dealing with Hoover in person found Tolson an authoritative, courteous substitute. Tall, softly-spoken and deferential (he usually called Hoover 'Boss', while Hoover called him 'Junior' despite the mere five years' difference in their ages), Tolson concealed behind his modest exterior a quick intelligence and an exceptional memory. He never returned Hoover's periodic insults, or flaunted his own skill. Alabama lawyer George Allen, several times an eyewitness of Tolson in action, recounted how sometimes the irritable Hoover

> would say 'My God, shut up, Junior, you're putting my
> ears out.' Clyde would say, 'Aah.' Paid no attention to
> him whatsoever ... you wanted to know about the sit-
> uation in, say, Guatemala, [you'd] call Clyde. He'd give
> it to you quicker than Hoover. And he wasn't jealous
> of Hoover, either. He never let anybody know how
> much he helped Hoover.

By 1930 Hoover and Tolson were taking their holidays together. Was theirs a full sexual union? Gossips abounded who maintained that it was, and who said so while both men lived. Those closer to Hoover – such as DeLoach – have emphatically denied that Hoover and Tolson were ever lovers, and have observed that much Hoover-related scandal-mongering displays attitudes which, if shown towards almost anybody except Hoover, 'would have been attacked by every politically correct reviewer in the country for being "homophobic"'. That a deep emotional bond existed between the two, no one can contest. Nonetheless it surely remains implausible that two devout men in love with power should have risked physical activity which not only broke prevailing laws in all states but, if discovered, would have ruined their careers for ever.

Anthony Summers, in his readable but predominantly spurious 1993 book *Official and Confidential*, makes much of photographs supposedly depicting Hoover and Tolson having sex; he insists that gangsters like Meyer Lansky used such pictures against Hoover for blackmailing purposes. But when criminologist Peter Maas tracked down individuals whom Summers cites concerning this assertion, he found them thoroughly sceptical about Summers' claims. One OSS member from the 1940s, John Weitz, told Maas merely that he once saw

[a] photograph … [that] seemed to show two men humping on a beach. Perhaps it was Hoover, perhaps not.

William Hundley, a prominent Justice Department official during the 1960s, bluntly observed of Summers' conclusion: 'It was baloney.' Most emphatic of the lot was Meyer Lansky's key subordinate, Vincent Alo, who when Maas asked him about the pictures Summers described, snapped: 'Are you nuts?' On this particular sand Summers has built his whole castle of conjecture concerning Hoover the active pæderast.

· · · · ·

Roosevelt's first term, 1933–37, was for Hoover the least politically active and the most generally rewarding period of his adult life. The Republicans remained in shock from the scale of their 1932 loss; and in his 1936 re-election bid, FDR carried every state except Maine and Vermont. Hoover remained free to concentrate on improving the bureau, confident that Roosevelt and the new attorney-general, Homer S. Cummings of Connecticut, would both support him.

Various improvements were already in place before Roosevelt became president. The bureau had established a National Division of Identification for fingerprint archives within a fortnight of Hoover's appointment to the directorship. On 24 November 1932 the bureau formally established its main laboratory. Not content with predictable forensic equipment, this laboratory acquired all sorts of painstakingly classified novelties. These included type specimens from most of the main brands of typewriter, no fewer than 42,000 examples of paper watermarks, and – lest its collection of fauna relics should otherwise seem too parochial – carefully preserved wallaby and wombat hairs. 'Before science,' Hoover habitually said, 'all must fall.' Yet, mindful that impressive bureau technology would be useless without comparable improvement in the human beings who operated it, Hoover also compelled specific schooling criteria for all agents. From the late 1920s onwards, every applicant for an agent's position (a very few, never publicised, exceptions were made) needed to have a degree in law or accounting, preferably from George Washington University itself. Before he got the job, his private life underwent strict bureau investigation; and if it emerged that he could not hold his liquor, or slept around, or had a criminal record, or even perused girlie magazines, his chances of acceptance were zero. Existing agents could be, and were, severely censured for the smallest solecism in their appearance: an unironed shirt (or an ironed shirt in any other colour than white), an unpolished shoe, a hasty shave, deferral of a haircut. Like that other publicity-conscious autocrat Louis XIV, Hoover realised that if you enforce discipline among courtiers on niceties of deportment, discipline on larger issues will to a pleasing extent take care of itself.

Meanwhile the bureau's larger role remained unclear. Advocates of a nationally coordinated war on crime received, admittedly, a great fillip from the nightmare of the Lindbergh baby's kidnapping and murder. Public outrage at this tragedy inspired the Lindbergh Law, which made kidnapping a federal offence. Irked at the delays in solving the Lindbergh case, Cummings proposed to merge the bureau with the Prohibition law enforcement staff; but with such vehemence did Hoover oppose this amalgamation – and its inevitable dilution of bureau standards – that Cummings demurely shelved his plan.

Clearly, the bureau needed a great crime-fighting success if Cummings' plan was to remain shelved. It achieved its first such success of FDR's reign in July 1933, when it captured George ('Machine-Gun') Kelly and his wife, both of whom had kidnapped oil tycoon Charles Urschel. Acting partly on guesses that Urschel had made about where his kidnappers had taken him, bureau agents tracked the Kellys down to a farm in Tennessee. There, along with Memphis policemen – who had, unlike bureau staff, the advantage of being permitted to carry guns – they surrounded the farmhouse. Eventually Kelly emerged and said, 'Okay, boys, I've been waiting for you all night'; but the bureau's journalistic *legerdemain* transformed this prosaic sentence into the far more memorable plea 'Don't shoot, G-men, don't shoot!' Thus the word 'G-men' – meaning government men, implying an incorruptibility that could belong to government alone – entered the language.

Machine-Gun Kelly's downfall inaugurated the great age of bureau victories against violent crime. Specifically, it enabled Cummings to sign into law a bill allowing bureau staff to bear firearms. During early 1934 John Dillinger became America's most famous outlaw since Wild West days, eluding capture like some five-and-dime Scarlet Pimpernel. After deserting from the navy, Dillinger had spent most of his twenties in prison. Once free, he founded the Dillinger Gang, partly to raise money for the release of other inmates. The gang included fellow charmers Pretty Boy (*né* Charles Arthur) Floyd – wanted primarily in connection with the machine-gunning of four policemen in the Kansas City Massacre of June 1933 – and Baby Face Nelson (*né* Lester Gillis). In the course of robbing a dozen banks, Dillinger's men killed sixteen innocent bystanders. Eventually Dillinger himself perished in bureau agents' gunfire outside a Chicago theatre in July 1934; his death mask took pride of place among the exhibits on Hoover's wall for as long as Hoover lived. Pretty Boy Floyd was fatally shot after a protracted battle with G-men in October 1934. The following month Nelson died even harder, slaying two agents before expiring from bullet wounds in an Illinois cornfield. Allies of the Dillinger gang, the Barker Brothers – whose kidnappings and robberies their indomitable mother Kate ('Ma') Barker planned – defied arrest for months before a January 1935 shoot-out in Florida, after which Ma Barker and two of her sons lay dead. Hoover regarded Ma Barker with especial detestation; it was as if her ragtime caricature of mother love shocked his deepest instincts.

Whole books have been written on the revolution in law enforcement's national image that the G-men's exploits of 1933–35 effected. When Cummings, on 1 July 1935, renamed Hoover's agency the Federal Bureau of Investigation – thus making 'FBI' one of the two or three best known acronyms in American life – he merely confirmed an established fact. Hoover-mania had set in, and whatever reservations the great American public might have acquired about his behaviour in old age, he could do no wrong in 1935.

Hoover profited, moreover, from his zeal to proclaim FBI triumphs via the cinema. He brought to Tinseltown the same evangelistic ardour that he brought to politics in general. Contemplating the dream factory's moral shortcomings, Hoover did not just rail at them, as did the 'radio priest' Father Charles Coughlin; he asked himself a variant of the question the Salvation Army's founder had once posed: 'Why should the devil have all the best *movies*?'

His enterprise's outcome was the gangster film genre, which from the mid-1930s enjoyed a decade and a half of vigour. Hays Office censorship requirements that villains be arrested or killed off in any gangster film's last scene helped, rather than vitiated, Hoover's cinematic crusade. Sometimes, as in *You Can't Get Away With It* (1936), Hollywood essayed the ultimate in *cinéma vérité*: it cast Hoover himself as Hoover, while other FBI staff impersonated other FBI staff with varying degrees of skill.

There remained one chink in the armour of Hoover's heroic image: he had not yet arrested a Public Enemy himself.

Goaded by a Tennesseean senator's taunt that Hoover had wasted agents' lives through his own timidity, Hoover determined to capture with his own hands the thief Alvin Karpis. Known as 'Creepy' after a less than satisfying encounter with a plastic surgeon, Karpis alternated between crisscrossing America on his bank-robbing raids, and sending Hoover letters that ridiculed the FBI's efforts to track him down. When (April 1936) Karpis was spotted in New Orleans, Hoover made the journey to meet him, and on seeing him,

> jammed a gun in Karpis's ribs. Karpis recognised
> Hoover immediately, put up his hands, and said, 'Well,
> you've got me, Edgar.'

Hoover's contributions to film history remain important less for their artistic standards (though their much-mocked moralising tendencies have surely been endemic to all governmental docudrama from *The Battleship Potemkin* onwards) than in their having established, by the near-delirious acclaim that they scored, a credit account of public goodwill for Hoover himself. On this account Hoover drew – sometimes judiciously, sometimes ill-advisedly – for the rest of his career.

Even during the 1930s, though, cavillers lamented, and not just on the left. Maverick right-wing columnist Westbrook Pegler dismissed Hoover as 'a nightclub fly-cop'. ('Pegler,' Hoover once observed in a rare flash of wit, 'has mental halitosis.') Since every policeman ever born prefers dramatically solvable crimes that look good in the statistics, it is scarcely surprising that Hoover fought murderous freelances like Dillinger more ably than he did the Mafia, the Camorra, and other such syndicates. (FBI dress requirements, as Maas admitted, limited effective undercover work of the sort that alone could have defeated organised crime.) He notched up his anti-syndicate successes even so, notably against 'Czar' Louis Lepke, boss of Murder Incorporated.

Impatient with Capone's Mediterranean theatrics and cottage-industry approach, the mild-faced Lepke brought to contract killing the same assembly-line techniques by which America dominated the world's automobile market: his exact number of 'hits' has never been known, but was probably more than one hundred. With his myrmidons he ran several labour unions for a decade. By 1939, however, he had lost ground and agreed to surrender on comparatively minor charges, where-upon the irrepressible journalist Walter Winchell arranged that Hoover himself could clap the handcuffs on Lepke. In 1944 New York State's Governor Thomas Dewey sent Lepke, for his Murder Incorporated role, to the electric chair – on a Saturday, despite or because of Lepke's Jewish background.

Three years after Lepke's surrender, two notorious Chicago gangsters broke out of Illinois State Prison. At first, since their escape had broken state rather than federal laws, G-men could do nothing. But eventually the FBI captured the escapees, having ingeniously concluded that both could be re-imprisoned for failing to notify the Draft Board of their most recent address change.

World War and Early Cold War: 1936–60

Almost everything that went right for Roosevelt's administra-tion (and by extension for Hoover) in his first presidential term went wrong in his second. From 1937 until Pearl Harbor America's jobless rate averaged – even on the govern-ment's own, presumably optimistic, figures – 18 per cent. The

Supreme Court and organised labour, hitherto docile, both began deploring Roosevelt's high-handedness. Roosevelt's obvious desire for a third term in office broke no law; but it violated political traditions that had remained in place ever since George Washington's reign. It failed even to do FDR any electoral good, since his 1940 success was a win on points rather than a total knock-out to match his 1932 and 1936 victories.

Moreover, the Communists had, for the first time, made Roosevelt nettled (no stronger word is adequate); his attitude towards them suggested a jilted lover wailing along the lines of 'After all I've done for you ...'. In August 1936 FDR assured Hoover in person that Communism threatened to become almost as great a danger to mankind as, well, Father Coughlin. (Soon afterwards Roosevelt – thoroughly rattled by Father Coughlin's openly declared interest in raising a Catholic fighting force against Mexico's anticlerical régime – sooled tax inspectors onto the radio priest's muddled book-keeping, and continued doing so for three consecutive fiscal years.)

Less than a year before FDR's fretting to Hoover, Communist strategy worldwide had made a 180-degree turn. Rather than continuing to chastise socialists, social democrats and liberals as 'social fascists', Communism now pleaded with all these groups to join with it in a Popular Front against Hitler, Mussolini and (from 1936) Franco. This rapprochement lasted until the Nazi-Soviet Pact of August 1939. This traumatised American 'progressive' opinion, but failed to startle Hoover, who had already recognised National Socialism and the international sort as two sides of the same pagan coin.

In his January 1940 report to the Congress budget committee, Hoover incautiously admitted that the bureau was monitoring persons whom it considered national security risks. A more cynical director would have simply concealed such activities from Congress, yet in some respects Hoover could reveal touching naïveté. He never anticipated what he actually incurred: a blast of invective from New York State's representative, Vito Marcantonio, veteran fellow traveller of Communists and (we now know) the subject of a 993-page FBI file on his political doings. Marcantonio charged Hoover with planning

> a blackout against the civil liberties of the American people, a system of terror by index cards such as you have in the Gestapo countries ... [and with] engendering a war hysteria which is a menace to the peace of the United States.

(Despite Nazi-Soviet rapport, Communism's American leadership continued to encourage anti-Hitler rhetoric: combined, if possible, with attacks on the alliance's opponents as warmongers.) How much substance did Marcantonio's 'Gestapo' allegation possess?

There is no denying that, in an age when TV cameras, Freedom of Information laws and suchlike constraints on executive action belonged to an unimaginable future, Hoover at times exceeded his legal powers. This fact has led to repeated denunciations of his 'fascist' activities, denunciations often given a veneer of academic enquiry by tomes with such breathless subtitles as *The Great American Inquisition* and *The FBI's War on Freedom of Expression*. It is worth examining what basis these and similar accusations have in practice.

Under Hoover, the FBI kept secret files not just on

America's chief legislators at both federal and state level, but on prominent scientists (the file on Einstein, who associated himself with no fewer than thirty-four Communist fronts, ran to 1,427 pages), on prominent entertainers (Groucho Marx, Lucille Ball) and, from the 1930s, on numerous authors as well. Normally an author would acquire a file only when he had made some overtly political statement. The usual procedure would be that when his name had appeared in newspapers or literary magazines in connection with some political activity, the FBI would start collecting press reports related to his life or work. In due course the press-cuttings would acquire more and more annotations by FBI staffers, at times by Hoover himself.

On occasions wholly or partly apolitical events which attracted authors from around the nation (poetry readings, for instance) would inspire the creation of fresh authorial files. One author thus belatedly memorialised in FBI archives was the Southern poet John Crowe Ransom, whose attendance in old age at a national poetry symposium prompted FBI archivists' startled discovery that the bureau had no previous documents related to his existence. Bureaucracy being what it is, Ransom's file 'was started because he didn't have a file'. T.S. Eliot's file arose because the Communist-run *Daily Worker* had repeatedly calumniated him over his public admiration for Ezra Pound. Far more often, though, the FBI maintained files on authors who signed public petitions urging aid to Republican Spain or some other left-wing demand; authors who, whether through genuine conviction or useful idiocy, attended public functions organised by the innocuous-sounding but Communist-controlled League of American Writers; authors who had actively and consciously assisted Communist penetration of Hollywood's screenwriting circles. The first two of these categories accounted for writers of major artistic importance: Scott Fitzgerald, John Steinbeck, Dashiell Hammett, William Saroyan, Dorothy Parker and Sinclair Lewis, to name a mere half-dozen. The third consisted mainly of Stalinist hacks like Donald Ogden Stewart, who from the 1930s to the late 1940s (when Congress cracked down on him and his fellow Tinseltown apparatchiks) laboured indefatigably for the Red dawn.

Stewart's case demonstrates that sometimes monitoring went well beyond the simple maintenance of data via print sources accessible in any large municipal library. From 1927 till at least 1944 the FBI regularly opened Stewart's incoming and outgoing mail. During World War II, mindful of the fact that even the Nazi–Soviet Pact had not ended Stewart's loyalty to Moscow, FBI agents kept up round-the-clock surveillance on Stewart's home: with the aid of such informants as a chambermaid and a cleaning firm's delivery boy. At a rather higher artistic level, the FBI regularly opened letters to and from Thomas Mann: not through any undue appetite for Germanic *Kultur,* but thanks to Mann's repeated public predilection for extenuating Stalin's atrocities. Transcripts of certain calls made to Sinclair Lewis' phone also found their way into FBI files. Mailing lists kept by that ancient *bête noire* of Hoover's, the American Civil Liberties Union, found their way into the bureau archives; the ACLU's Roger Baldwin inspired particular disgust in the FBI because he combined left-wing beliefs with an aristocratic background, his ancestors having arrived in America on board the *Mayflower.* Even the harmless short-story writer John Cheever had his phone briefly tapped: probably because of his long connection with *The New Yorker,*

rather than through any subversive elements in his own genteel and apolitical fiction.

Inevitably misjudgements occurred. Hoover once
described the columnist Murray Kempton as 'a stinking rat'.
This was grossly unfair. (While Kempton – a tweedy singleton
with self-confessed tastes for such un-American activities as
bicycling and listening to Elizabethan church music – had a
genius for backing malodorous *causes célèbres* from the Hollywood Ten to the Black Panthers, and several times mocked the
FBI in print,* rat-like cunning lay beyond his powers.) Nevertheless, errors arose at least as often from bungling as from
Hoover's thin skin.

FBI data on Clifford Odets, America's best known
playwright of the 1930s and an indefatigable fellow
traveller until after World War II, referred to him as 'O'Dets'.
Diana Trilling, literary critic and widow of fellow critic Lionel
Trilling, expressed surprise at how *little* her husband's FBI file
contained: at its omission of all references to several Communist-front campaigns in which her husband had been involved
(notably the committee to free the Scottsboro Boys, nine
black Tennessee youths sentenced to death on dubious charges
of gang-rape in the 1930s). The muckraking journalist Jessica
Mitford kept up her Communist Party membership for
years, but FBI phone-taps never caught her passing on any
information more incriminating than the recipes she
exchanged with friends. No less a figure than Roger Baldwin's
ACLU colleague Morris Ernst credited the FBI with 'a

---

* Kempton once, in a *New York Review of Books* article, described the FBI as
'an example of the triumph of the socialist idea'. This standpoint's originality
did nothing to endear Kempton to Hoover.

magnificent record of respect for human freedom'.* Readers must judge for themselves whether Hoover's actions justified Marcantonio's 'Gestapo' charge.

• • • • •

On 6 February 1940 in Detroit, G-men captured eleven left-ists who had recruited troops for the Spanish Republicans in 1936–39. Now that Hitler and Stalin had made up their quar-rel, such recruitment acquired in FDR's mind a retroactive significance. Detroit's city fathers, defying Hoover's instruc-tions, handcuffed the defendants to a chain in full view of press photographers. Wrongly but understandably, news-paper readers and leader-writers assumed that the FBI had chained the defendants up. Only ten days after the arrests, the attorney-general – by this time Robert Jackson of Pennsylva-nia – demanded that the indictments be thrown out; but such clemency by no means halted complaints against the arrests themselves.

By April 1940 the most determined of such attacks had fizzled out, thanks largely to Roosevelt continuing his co-operation with Hoover when he had been almost universally expected to throw Hoover to the wolves. At a Washington dinner on 16 March Roosevelt asked Hoover outright: 'Edgar, what are they trying to do to you on the [i.e. on Capitol] Hill?' 'I don't know, Mr President,' Hoover responded. Where-upon FDR smiled and gave a dramatic thumbs-down gesture

---

*   Ernst's support had perhaps less value to the FBI than this quotation sug-gests, given that Ernst privately wrote the following to Hoover: 'A lot of people think I am just a stooge for you which I take as a high compliment.'

that, since he had been seated on a platform, could be seen by the whole company. He said, 'That's for them.' Thus Hoover remained safe in his job; but the experiences of early 1940 had scarred him, to the extent that years later he observed: 'No one outside the FBI and the Department of Justice ever knew how close they came to wrecking us.'

Between March 1940 and Pearl Harbor almost two years later, Hoover ordered (notwithstanding America's continued neutrality) repeated investigations of German, Italian and Japanese consular activities. These – unlike the Spanish Republican agents' arrests – produced no indignation among the chattering classes. Neither did the FBI's crackdown on the fiercely anti-Roosevelt *Amerika-Deutscher Volksbund* (better known by its alternative title, 'German-American Bund'). During the late 1930s the Bund possessed a hard core of 6,500 activists, and had been able to draw thousands more to its rallies (one of these, held in March 1939 at Madison Square Garden, attracted a crowd of 20,000); but its upper ranks turned out to be swarming with FBI informers, who obtained – and passed on to head office – membership lists that accounted for almost every Bund adherent. Moreover, in 1942 (the exact date is unclear) Hoover established a 'Do Not File' category for especially sensitive FBI documents.

One form of statist activism, nevertheless, he refused to countenance. When, in Pearl Harbor's aftermath, Roosevelt demanded that 120,000 Japanese-Americans be arrested and confined to internment camps on the West Coast, Hoover made sharp complaints not solely against this move's callousness, but also against its political uselessness. In 1943 he treated FDR to a 480-page report expressing his view that the whole internment programme had been 'extremely unfortunate'.

• • • • •

From 1939 to 1945 Hoover bombarded Roosevelt with, on average, two security-related memoranda per day. Valuable and valueless fact jostled for prominence in these screeds, and one can only regret the opportunity Hoover wasted. Had he devoted some of his prodigious literary energies to enlightening Roosevelt about the true nature of Communism's dogmas, he might conceivably have done immense good. Alas, his loyalty to Roosevelt raised an insuperable barrier during the late 1930s and early 1940s to systematic warfare against the Soviet threat. He kept the House Un-American Activities Committee (HUAC) at a distance throughout this period, because it openly condemned not just Soviet infiltration but the New Deal itself. Similarly, when *Time* editor Whittaker Chambers forsook in disgust the Communist Party for which he had spied until 1938, his early exposés of Communist networks in the government found in Hoover a less than enthusiastic audience. If Chambers were justified, then FDR had been betraying national interests; FDR could not have been betraying national interests; therefore Chambers could not be justified. However apocalyptic his anti-Communist postwar moods, Hoover never brought himself to question this syllogism's implications. By the time Hoover appreciated Chambers' courage it was too late: the USSR had the Bomb, and its loyalists had gobbled up half Europe.

An equal myopia afflicted Hoover's view of Joseph Kennedy, bootlegging billionaire and former ambassador to Britain. Shrewd in much else, Hoover abandoned all judgement when subjected to Kennedy's toadying. In January 1942, indications as to the trustworthiness of Kennedy's brood emerged when twenty-four-year-old Ensign John F. Kennedy proved to be having a passionate affair with Inga Arvad, an unhappily married Danish newspaper columnist suspected of espionage. (With characteristic gallantry, JFK referred to Arvad as 'something I picked up on the road'.) FBI surveillance could never confirm that Arvad had snooped for the Axis, but any other serviceman in Jack's position would have been cashiered for such a reckless relationship. Fortunately for Jack, his father had paid *New York Times* manager Arthur Krock $25,000 to guarantee a deluge of sycophantic press for his clan. What afterwards changed Hoover's mind about Jack was, first, the realisation that the latter's security-jeopardising sex mania – initially attributable to youthful high spirits – increased with middle age; second, his predilection for gangsters' company; and third, the discovery that 'his' Pulitzer-winning book *Profiles in Courage* had in fact been ghost-written by the faithful Krock.

If Arvad gave Hoover a brief headache, Eleanor Roosevelt induced the equivalent of an epic migraine. The estrangement between top cop and First Lady had trivial origins. Eleanor wanted to eschew secret service protection; her husband reluctantly agreed to this, on condition that she learned how to use a gun. But her passionate friendship with Joseph P. Lash, an army captain with a long history of Communist-front activism, alarmed Hoover more lastingly. Hoover and several other leading FBI figures concluded that Lash was cuckolding the president. (FDR, according to Hoover, put his own gloss on the subject: 'the old bitch is going through the change of life'.) A Military Intelligence Division microphone hidden in a Chicago hotel room in March 1943 was thought at first to have captured the sounds of Eleanor and Lash copulating. These turned out to be, instead, of Lash and his fiancée thus occupied; but the original mistake travelled much faster than the correction. Probably Eleanor's affection for Lash never went beyond the indiscreet hand-holding and flowery correspondence which had aroused FBI suspicions, and which she lavished similarly on female friends. Usually quick to forgive antagonists, Eleanor harboured for Hoover an aversion that lasted until her death in 1962. Hoover, for his part, took special pleasure in rejecting Eleanor's subsequent requests for copies of FBI documents that interested her. His file on Eleanor was among the fattest and most detailed that he ever kept; and after the Republicans won back the presidency in 1952, Hoover provided data on the Lash–Eleanor connection for their perusal.

It could, for Eleanor, have gone still worse. For her cousin Kermit Roosevelt (Theodore Roosevelt's grandson), it dramatically did. One day in July 1941 Hoover received the news that Kermit had disappeared. FDR wanted him found, not least because Kermit from his extramarital trysts had contracted gonorrhœa. Hoover agreed to the FBI searching for, and monitoring, Kermit: but only with reluctance (as transcripts from the recording machine attached to his office telephone in February 1941 reveal), since the President had not directly asked Hoover himself, but had conveyed his request through an intermediary, and was perfectly capable of evading all responsibility for demanding the search if opponents had learnt of it and had made political capital from it. Still, the FBI soon discovered Kermit's whereabouts, reported on his daily activities for a month, and made FDR happy by keeping the black sheep's name out of the papers. (Kermit went on to a distinguished career in the CIA, his finest hour being the carrying-out of Operation Ajax, the coup that reinstated the Shah of Iran on his throne in 1953.)

Equally messy, but far less personal in its ramifications, was Hoover's campaign to deport Harry Bridges, the Australian-born Marxist union organiser who had led a great longshoremen's strike in the San Francisco Bay Area in 1934. The FBI eagerly sought, but failed to find, evidence that Bridges had actually joined the Communist Party (evidence which it needed to ensure Bridges' expulsion from America as an undesirable alien); and in 1945 the Supreme Court ruled that Bridges had a right to remain in the USA. As if this outcome did not embarrass Hoover enough, Bridges insisted on going public, to describe the FBI's surveillance of him. He told *New Yorker* readers of bureau methods that in their sheer clumsiness seemed to prefigure Inspector Clouseau:

> You look under the connecting door [between Bridges' own room and the room booked by FBI agents], and you listen. If you see two pairs of men's feet moving around the room and hear no talking, except in whispers, you can be fairly certain the room is occupied by FBI men … Of course, you can often see the wiretapping apparatus – the wires and earphones and so forth – all spread on the floor of this other room, and then you don't have any doubts at all.

At least with one of Hoover's other wartime concerns, the case of Sumner Welles, no one disputed the facts at hand. Only the appropriate response to the facts divided governmental opinion. Sumner Welles, a tall, charming, polyglot dandy, became FDR's under-secretary of State in 1937. For decades he kept secret his habit, when drunk, of proposition-ing any halfway personable male he saw. But in 1940 he attempted to seduce (on a train containing FDR and most of the cabinet) several black porters at the railway station of Jasper, Alabama. Cabinet solidarity remained so firm on the issue that it took three years for Welles' behaviour to damage him, although Hoover privately expressed consternation about it as early as 1941. Once a Republican senator got hold of it in 1943, Welles had to resign. Even then Hoover kept the topic under wraps, and it became public knowledge only in 1956, when the pulp magazine *Confidential* announced it.

• • • • •

A cerebral hæmorrhage killed Roosevelt on 12 April 1945, only five months after he had been re-elected for an unprece-dented fourth presidential term. During his last year of office he had only intermittently been well enough to function; growing befuddlement warred with congenital chicanery for dominance of his soul. Yet Harry S. Truman, vice-president since January 1945, was kept in the dark as to the gravity of Roosevelt's illness. Accordingly, Truman had made less effort than any other nationally renowned American politician to ingratiate himself with Hoover, or even to recognise Hoover's importance. Embarrassingly candid where Roosevelt had been habitually devious, Truman always found it difficult to conceal his dislikes. Within weeks of being sworn in as presi-dent, Truman (successfully) ordered the FBI to tap the phones of disloyal cabinet staff; but overall he tended to take Hoover for granted. One of Hoover's chief assistants, who periodically saw the Truman White House from the inside, spelt out the consequences:

> Hoover was frightened of his life with Truman, I know that personally. During his entire career in the White House, Truman had nothing to do with Hoover and wouldn't let Hoover get anywhere close to him.

As if in response to Truman's attitude, Hoover's anti-Communist principles – in abeyance since 1941 – emerged from their slumber. On 8 November 1945 Hoover complained in a memo to Truman about the Communist activities of Treasury official Harry Dexter White, who the previous year had helped to establish the International Monetary Fund. Truman ignored the warnings, and showed no more interest when Hoover finally admitted that Whittaker Chambers had been right to accuse Alger Hiss (then a State Department staffer) of spying for Moscow. Hoover failed to understand why Truman, willing to fight Soviet Communism abroad, scorned decent resistance to it on the home front. But Truman persisted in underrating the threat that Hiss and his fellow conspirators posed. When Chambers testified against Hiss before the House Un-American Activities Committee, Truman recklessly concurred with a journalist who on 5 August 1948 called the entire session 'a red herring to divert the public's attention from inflation'. During 1949 Truman gave serious consideration to dismissing Hoover from office, and abandoned this idea only when he realised that if Hoover lost his job, the Republican opposition would use his downfall for political point-scoring at the congressional elections of 1950 and the presidential elections of two years later.

Hoover took particular umbrage at an anti-FBI book which appeared at this time, and which seemed to him at least as subversive as anything the Communist Party did. He vented most of his resultant rage upon – and thereby reduced to tears – his chief press officer, Louis Nichols, whose devotion to Hoover's cause took so extreme a form that on this occasion he sobbed: 'Mr Hoover, if I had known this book was going to be published, I'd have thrown my body between the presses and stopped it.' (Notwithstanding his sycophancy, Nichols clearly aroused in Hoover genuine apprehension. When he left Hoover's employ in 1957, Hoover said: 'I never want another man to have such power in this organisation again.')

Even Truman, nonetheless, had to take notice when the FBI arrested Julius Rosenberg on 17 July 1950,* and Ethel Rosenberg a month later. The bureau alleged the couple's active participation in the wartime Soviet spy ring that had passed on to Moscow vital details of atomic bomb manufacture: details that the Soviets put to devastating use when they detonated a nuclear device in September 1949. Hoover, while conceding the Rosenbergs' guilt, displayed initial squeamishness about permitting Ethel to die. Then he learned that Ethel had chillingly dismissed her own sons as insignificant. 'Don't mention the children,' Ethel told her own mother. 'Children are born every day of the week.' Hoover was so shocked by

---

* In November 2001 Ethel Rosenberg's brother, David Greenglass, who famously testified against Ethel in 1951, publicly admitted for the first time that he had not been entirely honest in the witness stand. But he stopped well short of saying that Ethel had been wrongly convicted; and so did the historian Ronald Radosh, who in his 1983 book on the topic (*The Rosenberg File: A Search for the Truth*) demonstrated *both* Rosenbergs' guilt while deploring Ethel's execution.

this comment's absence of maternal feeling that he always spoke thenceforth of Ethel, as of her husband (both executed on 19 June 1953), with disgust.

Over Senator Joseph McCarthy, whose fame before 1950 had been strictly local, the normally decisive Hoover was in two minds. That which mainstream American scholarship never even began conceding till the FBI's Venona files on Soviet espionage entered the public domain in 1995, Hoover knew from the start. He knew that McCarthy told the truth; that in fact the senator *under*estimated the number of Soviet agents in American bureaucracies; that the Senator inspired outrage (as one recent observer puts it) 'not because he "smeared innocent people", but because he identified and exposed culpable ones'; and that the usual liberal complaint against McCarthyism – of 'giving anti-Communism a bad name' – achieved its greatest currency among those who wanted genuine anti-Communism to have a bad name anyway, whatever social snobbishness, irrelevant personal grievance, or (above all) sectarian rancour animated them. At the same time, McCarthy's reluctance to concede that discretion might be the better part of valour threatened to get Hoover into trouble. When, in 1953, McCarthy began treating the FBI as a glorified research library *cum* job employment agency, one that he could boast about to all comers, Hoover increasingly froze him out. The director valued secrecy too much to let even an otherwise sympathetic senator jeopardise it.

• • • • •

By the time McCarthy's career collapsed (1954), America had a new president in Eisenhower, who no more aroused

Hoover's devotion than Truman had done. As one biographer noted,

> [Hoover] was repeatedly taken aback by Eisenhower's casual cruelties, by his knowledge of the means of politics and ignorance of its ends.

At least neither of Eisenhower's attorneys-general – Herbert Brownell during his first term as president, William Rogers during his second – tried to depose Hoover, or to inhibit undercover domestic operations. On the contrary: Hoover's surveillance opportunities improved, thanks in part to Brownell's support, and in part to technological developments previously unavailable, such as robust tape-recorders and omnidirectional miniature microphones, which facilitated the bugging of suspects' homes and offices. In March 1954 Brownell did what Truman's attorney-general, J. Howard McGrath, had refused to do: he provided, in writing, specific authorisation for secret bugs.

Moreover, the immediate Communist peril at home receded dramatically during Eisenhower's administration. Yet Hoover always rejected assertions that Communism as a driving force was dead. It was supposed to have been equally dead after the events of 1919–20, after the widespread disillusionment that the Nazi–Soviet Pact had inspired, and after the 1947 Loyalty Program had begun. On none of those occasions had it actually died, and Hoover saw no reason to believe that it was about to die in the 1950s. His fear of a Communist renaissance inspired him in August 1956 to set up COINTELPRO, an FBI subdivision with the specific role of domestic intelligence-gathering on subversive (primarily

Communist and crypto-Communist, though also Puerto Rican tribalist and white-supremacist) activities.

For much of its life COINTELPRO's boss was William Sullivan, a bookish and intellectually restless agent seventeen years Hoover's junior, whom 'the old man' treated at first like a son. Hoover even let Sullivan dress like a scarecrow out for a walk; any other G-man similarly attired would have faced the mother of all tongue-lashings, if not immediate retrenchment. It would be idle to pretend that COINTELPRO always behaved according to the Sunday school principles which Hoover had once articulated. Sometimes COINTELPRO staff would break into suspects' offices and steal documents ('black-bag jobs'). On other occasions their surveillance took the form of sending unsigned letters to young activists' parents, 'reporting on their sons' or daughters' premarital sexual activities and use of illicit drugs'. Such measures might in certain circumstances have been necessary; it is less obvious that national interests were served by another COINTELPRO campaign of the period, whereby agents hoping to disgrace certain fashionable leftists arranged for them to be entertained by whores who carried venereal disease.

When Adlai Stevenson became the Democratic candidate for two successive presidential elections – 1952 and 1956 – Hoover suspected Stevenson of being soft on Communism, and noted this suspicion in Stevenson's FBI file. The truth was that Stevenson's softness on Communism reflected his softness on almost everything. That anger at Hoover's enmity goaded such a man into calling Hoover 'that bastard in the Bureau' indicates how much the director had frightened him. His fright's origins were not necessarily political in the strict sense. Stevenson never successfully dispelled accusations that he preferred men to women; and in a Hoover card-index entitled 'Sex Deviates', Stevenson's name and putative eroticism figured prominently.

Not every politician in Eisenhower's America, however, trembled at the thought of Hoover's files. Congressman Adam Clayton Powell achieved, in his colourful – some would say lurid – political career, the possibly unique distinction of laughing at them. Before Martin Luther King, before Malcolm X, and long before Jesse Jackson, there was Powell, the first black activist for civil rights to obtain a mass national following. Powell combined his successors' rhetorical mastery with two characteristics they never shared: innate impishness, and love for number-crunching.

In 1944, aged thirty-six, Powell became New York State's first black member of the House of Representatives. When Mississippi Congressman John Rankin made a speech freely punctuated with the term 'nigger', Powell silently rose from his chair, and gave Rankin a mighty punch to the side of the head. The blow that Powell had, in the most literal fashion, struck for his race established him as a formidable Washington operator, whom Hoover would be crazy to overlook.

Hoover comforted himself with the fact that Powell, as well as having courted Communists, maintained an exhaustingly elaborate sexual life. Alas for Hoover, Powell so boasted of his womanising that Hoover was defeated before he had started. Once Powell even called a press conference to reveal that he would be taking with him two gorgeous secretaries – one of them a beauty contest winner, and white – on a taxpayer-funded overseas study tour, travelling (naturally) first-class. The threesome would, he po-facedly told journalists, 'investigate women's working conditions at some of the best restaurants, hotels and night clubs in Europe'.

Doggedly Hoover tried. One evening Powell came home to discover that all his belongings had been ransacked, but that nothing had been stolen. Realising that the FBI was behind this, he did the unthinkable: he obtained Hoover's telephone extension, and twitted him. 'Edgar, your boys seem to have paid me another visit,' Powell chortled. Hoover took several seconds to recover from the shock of being addressed on first-name terms, by a black man at that. 'Well, Adam, as you know,' he improvised, 'there have been threats against your life, and we have to take every precaution to protect you.' The more Hoover fumed, the more Powell chuckled. After that Hoover let Powell alone.

'No One Can Say We Democrats Don't Have Fun': 1960–64

Unpleasant though Hoover found the Eisenhower years at the time, they came to appear like distilled prelapsarian joy compared with Kennedy's Camelot. Whilst neither by temperament nor by conviction was Eisenhower the type of president whom Hoover would have wished, at least he could be recognised as an adult human being. And then, by contrast, there was the Kennedy tribe.

In 1956 Stevenson had blandly described Democratic infighting with the words 'No one can say we Democrats don't have fun'; but the Kennedys elevated this off-hand comment to a veritable religion of hedonism, allied to an outlook that made image-mongering the universe's very centre. Old Joe Kennedy had warned that his son would attain supreme office on pure Madison Avenue principles: 'We're going to sell

Jack like soap flakes.' Hoover was determined to make Jack sweat, not only (or primarily) on the issue of the vote fraud of 1960, but also on the Inga Arvad question. Jack asked Hoover to provide, in writing, a formal statement exonerating Arvad of Nazi espionage. Hoover refused, aware that the FBI still had the recordings of Kennedy and Arvad's pillow talk, and that he would be stupid to relinquish the potential power over the new chief executive which the recordings' survival gave him. To a friend who suggested that Jack dismiss Hoover, Jack retorted: 'You don't fire God.'

Still, Jack probably never realised – and certainly never admitted – how many hostages to fortune his behaviour over the preceding two decades had given Hoover. Indeed, perhaps the most striking single aspect of Jack's whole political career is not how much Hoover persecuted him, but how little. It took till 1961 for Hoover to confirm the truth about Jack's clandestine 1947 marriage to a Florida lady (her divorced status failed to deter the ostentatiously Catholic Jack); and when apprised of it, he spoke of it to Jack as a foolish journalistic conjecture which he scorned, rather than as established fact. Had voters in 1960 been aware of this marriage, Jack's presidential campaign would have ended in minutes.

For Hoover (as for many others), Jack at least had the partially redeeming virtue of intellectual laziness that lessened his rancour. Not so his brother Robert – 'Bobby', as most people called him – whom in 1961 Hoover recommended to the post of attorney-general; 'worst damn mistake I ever made', Hoover afterwards assured DeLoach. Jack decked political opponents in the half-genial expectation that they would get up again and dust themselves off; Bobby always hit to hurt.

When temporarily frustrated in a football game, Bobby, unlike Jack, would kick and gouge opponents until separated from them by superior force. One of Vice-President Lyndon Johnson's advisers, John P. Roche, observed of Bobby: 'He couldn't distinguish a principle from a fireplug.' It might be truer to say that Bobby made his antipathies *into* a principle: that for him, opposing football players represented cosmic evil while, and only while, he was pummelling them. The approach that worked so well on the football field he carried over in political life, forever letting his emotions show, which exposure was at once his strength and his weakness. He did not so much enunciate policy as expectorate it forth. Whereas Jack often soothed, Bobby always nagged. He nagged Hoover about the FBI's failures in combating organised crime: a particularly audacious accusation coming from Bobby. While Bobby hounded individual rogues like the trucking-union boss Jimmy Hoffa – who at least had battled against intra-union Communists – he took no serious action against the Mafia. Illinois Mafioso Sam Giancana told the mistress he shared with Jack: 'Listen, honey, if it wasn't for me your boyfriend wouldn't even be in the White House.' And a temporary rebuff drew from Giancana a plaint warranting immortality: 'They can't do this to me,' he whined, 'I'm working for the government.'

Hoover never needed Bobby to teach him how to fight mobsters. That the FBI could, and should, have done better in this fight is undeniable. It might have done, but for what DeLoach acutely called

his [Hoover's] profound contempt for the criminal mind ... [which] persuaded him that no such complex

299

national criminal organisation [as the Mob] could exist without him knowing about it.

Nevertheless, Hoover had put in an impressive, sensible performance at the 1951 Senate Commission into gangsterism (among the first American political events to be nationally televised); and his characteristic staccato hectoring made him a natural TV performer, one skilled at offering sound-bites four decades before the word 'sound-bite' had even been invented. Besides, when (in September 1962) ex-mobster Joe Valachi delated to the authorities the nature and structure of La Cosa Nostra – information hitherto unknown, outside the Mob itself, in any but the most fragmented manner – he confided his admissions to Hoover's FBI, not to Bobby or his associates. Bobby happily tried to hog credit for the resultant revelations, but only after the FBI had done the legwork. It constituted a typical performance for one whose place as America's least competent attorney-general remains unchallenged.

Had Bobby contented himself with making a hash of his own job, he might still have salvaged some useful results from his term in office; regrettably, he also thought himself a better and cleverer Hoover than Hoover. Thus, whereas both of Eisenhower's attorneys-general had merely acquiesced in dubiously legal or downright illegal electronic surveillance on Hoover's part (telephone company executive Horace Hampton estimated the annual number of Hoover-initiated wiretaps as approximately one hundred in pre-Kennedy years), Bobby initiated extra surveillance, in October 1963, at his own command. Bobby, who in DeLoach's bitter words 'never saw a wiretap he didn't like', predictably kept this command top-secret (as it remained until June 1969, by which time he had been dead for almost a year). One difficulty if you institute wiretaps – a difficulty that Bobby seems never to have contemplated in his initial enthusiasm for snooping – is the danger of thereby capturing material personally offensive to yourself. He found out this truth the hard way after his brother's murder, when FBI microphones captured the chitchat of an internationally celebrated leader, watching on television a rerun of Jack Kennedy's funeral. As the TV screen showed Jacqueline Kennedy kneeling before her husband's casket, the leader in question said of the grieving widow: 'Look at her – sucking him off one last time.'

Hoover took considerable pleasure in showing Bobby the transcript of that particular observation. The leader who had thus accused Jackie was none other than Nobel Peace Prize winner Martin Luther King.

• • • • •

Of all Hoover's sins, real and fictional, his harassment of King harmed him most in posterity's eyes. Now that King has become the opiate of post-Christian America's masses, two simple truths extremely well known to Hoover and to almost every other 1960s bureaucrat have dropped down the memory hole: King's comparatively humble position in black politics for most of his life (even at his zenith he was merely *primus inter pares*); and his seemingly incessant Communist associations. The facts indicate that both Hoover and King behaved deplorably towards one another, King's behaviour being rather worse than Hoover's.

Like most Americans, Hoover knew little about King

before March 1956, when King had emerged from obscurity
to lead the boycott of segregated buses in Montgomery,
Alabama. Initially neither Hoover nor FBI agents actually
in the field had cause to suspect King of fellow travelling.
One memo from Washington, DC to the FBI's Atlanta office
(20 September 1957) went so far as to say:

> In the absence of any indication that the Communist
> Party has attempted, or is attempting, to infiltrate this
> organisation [the King-controlled Southern Christian
> Leadership Conference, or SCLC for short], you
> should conduct no investigation in this matter.

This changed between 1958 and 1961. During those
years FBI files noted King's meetings with black Communist
leader Benjamin Davis (who donated blood at the nearest
clinic in 1958 when a mental patient wounded King with a
knife); his praise for the Socialist Workers' Party; his arrest in
Georgia on a dangerous driving charge; and his complaint (in
Nation magazine) that FBI job policies discriminated against
blacks. Still, even with these provocations, the FBI considered
it best not to rebuke King directly. An internal report convinced DeLoach – not that he needed much convincing – to
overrule any calls for the FBI to correct King's factual mis-
statements, since King 'would only welcome any controversy
or resulting publicity that might ensue'.

Only from 1962 did Hoover worry much about King's
activism. The FBI had discovered, and in January 1962
Hoover reported to Bobby Kennedy, King's close and deep
friendship (of at least four years' standing) with Stanley Levison. A New York Jewish lawyer, the mysterious and sinister

Levison – whose death in 1979 deprived historians of many a detail concerning the CPUSA's American power struggles – had during the early 1950s been one of the party's most active and skilled treasurers. The bureau, believing that he had become disillusioned with Communism, even approached him (in 1959, without success) as a suitable informant on CP activities. By 1959 Levinson's Svengali-like role in King's life included writing speeches for King (one of which King gave to America's highest labour union forum, the AFL-CIO); helping to edit the manuscript for King's first book, *Stride Toward Freedom*; and even protecting King from the latter's own financial ineptitude. Like many brilliant rhetoricians, King suffered from spectacular administrative and legal ignorance, so that his utopian visions would regularly be interrupted by his inability to return a vital phone call or to submit an income-tax form. Enter Levison, who knew exactly how to appease a bumptious civil service clerk, design a publishing contract, and win over a deeply anti-Communist union leader or a deeply uncommitted TV host.

This all raised, to Hoover, the fearful possibility that Levison's ostensible split with the party in 1956 had been a feint, and that through him the CP could do what it liked with King's crusade. Possibility began to resemble probability when Hoover learned, also in 1962, that one of King's young protégés – Jack O'Dell, who owed his job at the SCLC's New York branch to Levison's recommendation – had been involved with the CP for years. King, for his part, had burbled Marxist sentiments to academic supervisors, close friends, SCLC staffers, and sometimes entire congregations, ever since the early 1950s. A term paper he wrote in his undergraduate days referred to 'my present anti-capitalistic feelings', though these feelings never prevented King himself from pitiless copyright control over his public utterances. To (presumably astonished) readers of *Ebony*, a middle-class periodical advocating black economic self-help, King announced: 'Southerners are making the Marxist analysis of history more accurate than the Christian hope that men can be persuaded through teaching and preaching.'

By this stage, one hardly needed the late Joseph McCarthy's outlook to fear that King might be a Communist dupe or worse. King denied ever having been told about any possible Communist infiltrators except O'Dell, whereas the FBI had files to reveal that it had warned King about Levison's background too. When *The New York Times* quoted, on 18 November 1962, King's complaint that the FBI was crawling with white Southern bigots, the FBI took him seriously. Had King bothered to obtain the relevant statistics from those investigative officers whom he regularly disdained except when he needed to be rescued from lynch-mobs, he would have discovered that his charge of Southerners dominating the FBI's Southern operations was false. DeLoach, hoping to put King right on the topic, tried to arrange at least one meeting; but he underestimated King's indolence. King failed to return DeLoach's telephone calls, and left DeLoach with the impression of the FBI being deliberately snubbed. Unlike King, Hoover knew how to bide his time.

Then came Bobby's authorisation to Hoover for wire-tapping of King's office, followed by similar permission for bugging King's home and any hotel rooms he used. Hoover now felt the heat from both sides. Under these conflicting pressures, Hoover blurted out his true feelings towards King on 18 November 1964, at – of all places – a press conference.

Normally press conferences ranked in Hoover's opinion only one step morally above Communist rallies; but on this occasion his hearers were mostly members of the National Women's Press Club, and therefore (he assumed) too ladylike to cause him trouble. After a boring recitation of crime statistics, Hoover raised the matter of King's misconceptions as to Southerners in the FBI. 'In my opinion,' Hoover went on to announce, 'Dr Martin Luther King is the most notorious liar in the country.'

Thrice DeLoach, seated on the platform, frantically scribbled messages to Hoover urging that he declare his accusation off the record. Thrice Hoover refused. 'DeLoach,' he finally proclaimed,

> advises me to tell you ladies that my calling Dr King a notorious liar should be off the record. I won't do this. Feel free to print my remarks as given.

On that day Hoover became publicly vulnerable as he had never been before. He had managed the impossible. In one sentence he had handed over the moral high ground to a demagogue who thought it comical to accuse a widowed First Lady of necrophiliac fellatio; to an ordained clergyman who, at moments of erotic climax with prostitutes, would scream 'I'm f__king for God!' or (still more revealingly) 'I'm not a Negro tonight!'

After 18 November 1964, then, Hoover remained on the permanent defensive. But as his national influence weakened, little by little, so – for different reasons – did King's. Increasingly denounced by black conservatives like George S. Schuyler for his sympathies with Moscow and Hanoi

(Schuyler likened King to 'some sable Typhoid Mary'), increasingly mocked by Black Power and Nation of Islam leaders as an Uncle Tom, King spent his post-1964 career trying in desperation to outbid the hard left without stooping to violence. It did him no good. Lyndon Johnson, the most impassioned champion blacks had had in the White House for a century, wanted nothing to do with King's rants. King was dead politically for three years before the sniper fire of drifter and drug-peddler James Earl Ray, on 4 April 1968, killed him physically.

Had Hoover but known it, he could have destroyed King's power base without a single public insult, let alone sustained electronic surveillance. From 1987 it emerged that King was, throughout his adult life, a plagiarist. In particular King stole his doctoral thesis material from others, and stole from a fellow black preacher his 'I have a dream' speech. During King's lifetime – as opposed to the present day – the merest hint of plagiarism could, and did, regularly destroy careers, above all academic careers. Unrepentant King apologist Gerald McKnight conceded:

> Had the FBI discovered King's plagiarism … it is hard to see how King could have continued as an effective public figure …
>
> That the bureau missed this singular window of opportunity to destroy King diminishes the carefully cultivated image of the Hoover-era FBI as omnipotent and omniscient.

Ozymandias in Washington: 1965–72

'Look on my works, ye mighty, and despair': Hoover's last years made him resemble an Ozymandias straight from Central Casting. They witnessed almost unrelieved political decline, cruelly coexisting with alert mental function till the end. Decline, admittedly, did not seem imminent at first. Conservative philosopher Russell Kirk recommended that President Johnson appoint Hoover attorney-general once Bobby, in a characteristic tantrum, had stormed out of the job. This suggestion Hoover rejected; forty years possessing power's substance had left him ill-fitted for power's legal shadow, although Kirk's warm admiration pleased him. He showed no pleasure when Alabama's Governor George Wallace, campaigning for the presidency in 1968 as a law and order independent, asked him to be his running mate. (Hoover continued to resent Wallace's failure to rid Alabama's essential services of Klansmen at the FBI's urging.) Yet the notion that powerful individuals saw him as a future vice-president could hardly fail to tickle his vanity.

In 1965 America's television screens began transmitting episodes of *The FBI*, starring Efrem Zimbalist Jr; these brought the crime-fighting feats of Hoover and his organisation to the notice of millions far too young to have attended prewar picture theatres, and gave Hoover an Indian summer of glory before the film cameras. (Improbably enough, *The FBI* continued in production until 1974.) What was more, Johnson issued, in plenty of time for Hoover's seventieth birthday, Executive Order No. 10682, the wording of which DeLoach had drafted. This order specifically decreed that the normal federal civil service retirement age of seventy did not apply in Hoover's case. Johnson is supposed to have justified his action by saying 'I'd rather have him [Hoover] inside the tent pissing out, than outside the tent pissing in.' Cheated thereby of his own hopes for the FBI directorship, DeLoach continued nevertheless to serve Hoover faithfully and shrewdly, until a job offer by the Pepsico firm in 1970 enticed him from Hoover's entourage.

William Sullivan's departure from the FBI occurred in less agreeable circumstances. Secure, as he thought, in Hoover's esteem, Sullivan more and more ran COINTEL-PRO as an independent operation with only the most tangential reference to FBI practices. When he considered that Hoover was letting King off far too lightly, he sent King (only three days after Hoover's 'notorious liar' accusation) an anonymous letter purporting to come from a disappointed black, and urging King to commit suicide. Accompanying the letter was a tape of one of King's more strenuous bump and grind sessions, captured by FBI recording devices. Sullivan took great care to conceal from Hoover his connection with this epistle, but freely admitted his belief that Hoover was past it. In 1970 Sullivan turned up to his office one morning only to discover that he no longer had a job. Hoover had not actually dismissed him; he had simply ordered the lock on Sullivan's door changed overnight. After this blow, Sullivan laboured away at the memoirs by which he hoped to establish himself as the supreme anti-Hoover historian. These appeared in 1979, but he could no longer benefit from them. On 9 November 1977 he had perished in a bizarre, but apparently genuine, hunting accident.

Had Sullivan been alone in his impatience with Hoover the septuagenarian, the latter's last years would have been happier. Unfortunately for Hoover, every objection Sullivan had

308

made to Hoover continuing as FBI director found its echo, point by point, in White House advisers' counsel once Johnson had stepped down from the presidency in favour of Richard Nixon. With Johnson, as with no other president after FDR died, Hoover enjoyed a certain intimacy. Johnson sometimes invited Hoover to his Texas ranch, and Hoover came to play an avuncular role in the lives of Johnson's daughters, commiserating with them in their teenage griefs, playing boisterously with their pet dogs. (He seemed less avuncular when subjecting their boyfriends and husbands to FBI wiretapping, but maintained cordial dealings with Johnson even so.)

By Nixon – who harboured sour memories of applying for an FBI job in 1939, only to suffer rejection on the grounds of 'lacking aggressiveness' – Hoover found himself again sidelined. The Nixon circle believed that age had blunted Hoover's intellectual powers. By 1971 Nixon himself, although appreciative of Hoover's past services, had come to agree. America's internal issues bored Nixon anyhow (on one Watergate tape, he eloquently referred to domestic political processes as 'building outhouses in Peoria'); and even if the home front had been among Nixon's all-consuming concerns, Hoover was no longer the man to improve it. Hoover's bugging propensities had already attracted unwelcome legal publicity in the case of Fred Black, a Washington lobbyist who appealed against his 1966 conviction for tax fraud on the grounds that the evidence against him had been illegally obtained through FBI microphones. The Supreme Court not only agreed with Black, but soothed his hurt feelings by ordering the FBI to pay him $900,000.

In 1972 Presidential Assistant Tom Huston flatly

informed White House Chief of Staff H.R. Haldeman: 'At some point, Hoover has to be told who is President. He has become totally unreasonable.' Future Watergate burglar G. Gordon Liddy – himself an erstwhile FBI agent, who had acquired the melancholy distinction of failing to convict Timothy Leary for illegal drug use – wrote a confidential report concerning ever-poorer FBI morale. Moved by the urgency of the circumstances to quote Tennyson's *Idylls of the King* ('The old order changeth, giving place to new'), Liddy also described Tolson as having said on 30 June 1971, with untypical bluntness: 'Hoover knows that, no matter who wins in '72, he's through.' Eventually Nixon decided that Hoover should retain his job till the 1972 election; after that, he would need to go.

DeLoach – who concluded independently of the White House that Hoover had grown set in his ways and had outlived his prime – advised the cabinet to handle 'the old man' gently, and to allow Hoover most of his existing privileges, including a bullet-proof limousine. Not that the cabinet's members needed much urging to handle Hoover gently; rather, it required stomach-churning fortitude on their part to contemplate handling Hoover at all. The President entreated DeLoach to give Hoover the bad news in person: something DeLoach refused, and Nixon feared, to do. Then Attorney-General John Mitchell determined to bite the bullet – a metaphor singularly appropriate in the FBI's context – and tell Hoover himself. At the crucial moment Mitchell's courage also failed. So nobody dared to give Hoover the sack. His career ended only when the Grim Reaper called on him, sometime during the night of 1–2 May 1972.

Postlude

Tolson, to whom Hoover left most of his $600,000 estate, survived his friend by less than three years. When he died, on 14 April 1975, he remained so little known outside criminological circles that careless *Washington Post* feature-editors supplemented the newspaper's obituary of him with a picture of Louis Nichols instead. Meanwhile five congressional committees, still flush with triumph from Nixon's resignation, were simultaneously examining abuses of power by Tolson and Hoover's FBI: particularly the assertion that Hoover had kept seventeen top-secret folders on peccant congressmen. This last activity of Hoover's inspired congressional shock greater than anything his previous wrongdoings had induced. Ovid Demaris declared, with pardonable annoyance:

> It was perfectly fine for the FBI to have 6.8 million files and 55 million index cards on private citizens, but seventeen folders on the philandering and drinking habits of lawmakers heralded nothing short of the 'destruction of our forms of government' ... Politicians are notoriously thin-skinned, but there is nothing wrong with their instinct for the jugular.

The allegation which stuck the longest in Congress's craw came from a retired FBI agent named Arthur Murtagh, who in his committee testimony accused DeLoach of having blackmailed a senator who wanted FBI funding cut. According to Murtagh, DeLoach announced to various journalists:

> The other night, we picked up a situation where this senator was seen drunk, in a hit-and-run accident, and

some good-looking broad was with him. We got the information, reported it in a memorandum, and by noon the next day, the good senator was aware that we had the information, and we never had trouble with him on appropriations since.

DeLoach always denied saying anything of the sort; and given his well-authenticated distaste for vulgar language in any form (let alone terminology like 'broad'), his denials are eminently believable. Yet the words attributed to him were so obviously things which the Hoover acolytes of 1970s leftist mythology *would* have said, that it required only a small leap of faith for Congress to conclude that Hoover acolytes *did* say them. The dividing line between reality and mass media fairytale has long tended (at least since JFK's accession) to be thinner in America than elsewhere; and if the fairytale demanded that Hoover be cried up as an omnipotent bogeyman continuing to torment harmless politicos three years after he had died, then so much the worse for reality.

By 1977, when Nixon's successor as president left the White House, it was as if Hoover – once the possessor of 'a name at which the world grew pale' – had never been: save 'to point a moral or adorn a tale'. The tale that gained most currency was Summers' 1993 allegation that Hoover had enjoyed wearing women's clothes. His sole source for this canard was an assurance to this effect by a convicted perjurer (who wanted to revenge herself on her ex-husband, a Hoover ally) that at a private New York party she had seen Hoover camping around in a dress and a feather boa. Even hard-core left-wingers dismissed the arraignment as pure fantasy. Summers alone believed it. He failed to adduce a scrap of proof for it, but it acquired the character of a Jungian archetype, the stuff of late-night comedians' wisecracks. As a consequence, the very name 'J. Edgar Hoover' now conjures up the word 'transvestite' as readily as 'Rolls' suggests 'Royce', or 'Laurel' evokes 'Hardy'.

Though a sad end for the repute of a man who for all his conspicuous faults deserved better of his compatriots, it was not much crueller a fate than Hoover would have predicted for himself. He knew the provisional nature of his achievement, and of civilisation as a whole: the difficulty with which man has extricated himself from the cave, and his readiness to revert to savagery at the first chance he gets.

No subsequent FBI chief has shown a scintilla of Hoover's political adroitness, media mastery, or temperamental independence. The FBI's post-1972 decline has been, by any yardstick, spectacular. It has involved not only such conventional rackets as hiring employees in accordance with racial quotas, and paying damages to staff dismissed for homosexual acts, but the more creative procedure of mislaying 3,135 crucial documents appertaining to Oklahoma City bomber Timothy McVeigh, as well as public breast-beating over FBI computer systems' obsolescence. When in February 2001 FBI agent Robert Hanssen pleaded guilty to having spied for Moscow since at least 1985, the wheel of FBI-CIA antagonism came full circle. Hoover had openly abhorred 'Wild Bill' Donovan, apparently keeping several thousand pages' worth of confidential files on him (though only a few hundred pages survived Hoover's death); and now at least one FBI staffer had proved himself fully the equal of any CIA operative in high treason. By this collapse in FBI self-confidence Hoover would have been saddened, but scarcely surprised.

Of all twentieth-century tragic figures (and his lapses from the high standards which he set himself ensure that the adjective 'tragic' cannot, in all conscience, be denied him), Hoover perhaps most resembles a leader with whom he would have shuddered at the very notion of being linked: Marshal Pétain. The comparison, though in some respects inept – not least *vis-à-vis* the respective positions of Jews in Pétain's France and Hoover's America – warrants pursuing. Both men possessed scientific and soldierly, rather than contemplative, minds. Both men, despised by most intellectuals, enjoyed near-regal acclaim among the middle classes. Both men loathed Communism as profoundly secularist and, indeed, secularism as profoundly Communist. Both men despised vote-catching politicians. Both men placed undue trust in juniors who alternated between sycophancy and hostility (Hoover in Sullivan, Pétain in his Prime Minister Pierre Laval). Above all, both men lived too long. With justice, Hoover biographer Richard Gid Powers cited a lament that Cato the Elder, as described by Plutarch, uttered in his last years:

> It is hard that I, who have lived with one generation, should be obliged to make my defence to those of another.

afterword

It is curious to realise, from the foregoing chapters, how the same personality types recur in the most disparate settings: even when conscious influence of one setting upon another can be ruled out. Stalin admittedly revered Fouché, and Göring admired Dzerzhinsky; but Fouché owed nothing at a conscious level to Walsingham or Salisbury, and Hoover had no discernible interest in any of his police predecessors.

Most of those who ran surveillance operations have been far more interested in power than in money or sex. Fouché and Hoover ended their days in comfortable circumstances, but the desire for riches drove neither man. Walsingham died in debt, and lived – as Dzerzhinsky and Andropov would do more than three centuries later – by the most uncompromising ethical code. The maggots in Himmler's head did not include greed or lust. Of this volume's protagonists, Beria stands out from the others by his demented and criminal eroticism.

The protagonists share other temperamental features also. All were primarily autodidacts. When they undertook higher education at all, they did so at instrumentalist, unglamorous institutions (where they studied such disciplines as pharmacy, accountancy and engineering). None of these figures came from the cream of the educational crop, in the way that Cambridge's Soviet spies were to do during the 1930s. All of them made the greater part of their own good luck. Three of them – Walsingham, Dzerzhinsky and Göring – spent years in exile. A tendency to squeamishness when it came to inflicting physical violence on persons commonly occurred: the exceptions being Dzerzhinsky and Beria, who in their torture sessions led by example. Several possessed deeply religious backgrounds: Walsingham the doctrinaire Puritan, Dzerzhinsky planning at first to enter the priesthood, Hoover the untiring Sunday-school teacher. Only Dzerzhinsky and Salisbury belonged by birth to the upper classes, though Göring married into them (and Salisbury's noble status was of a strictly *nouveau-riche* kind, while Dzerzhinsky's aristocratic rank coexisted with galling hardship). Salisbury, Göring, Himmler and Hoover all had fathers in government employ. A pattern therefore emerges from their origins: not uniformly consistent, but present even so.

In all but one of the cases described in this book, revolution formed the prelude to surveillance: whether the religious revolution that propelled a Walsingham to high office, or the political revolutions that brought Fouché, the Bolsheviks and the National Socialists to the top. Only Hoover achieved his authority without an overt revolutionary process; and even he, like many another American official in 1919, feared that revolution would break out on American soil.

· · · · ·

This book was in its final stages when the 11 September terrorist attacks on America appalled the world. These crimes have served, as nothing less horrible could, to make still more urgent the most elementary questions about what level of government surveillance on the citizenry we are stuck with, what level we actually require, and what level will extinguish every hard-won freedom which remains to us as private individuals.

To a certain extent, the very fact of living in a Western society with liberal traditions would have forced such questions on us in any event (Taliban or no Taliban, Cold War or no Cold War). They occur to anyone who reads of Hoover's doings, for example. The top-secret files Hoover kept upon the misdeeds of friend and foe alike, be that foe the American President himself, eventually incurred scathing media criticism. In Walsingham's circumstances, or Fouché's (to say nothing of Beria's or Göring's), *failure* to keep such files would have seemed the truly heinous offence. Were the objectives of Hoover's FBI compatible with a free press, an independent judicature, alert republican citizens, and the Jefferson Project in general? Is the Jefferson Project itself compatible with superpower status?

The FBI's post-Hoover failures derive directly from the complete absence (either within the Bureau's own ranks or, more to the point, within the ranks of the society it serves) of consensus as to what it should, and should not, be doing. Even now that the physical safety of Americans *en masse* is imperilled as it has never been imperilled before, the loudest voices in America's political discourse make demands which appear, and presumably are, mutually incompatible. They want the maximum of personal liberty *and* the maximum of governmental interference in the running of public places like airports; they want low taxes *and* up-to-the-minute bureaucratic technology to thwart future terrorists; they want America's enemies walloped in battle, *and* all possible assurances that American mothers' sons will not come home in body-bags; they want due process of law observed towards civilian suspects, *and* the electoral credit for toughness. If they would all at least want the same thing – however ludicrous – without simultaneously wanting its diametrical opposite, America would be easier to govern. Yet since they disdain elementary logical consistency, they must hope that sheer governmental vigour will see them through.

As these words are being written, the White House is promising with every appearance of relish the reintroduction of wartime courts-martial, with no pettifogging rubbish about formal warrants for such practices as tapping defendants' phones. Well before the World Trade Center and Pentagon attacks, the FBI had been considering in all seriousness (and since the attacks it has been shamelessly using) an e-mail monitoring programme called Carnivore. In October 2001, FBI agents acquired the legal right to place a 'roving wiretap' on every phone a suspect uses (as opposed to a conventional wiretap, which monitors only a specific phone number); two months later California's governor formally sought similar powers from his state's legislature. Britain's Government, for its part, rammed through the emasculated House of Lords in 2000 its own Regulation of Investigatory Powers Bill: requiring all the country's Internet service providers to monitor all data traffic and report it, on demand, to the British secret service department MI5. Predictably enough, the mass media's alleged 'adversary culture' has not – with a handful of honourable exceptions in the form of individual commentators – seen fit to strike adversarial attitudes towards all this Orwellian behaviour. One of this behaviour's few sustained critics has been journalist and historian Philip Jenkins, who in the November 2001 issue of the Illinois monthly magazine *Chronicles* made several pertinent points, applicable outside as well as within the USA:

> Random trawls [whether in cyberspace or of flesh-and-blood suspects] can even do more harm than good. Basically, too much information can overwhelm a system, even if the individual pieces of information are priceless. ... Time and again, security forces have tried to pull in hundreds or even thousands of suspects, who are either not interrogated thoroughly, or who produce so much information that the system is swamped. Far better to round up a dozen or so activists who can be interrogated in depth, with the information properly analysed and assimilated.

Are we witnessing the re-emergence of outright secret police terror, all carried out – but of course – in the name of wartime 'emergency' powers? This question will be easier to answer in a decade's time; much will depend upon whether it can even be asked. In the meantime, Benjamin Franklin's words from 1759 are at least as pertinent in a War on Terror environment as they were in the comparatively civilised conflicts of Franklin's own America: 'They that give up essential liberty to obtain a little temporary safety deserve neither liberty nor safety.'

Robert J. Stove
Ascot Vale, Victoria, December 2001

acknowledgments

To Michael Duffy, whose idea it was; and to Anthony Adair, who did so much to make the idea a reality.

To Peter Coleman, Peter Day, Dr James Franklin, Dr L.K. Howell, Robin Marsden, and Sophie Masson: all of whom read the original manuscript in its daunting entirety, saved me from various factual errors, and suggested useful improvements. These individuals – none of whom, of course, should be blamed for shortcomings in the final product – have earned especially lively gratitude.

To Dr I.C.F. Spry QC, Editor of *National Observer* (Melbourne), and Fr Paul Stenhouse MSC, Editor of *Annals Australasia* (Sydney), where some of this material first appeared in print.

To the staff of the State Library of New South Wales (Sydney), the State Library of South Australia (Adelaide), the State Library of Victoria (Melbourne), the National Library of Australia (Canberra), and the University of Sydney's Fisher Library: who invariably provided unstinting help in obtaining hard-to-find documents, often at notice so short as to be punitive.

And to Norma Scott of the Australian Picture Library (Sydney). Her unfailing patience, good manners and professionalism in answering even, or especially, the least considerate and most frantic of authors' requests for pictorial material is unmatched in my experience.

R.J.S.

notes

Chapter One
page 10
her lippes ... hour   Singh, p. 44
page 11
as grey ... old   Plowden (1984), p. 218
which was ... noted   Singh, p. 44
God ... conscience   Fraser, p. 529
page 12
How fond ... life   Sitwell, p. 360
My Dear Brother ... it not   Marcus, Mueller and Rose, p. 296
page 14
without translating somewhat   Read, Vol. 1, p. 18–20; Williams (1998), p. 272
page 15
Christ ... agree   Plowden (1984), p. 183
For the ... prescribed   Read, Vol. 1, pp. 286, 289
page 16
the one wholehearted ideologue   MacCaffrey, p. 441
Elizabeth's slipper thrown at Walsingham   Hibbert, p. 115
Lie there, Lord Treasurer   Sitwell, p. 55
2,500 individual bureaucrats   Williams (1998), pp. 157–158
page 17
make ... men's hearts   Hibbert, p. 89
page 18
one of the diamonds of England   Waugh, p. 53
page 20
Her Majesty ... vermin   Haynes (1992), p. xix; A.G. Smith (1934), p. 143
Some few of them suffered   Haynes (1992), p. xix; A.G. Smith (1934), p. 142
Walsingham and Irish archbishop   Haynes (1992), p. 25
page 21
Walsingham's fluent Italian   Haynes (1992), p. 25
page 22
Ridolfi in Walsingham's pay?   Kamen, p. 134; Plowden (1991), p. 44
page 23
the Pretended ... to her   Hibbert, p. 73
Complaints by Philip II, Alva, Maximilian II   Waugh, p. 40
he meant ... country's   Waugh, p. 41
page 24
any bull ... Rome   Waugh, p. 87
take ... protection   Sitwell, p. 280
preferred ... pillow   Hibbert, p. 172

page 25
You will ... torture   Haynes (1992), p. 52
page 26
come ... consolation   Sitwell, p. 289
comfort himself in God   Sitwell, p. 288
Lord! ... ambassador!   Fraser, p. 146; Plowden (1991), p. 43
page 27
Serve ... devil   Sitwell, p. 449
page 28
I think ... friends   Plowden (1991), p. 51
page 29
Towns containing Walsingham's agents   Jardine and Stewart, p. 44
He would ... servants   Lloyd, p. 516
demographic ... kill them   Haynes (1992), p. 46
page 30
Bacon's £30 debt   Jardine and Stewart, pp. 47–50
If there ... the better   Haynes (1992), p. 92
page 31
Rogers in Castel Sant'Angelo   Read, Vol. 2, p. 331
distributor ... letters   Haynes (1992), p. 44
Stafford playing courtier with alcohol   Haynes (1992), p. 45
Standen, Walsingham, Philip II   Jardine and Stewart, p. 126
Ratcliffe and Don John   Petrie, p. 249
page 32
Walsingham's pay for agents   Haynes (1992), p. 242
Intelligence is never too dear   Hibbert, p. 116
page 33
Campion's expression of alarm in Rome   Waugh, p. 73
If the object ... authorities   Waugh, p. 95
It was ... as evidence   Waugh, p. 137
page 35
In condemning ... ancestors   Williams (1998), p. 202
Wherein ... prosperity   Waugh, pp. 165–166
page 36
It would ... public   Somerset, p. 392
If instead ... we lack   Somerset, p. 395
One third of each fine to informer   Waugh, pp. 87–88
page 37
that the blood ... bodies   Plowden (1991), p. 135
Topcliffe's allegations of sex with Queen   Somerset, p. 396
page 38
and Bassett ... prosperity   Waugh, p. 89
to make ... with joy   Waugh, p. 89
such ... hear it   Plowden (1991), p. 135
Let a woman show her throes   Plowden (1991), p. 56
page 39
Giordano Bruno   Bossy (1991a), pp. 83–183; Bossy (1991b), p. 19
six ... against   Hibbert, p. 200

notes

I have ... resolution   Read, Vol. 2, pp. 382–383

Walsingham's insults of Mendoza in Italian   Hibbert, pp. 201–202

You cannot ... forgive them   Sitwell, p. 326

page 40

Parry's relations with stepdaughter   L. B. Smith, p. 12

full of blood ... subjects   Sitwell, p. 333

page 41

I see ... amongst you   Camden, pp. 426–430

page 42

that the ... immortalised   Sitwell, p. 329

inclined to papistrie   Hibbert, p. 205

Correspondence in beer barrel   Singh, p. 36

page 43

Gifford's choirboyish appearance   Hibbert, pp. 204–205

I have ... no scruples   Singh, p. 39

Backlog of Embassy mail   Singh, p. 36

Myself ... execution   Singh, p. 37

page 44

of low ... smallpox   Singh, p. 40

any man's ... writ it   Singh, p. 41

page 45

I would ... hereunto   Singh, p. 41

page 46

Ballard's clothes   Sitwell, p. 330

Babington's walnut juice   Singh, p. 42

A gallous ... boweled   Camden, pp. 644–645

Mary's legal rights violated   A.G. Smith (1936), pp. 226–227

page 49

What a wife ... world   Weir, p. 399

page 51

Lopez and Essex's syphilis   Lacey, pp. 201–202

page 52

I have ... manner poison   Lacey, p. 119

It appears ... Inquisition   Hume, p. 35

page 53

Mirth at Lopez's declaration   Camden, p. 676; Lee, p. 195

page 54

Ciphers in Cecil's correspondence   Plowden (1991), p. 132

Cecil's pet parrot   Hibbert, p. 242

all deformed ... magistrates   McNeill, p. 125

page 55

Bacon and torture   Hall, p. 315; Sessions, pp. 269–289

Coke and torture   Hall, p. 304

Rosaries, hairshirt, scourges, books   Haynes (1989), p. 33

Challoner's function   Plowden (1991), p. 142

page 56

Cecil's acceptance of bribes   Cecil, pp. 136–137

Burghley's rejection of sweeteners   Somerset, p. 549

the unsleeping eye

page 59
My lord ... yowe Plowden (1991), p. 146
page 60
Catesby as double agent? Haynes (1996), p. 45
a few ... enough Plowden (1991), p. 147
page 62
Garnet and Byrd Caraman, p. 33
Stonor House's printing press Caraman, p. 43
page 63
been found ... equivocation Huntley, p. 390
Garnet's rumoured conversion to Protestantism Caraman, p. 433
This is ... equivocation Caraman, pp. 435–436
page 64
I maun hae ... Carr Irwin, p. 225
page 65
It was ... Thurloe Plowden (1991), pp. 150–151

Chapter Two
page 68
Suddenly ... oath Chateaubriand, Vol. 2, pp. 331, 335; Mansell, p. 256
certainly ... lot Hilt, p. 70
the eye of surveillance Singer, p. 177
page 70
Huic ... præbet Huxley, p. 182
Où est mon appui? Huxley, p. 259
Cabinet Noir's size Deacon, pp. 20–21
His secret ... factions Bailly, p. 204
page 72
Brissot's career Darnton, pp. 43, 58
Marat's presses smashed Loomis, p. 91
crouched ... buttock Loomis, p. 91
page 73
a pedant ... of air Loomis, p. 179
Roland's domestic informers Bernardin, pp. 402–409; Bosher, p. 253
Everything's going ... virtuous Roland Cobb, p. 52
page 74
Père Duchesne's 200,000 readers Cobb, p. 52
It was ... for her Loomis, p. 218
It's not ... Agrippina Loomis, p. 278
page 75
Héron and Committee of General Security Deacon, pp. 44–45
page 76
in a hundred ... lavatories Cobb, p. 52
even ... imprudence Cobb, p. 51
Agents' reportage Cobb, p. 51
page 77
Controversy over year of Fouché's birth Madelin, Vol. 1, pp. 2–3; Tulard, p. 18
Beauharnais and Jérôme Bonaparte Schom, p. 251

notes

page 79

criminal irresolution   Forssell, p. 46; Macaulay, p. 308

Fear of aggravating royal victim's suffering   Forssell, pp. 52–53

Fouché's atheism   Forssell, pp. 57–58

page 80

La mort ... éternel   Tulard, p. 47

Treatment of Catholic priests   Doyle, p. 259

Fouché charged with diverting gold and silver   Buisson, pp. 137–138

Fouché as proto-Communist?   Cole, p. 52

My death ... dear   Carlyle, p. 610

Anacreon of the guillotine   Macaulay, p. 330; Palmer, p. 394

Let the plough ... no more   Macaulay, p. 313

page 81

housed ... head   Carlyle, p. 644

Couthon fiercely rebuked in Paris   Forssell, p. 71

Collot d'Herbois laughed off stage   Carlyle, p. 645

page 82

levelling ... countenance   Carlyle, p. 645

Lyonnais death-toll   Buisson, pp. 130–131

Fouché gazing on butchery   Schom, p. 254

Presumptuous ... death   Rice-Oxley, p. 53

Mark her ... blood   Rice-Oxley, p. 177

page 83

When ... but once   Forssell, p. 76

Citizen ... Fouché   Schom, p. 254

page 84

Firing squads disbanded   Hilt, p. 72

allow ... fate   Hilt, p. 73

Nun's decapitation   Schom, p. 254

Executioner and assistant killed   Buisson, p. 133

Barras' and Tallien's fear of Robespierre's dictatorship   Cole, p. 70; Palmer, p. 377

page 85

Fouché's changes of lodgings   Cole, p. 76

Robespierre ... list   Loomis, p. 376

Committees' arrests compared   Godechot, p. 313; Jordan, pp. 207, 291

Down with the tyrant!   Cole, p. 86

Fouché readmitted to Jacobin Club   Cole, p. 87

page 86

little whelps ... mercy   Loomis, p. 288

Prisoners lashed together in pairs   Loomis, p. 289

page 87

New, separate Police Ministry   Bosher, p. 254; Church, p. 159

I was ... only   Hilt, p. 74

a director of public opinion   Deacon, pp. 46–47

Nine Police Ministers   Schom, p. 255

page 88

182 royalists on Council   Rapport, p. 15

Imbecile! ... warn you   Madelin, Vol. 1, p. 251; Schom, p. 255

page 89
without money … State Hilt, p. 74
page 90
Joséphine's secret information Schom, p. 256
He … like this Schom, p. 257
page 91
Barras arrested in bath Hilt, p. 75
page 92
Every government … influence Hilt, p. 77
page 93
a well-dressed person … hands of the government Macaulay, pp. 330–331
page 95
Where three … listening Forssell, p. 169; Hilt, p. 80
Every conspirator betraying the others Forssell, p. 169
Joséphine paid 1,000 francs daily Richardson, p. 200
Fouché and Richelieu compared Deacon, p. 50
page 96
Cook's reports to Fouché Hilt, p. 83
Foreign cities Schom, p. 259
regulateurs … Paris La Clère, p. 100
page 97
That … Your Majesty Hilt, p. 82; Schom, p. 272
page 98
I ought … opinion Hilt, p. 81; Schom, p. 272
Napoleon's two-timing paramour Cole, p. 138
page 99
Qui a chouanné, chouannera Forssell, p. 161
page 100
We have … emperor Cole, p. 150
C'est plus … une faute Tulard, p. 170
page 102
the supreme … life Schom, p. 267
that a woman's … values Madelin, Vol. 1, p. 388
It was … lacked Tulard, p. 222
page 103
running sore Fletcher and Cook, p. 17
Let us … enemies Zweig, p. 198
page 104
So it's you … scaffold! Cole, p. 199
If you … you Cole, p. 200
did no … required Hilt, p. 81
If I … hesitate Hilt, p. xviii
If the Emperor … veut ainsi Tulard, p. 260
page 105
Do you know … police Cole, p. 218
page 106
yes, the whole … succeeded Cole, p. 218

page 107
we shan't ... year   Hilt, p. 84
In the best ... farce   Hilt, p. 84
page 108
Misfiling crucial documents   Deacon, p. 54
Shrieking rage lasting an hour   Hilt, p. 85
page 109
Unfortunate ... pardon me   Hilt, p. 85
the only ... family   Hilt, p. 85
page 110
time ... prejudices   Cole, p. 307
page 111
I wish ... rescued me   Cole, p. 311
conducive ... memoirs   Hilt, pp. xxviii–xxix
Heine on Fouché's autobiography   Zweig, p. 232

Chapter Three
page 113
the embodiment ... hopes   Fuegi, p. 541
page 115
clutched ... stop   Hingley (1970), pp. 164–165
a demeritocracy ... talents   Hingley (1973), p. 38
page 116
This crueltie ... nobilitie   Ruud and Stepanov, p. 4
a kind ... slander   Ruud and Stepanov, p. 4
page 117
Ivan and St Bartholomew Massacre   Plowden, p. 102
page 118
Viazemskii's fate   Hingley (1973), p. 43
Malyuta ... people   Staden, pp. 35–36
page 119
Capital crime to mention Oprichnina   Ruud and Stepanov, p. 5
page 120
Semen Godunov strangled   Grey, pp. 158–159, 175
no little ... autocrat   Hingley (1973), p. 67
Alexis and failure to denounce treachery   Hingley (1970), p. 7
page 121
His Majesty ... liquor   Hingley (1973), pp. 78–79
How often ... limb   Anderson, p. 148
page 122
passed ... clock   Ustinov, p. 68
page 123
Sheshkovsky's torture methods   Hingley (1970), p. 19
page 124
Misunderstanding about Constantine's wife   Hingley (1970), p. 195
Mes amis du quatorze   Hingley (1973), p. 198
My God ... Russia   Hingley (1973), p. 197

page 125
Forty full-time officials   Squire, pp. 95, 105, 183
Sixteen full-time officials   Deacon, p. 48
Benckendorff's forgetfulness and visiting-card   Hingley (1970), p. 32
all matters whatever   Hingley (1970), p. 39
Libraries, grand pianos   Hingley (1973), p. 198
Its ... spied on   Hingley (1970), p. 36
They ... technique   Custine, p. 230
page 126
the cleverest man in Russia   Hingley (1973), p. 209
General's severe stutter   Hingley (1970), p. 46
page 128
a running ... aims   Hingley (1970), p. 58
Umbrella and Mesentzov's guard   Schebeko, pp. 30–31
page 129
Ochrana's 20,000 staff   Taylor, p. 177
Tsar's slush fund   Taylor, p. 177
New executive directors   Deacon, p. 70
a type ... member   Deacon, p. 72
Ochrana absolved of blame for *Protocols* forgery   Ruud and Stepanov, pp. 203–215
page 130
the most ... immediately   Deacon, p. 74
page 131
Garasimov's infiltrations   Hingley (1970), pp. 99–100
In a ... professional   Hingley (1970), p. 99
page 132
a blood-stained creature   Massie, p. 97
soul-murderer ... empire   Mazour, p. 356
page 133
Gapon's corpse   Harcave, p. 95; Mazour, p. 357
a whirlwind of energy   Massie, p. 206
the Stolypin necktie   Massie, p. 206
page 134
Robespierre plus Napoleon   Taylor, p. 282
We stand ... innocent   Hingley (1970), p. 122
page 136
Zosia Kaszprzak affair   Bromage, p. 152
shook ... throw   Bromage, p. 114
page 137
the dreary ... bricklaying   Bromage, p. 117
page 138
all ... Class Enemy   Bromage, p. 153
Dzerzhinsky's workload   Leggett, p. 253
Beating up inmates   Bromage, p. 153
page 139
Dzerzhinsky and boozing official   Bromage, pp. 146–147
I have ... shoot me now   Leggett, p. 251; Lindemann, p. 442
only saints ... scoundrels   Conquest, p. 544; Leggett, p. 266

notes

Remember? … pincers Lyons, pp. 470–473
page 140
However … its mark Leggett, p. 162
Vodka rations Leggett, p. 201
Victims' gold teeth Bromage, p. 156
Do not … character Conquest, p. 544; Leggett, p. 201
Kedrov and Deich Leggett, p. 201
page 141
justified … counter-revolution R. Medvedev (1972), p. 183
Loans to hard-up Chekists Bromage, p. 162
Belonging … duties Bromage, p. 160
Special vengeance Bromage, pp. 202–203
page 142
Lenin spying on Dzerzhinsky Bromage, p. 154
Cheka staff numbers Leggett, pp. 232–233
spiritual welfare Bromage, p. 156
page 143
Dzerzhinsky and Popov Bromage, p. 186
Are we … the others? Heller and Nekrich, p. 204
Dzerzhinsky's other jobs Heller and Nekrich, p. 140
page 144
You all … destroyed Bromage, pp. 204–206
page 146
We, the occupants … Socialism Bromage, p. 207
page 147
Chekists' murder rate Leggett, p. 467
Spiridonova's hospitalisation Courtois, p. 84
White Guard lice Courtois, p. 84
moved vaguely … Dzerzhinsky Lyons, p. 263
page 148
OGPU's monitoring Courtois, pp. 133–134
5,078,174 letters Courtois, p. 135
Article 58 Courtois, p. 136
I humbly request Andrew and Gordievsky, p. 80
page 149
the elimination … class Courtois, p. 147
140,000 kulaks Courtois, p. 203
with the … appropriation Courtois, p. 204
1930 kulak revolts Danilov and Berelovich, pp. 671–676
page 150
Stalin, Churchill and Ukrainian famine Churchill, Vol. 4, pp. 477–478
Six million famine victims Blum, p. 99
Life … merrier R. Medvedev (1983), p. 37
Lies from Stalin's Western apologists Dalrymple, pp. 250–264;
    Muggeridge, pp. 18–26; Sobran, pp. 3–4
a garden in full bloom Kupferman, p. 88
Gorky's secretary and Yagoda Hellar and Nekrich, p. 272
engineers of human souls Hellar and Nekrich, p. 274

page 151

the most ... literature   Hellar and Nekrich, p. 274

clearly ... proletariat   Hellar and Nekrich, p. 276

the crime of the century   Conquest, p. 43

page 152

This was ... minutes   Knight (1999), p. 206

Ninety Kirov murder suspects executed   Hellar and Nekrich, p. 279

Kirov's oratorical skill   Conquest, p. 14

page 153

He tricked ... everyone   Hellar and Nekrich, p. 302

conducting ... Fouché   Krivitsky, p. 168

page 154

Yezhov a mere five feet tall   Conquest, p. 16

In my ... a villain   Andrew and Gordievsky, p. 104

page 155

Each morning ... and slept   Andrew and Gordievsky, pp. 107–108

Does Comrade ... dog's disease   Vaksberg, pp. 34–35

page 156

The entire ... their toes   Hingley (1970), p. 163

You're ... Grigoryevich!   Andrew and Gordievsky, p. 101

page 157

We deem ... this matter   Hingley (1970), p. 163

page 158

proof ... guilty   Andrew and Gordievsky, p. 113

Statistics on defence manpower losses   R. Medvedev (1983), p. 14

The very ... minds   R. Medvedev (1983), p. 15

page 159

Yagoda's and Yezhov's top NKVD officials slain   Andrew and Gordievsky, p. 107

page 160

Kedrov's complaint about Beria   Knight (1995), pp. 22–23

Beria and Mogilevsky's plane crash   Knight (1995), p. 35

page 161

Beria and Khandzhian's 'suicide'   Knight (1995), pp. 70–71

Pimping for Beria   Volgokonov, p. 333

Beria's admission of syphilis   Knight (1995), p. 97

page 162

vulture face ... the night   Hingley (1970), p. 222

Shostakovich and NKVD   Macdonald, p. 105

page 163

NKVD's torture methods   Hingley (1970), pp. 174–176

We were ... in school   Mendelstam, p. 222

page 164

4,433 Polish officers   Zawodny, p. 24

Münzenberg's murder   Conquest, p. 430

page 165

Stalin's accusation to Beria   Volgokonov, p. 381

page 166

a pursuit ... preparation   Hingley (1970), p. 192

Beria and the atom bomb programme   Knight (1995), pp. 124–130
page 167
Stalin's distrust of the Jew   Lindemann, p. 452;Vaksberg, pp. 19, 197
Jews in Soviet leadership and administration   Vaksberg, p. 60
Jews in Ukrainian Cheka   Lindemann, pp. 443–444
the most … cannibalism   Vaksberg, p. 186
page 168
Stalin and Malenkov in 1944 on Jews   R. Medvedev (1983), p. 146
Was Beria Jewish?   Knight (1995), p. 147
page 169
Beria, Merkulov, Abakumov denounced   Knight (1995), pp. 170–171
Morozov play, Timashuk's Order of Lenin   Hingley (1970), pp. 217–218
Dispute as to when Stalin fell fatally ill   Knight (1995), pp. 176–178
Beria at Stalin's death-bed   Andrew and Gordievsky, p. 347
page 170
passed … another   Fuegi, p. 549
Beria versus Molotov on East Germany   Andrew and Gordievsky, p. 350
page 171
Charges laid against Beria   Knight (1995), p. 211
Beria's sheer vulgarity   Stickle, p. viii
even under … dachas   Knight (1995), p. 221
page 172
to cut out … ice floe   Hingley (1970), p. 223
page 173
Kiss of career death   Plate and Darvi, p. 100
KGB's legal obligation   Hingley (1970), p. 224
One would … convenient   Penkovsky, p. 193
page 174
knows only … shoot them   Penkovsky, p. 93
Iron Shurik   Andrew and Gordievsky, p. 398
request', 'demand   Andrew and Gordievsky, p. 378
page 175
Even a pig … eats   Andrew and Gordievsky, p. 397
page 176
Jews put to death in disproportionate numbers   Hingley (1970), p. 238
page 177
Andropov and hangings from lamp-posts   Andrew and Mitrokhin, p. 7
I had … every move   Andrew and Gordievsky, p. 396
If Khrushchev … 1937   Andrew and Gordievsky, p. 397
page 178
Semichastny's refusal to kill Khrushchev   Andrew and Mitrokhin, p. 471
Private massage parlour   Andrew and Mitrokhin, pp. 6–7
Shelepin and Brezhnev's stroke   Z. Medvedev, pp. 66–67
page 179
Andropov and Glenn Miller   Andrew and Mitrokhin, p. 8
New York Times on Andropov   Hellar and Nekrich, p. 705
page 180
our Sasha   Hellar and Nekrich, p. 705

the unsleeping eye

page 181
Soviet psychiatric diagnoses   Andrew and Mitrokhin, p. 326
sulfazine ... disease   James, p. 253
Stasi staff and informers   Kohler, p. 8–9
KGB staff in Stasi offices   Kohler, p. 74
page 182
Berlinguer, Marchais, Ibarurri   Andrew and Mitrokhin, pp. 392–393, 396–397
Importing Western computers   James, p. 267
page 183
Details of identity book   Fremantle, p. 27
that the ... imagination   Andrew and Mitrokhin, p. 10
page 184
Chebrikov, Sakharov, Bonner   Andrew and Mitrokhin, p. 432
page 185
military-political ... imperialism   Kohler, p. 75
Miss KGB   Knight (1997), p. 15
May 1991 legislation   Knight (1997), pp. 16, 256
page 186
I am ... up   Andrew and Mitrokhin, p. 511
a heavy ... him away   Andrew and Mitrokhin, p. 512
Bakatin's dismissal of his son   Safire, p. 11
page 187
Dzerzhinsky ... French Revolution   Anon, p. 11
Interview with Semichastny   Dobryukha, p. 6
page 188
For the ... the same   Albats, pp. 309–310

Chapter Four
page 190
naturally ... fellow-countrymen   Petrie, p. 184
page 192
Chastity Commission   Crankshaw (1971), p. 168
Geheime Kabinets-Kanzlei   Singh, p. 59
page 193
reliable ... public safety   Padover, pp. 132–133
Six-thousand-odd edicts' arcana   Brook-Shepherd, p. 29
servants ... everyone   Brook-Shepherd, pp. 29–30
page 194
In me ... police   Seward, p. 191
Small size of Metternich's staff   Seward, p. 192
Metternich and Pellico   Seward, p. 142
Copies from Germany or Belgium   Seward, p. 232
page 196
Kaiser, as head of Lutheran Church, rejects suicide   E. Taylor, p. 317
page 197
Would our ... workers   Masur, p. 292
Lipp's eccentricies   Toland, p. 80
GERMANY ... TO REPORT   Toland, p. 79

page 199
Jews' role in 1918–19 revolutions   Toland, p. 79
twelve ... poison gas   Kershaw (1996), p. 152
page 200
Hindenburg's hopes of Hohenzollerns' return   Dorpalen, pp. 477–478; Petrie, p. 191
page 201
Göring's lioness and its fresh meat   Lattimer, pp. 72, 75
page 202
Himmler on Japanese as 'Aryans   Crankshaw (1956), p. 22
page 203
my financial ... reluctantly   Brissaud, p. 21
In the SS ... beer-halls   Brissaud, p. 22
Heydrich, navy and fiancées   Whiting, pp. 5–6
page 204
real wolf's eyes   Brissaud, p. 24
I want ... minutes   Brissaud, p. 25
page 205
Weimar Republic's police   Browder, p. 33
Gestapo staff numbers   Browder, pp. 35–36
page 206
Diels' secret archives and Röhm's letters   Brissaud, p. 34
page 207
Heydrich and Himmler's underpants   Schwarz, p. 59
Röhm and eighty-four others   Irving, p. 149
page 208
Kahr's murder   Irving, p. 148
Music critic mistaken for SA officer   Toland, p. 347
Bose's murder   Irving, p. 148
Sense of German relief   Toland, pp. 346–347
Frick on SS   Browder, p. 148
Heydrich's recommendation to Göring re Gestapo   Browder, p. 145
the proud ... distinction   Crankshaw (1956), p. 18
page 209
commit ... property   Baker, p. 215
Pentecostals ... dissident Lutherans   Hillenbrand, pp. 58, 101
page 210
social fascists   Burleigh, p. 136
Niemöller's support for NS while objecting to Party interference
   Bentley, pp. 41, 57–58
Niemöller's five brief imprisonments   Bentley, p. 131
Niemöller's solitary confinement   Bentley, p. 142
page 211
Bavarian KZ statistics   Browder, p. 77
I'm sorry ... the same!   Hillenbrand, pp. 59, 112
Shall I ... right now?   Hillenbrand, p. 56
Malicious gossip' arrests   Browder, p. 82; Burleigh, p. 182
Diels' postal monitoring   Browder, p. 61
No Himmler or Heydrich jokes   Hillenbrand, p. 58

the unsleeping eye

page 212
Prussia's Gestapo legislation   Crankshaw (1956), p. 89
Hamburg's Gestapo and coroners   Burleigh, p. 184
Gestapo interventions against SS thugs   Browder, p. 80
Bavarian Gestapo statistics   Gellately, pp. 162, 164
page 213
Forschungsamt's status   Browder, p. 61
hated ... the tap   Irving, p. 124
an engineer ... method   Burleigh, p. 183
Blick in die Zeit suppressed   Gill, p. 25
page 214
40,000 staff?   Crankshaw (1956), p. 16
7,000 in Gestapo   Browder, p. 63
5,000 in SD   Burleigh, p. 182
Himmler and Henry I   Brissaud, p. 180
The Volk *... dictators*   Browder, p. 158
page 216
Blomberg's disgrace   Brissaud, pp. 186–187; Kershaw (2000), pp. 52–53
pervert, liar   Brissaud, p. 188
Fritsch's death in battle   Brissaud, p. 211; Gill, p. 73
page 218
a giant ... top   Douglas, Vol. 1, p. 116
one should ... sky-high   Burleigh, p. 191
Nebe's courage under torture   Gill, p. 141
page 219
Himmler's séance   Brissaud, pp. 271–272
page 220
Himmler's kicking of Elser   Toland, p. 593
to cut ... prematurely   Brissaud, p. 286
page 221
to destroy ... people   Frei, pp. 114–115
be ... from above   Frei, p. 115
page 222
Hübener's execution   Gill, p. 197
page 223
Rote Kapelle's motives unclear   Brysac, pp. 369–371
The person ... literature   Gill, p. 187
Shaw mistaken for a Jew   Gill, p. 185
page 224
We must ... extending it   Gill, p. 186
page 225
our Vyshinsky   Toland, p. 818
page 226
Origins of Kaltenbrunner's scars   Lattimer, p. 175
page 227
Canaris hated ... the Führer   Gisevius, pp. 443–445
page 228
Dohnányi's inability to turn over in bed   Snyder, p. 143

page 229
Goerdeler's protest over Mendelssohn monument   Snyder, p. 58
page 230
Stauffenberg and Stefan George   Hoffmann, pp. 33–37, 45, 75
page 232
there was … asset   Irving, p. 432
Beck's death   Kershaw (2000), p. 682
hung up like meat-carcasses   Kershaw (2000), p. 682
page 233
Did Hitler watch film of executions?   Kershaw (2000), p. 1006; Toland, p. 818
the German … resist   A.J.P. Taylor, p. 188
page 234
better off … assassinated   Klemperer, p. 347
page 235
Other prisoners … minds   Lattimer, p. 178
Müller's post-1945 fate   Douglas, Vol. 2, pp. 19–23; Hamilton, Vol. 2, pp. 167–168

Chapter Five
page 238
J. Edgar Hoover … beginning   Gentry, p. 29
page 239
We … mortal   Gentry, p. 28
He was … to be   Cooke (1988), p. 215
[a] political … Bill of Rights   Gentry, p. 28
J. Edgar Hoover … seventy-seven   Gentry, p. 34
page 240
was one …country   Gentry, p. 721
Jesus … cocksucker!   Gentry, p. 28
Annie Hoover's ancestry   Powers (1987), p. 9
page 241
'Onward Christian Soldiers', 'Jesus Wants Me For A Sunbeam'   Powers, p. 20
a crime prevention laboratory   Lynn and Wright, p. 97
Secularism … secularism   Powers (1987), p. 311
page 242
At the age … spat on it   Powers (1987), p. 311
As a youth … Bible   Powers (1987), p. 5
Hoover's stammer   Demaris (1975), p. 7
page 243
Hoover's *Weekly Review*   Powers (1987), pp. 20–22
Demaris and Hoover's cousins   Demaris (1974), p. 73
page 244
I became … then?   Toledano, p. 31
I've often … forever   DeLoach, p. 90
page 245
Hoover and the mentally aberrant   Powers (1987), p. 39
Hoover's work on Sundays   Demaris (1974), p. 73
Justice Department expenditures   Powers (1987), p. 44

page 246
Hoover and German women   Powers (1987), pp. 53–54
page 249
Communist revolution ostensibly imminent   Howe and Coser, p. 67
desperately ... Central High   Demaris (1974), p. 73
page 250
Goldman's apprehension and McKinley connection   Whitehead (1957), p. 57
page 251
All ... ark   Murray, p. 218
Centralia shoot-out and hanging   Gilje, p. 137; Toledano, p. 51
page 252
Tulsa massacre   Gilje, pp. 113–114
Plunge in Communist Party membership   Howe and Coser, pp. 91–92
page 253
Palmer, 'thee' and 'thou'   Powers (1987), p. 60
page 254
Deportation of 446 aliens   Toledano, p. 63
Hoover's recognition of Sacco and Vanzetti case as PR disaster
   Powers (1987), p. 126
page 255
Bureau plans to deport defendants   Powers (1987), p. 126
Burns beating up newspaper critics   Anthony, p. 295
Those of us ... worked   Anthony, p. 295
page 256
had ... Federal law   Lewis, p. 181
Hoover noting Garvey's pro-Moscow announcement   Lewis, p. 150
Plan to charge Garvey with tax evasion   Lewis, p. 182
page 257
People ... respect   Whitehead (1970), p. 18
page 258
Truman's KKK involvement   McCullough, pp. 164–165; Tucker, p. 6
page 258
Klansmen intercepting mail and monitoring phone calls   Chalmers, pp. 62–63;
   Toledano, p. 68; Whitehead (1957), p. 68
Clarke's gaoling and loss of influence   Powers (1987), p. 140;
   Whitehead (1957), p. 62
page 259
Stephenson's fate   Tucker, pp. 137–141
Klan formally dissolved   Whitehead (1970), p. 21
When ... named Hoover   Whitehead (1957), p. 73
page 260
did ... Good-day   Demaris (1974), p. 73
not ... deadbeat   Demaris (1974), p. 73
page 261
Hoover's dislike of drawing   DeLoach, facing p. 216
page 262
the first ... police   Cooke (1988), p. 214

page 263
White Slave Trade   Whitehead (1957), p. 37
page 264
a guy ... talking about   Demaris (1974), p. 77
Reductions in Bureau staff   Powers (1987), p. 148
Agents' rules   Whitehead (1957), p. 62
page 265
the most ... met   Anthony, p. 295
Means selling Bureau files   Gentry, p. 118
while ... course   Gentry, p. 120
Three servants, chauffeur-driven Cadillac   Gentry, p. 118
page 266
There was ... of its own   Hodgson, pp. 57–59
page 267
the Government ... for it   Whitehead (1957), p. 77
Prohibition and Treasury   Whitehead (1957), pp. 85, 91
page 268
Union leaders, ACLU, Friends of the Lictor, Navy League
   O'Reilly (1983), p. 18–20
Enrique Estrada   Whitehead (1957), pp. 86–87
page 269
There is ... Communists   Benoit, p. 168
page 270
more than ... people   DeLoach, p. 88
page 271
would say ... helped Hoover   Demaris (1974), p. 160
Gossips on Hoover-Tolson relationship   Buckley, p. 62;
   Theoharis (1991), pp. 346–356
page 272
would have ... "homophobic"   DeLoach, p. 66
[a] photograph ... not   Maas, p. 57
It was baloney   Maas, p. 57
Are you nuts?   Maas, p. 57
page 273
National Division of Identification   Toledano, p. 84
Wallaby, wombat hairs   Whitehead (1957), p. 141
Before ... fall   Powers (1987), p. 183
page 275
Don't ... shoot!   Powers (1987), p. 188
Kansas City Massacre   Unger, *passim*
page 277
jammed ... Edgar   DeLoach, pp. 93–94
a nightclub fly-cop   Cooke (1980), p. 28
Pegler ... halitosis   Toledano, p. 148
page 278
FBI dress requirements   Maas, p. 58
Winchell and Lepke   Toledano, p. 145
Chicago gangsters' re-imprisonment   DeLoach, p. 304

page 279
Coughlin against Mexican régime   Theoharis (1991), p. 180;
    Theoharis and Cox, p. 150
Tax inspectors against Coughlin   O'Reilly (1983), p. 144
page 280
a blackout ... United States   Whitehead (1957), p. 162
page 281
was started ... file   Robins, p. 440
Eliot and Pound   Robins, p. 424
page 282
Stewart's mail opened   Robins, p. 93
Chambermaid, delivery boy   Robins, p. 94
Mann's mail opened   Robins, p. 434
Lewis' phone transcripts   Robins, p. 100
Baldwin and the *Mayflower*   Gentry, p. 141
Cheever's phone tapped   Robins, p. 423
page 283
a stinking rat   Buckley, p. 63
O'Dets   Robins, p. 91
Diana and Lionel Trilling   Robins, p. 304
Jessica Mitford   Robins, p. 249
page 284
a magnificent ... freedom   Ernst, p. 139
Edgar ... That's for them   Whitehead (1957), p. 172
page 285
No-one ... wrecking us   Whitehead (1957), p. 161
6,500 Bund activists   Herzstein, p. 189
Crowd of 20,000   Gentry, p. 205n
extremely unfortunate   Powers (1987), p. 250
page 287
something ... road   Hamilton, p. 449
Krock paid $25,000   Hamilton, p. 212
Profiles in Courage ghost-written   Theoharis (1991), p. 33
the old ... life   Gentry, p. 297
page 288
Lash and his fiancée   Theoharis (1991), p. 64
Rejecting Eleanor's requests   O'Reilly (1983), p. 147
File on Eleanor   Gentry, p. 301
Lash-Eleanor connection and Republicans   Theoharis (1991), p. 64
Kermit Roosevelt   Theoharis (1991), pp. 331–334
page 289
You look ... at all   Gentry, p. 246
page 290
Welles at Jasper   Welles, pp. 2–3
Hoover's consternation about Welles affair   Gellman, pp. 235–237
page 291
Hoover was ... to him   Demaris (1975), p. 288
a red ... inflation   Powers (1987), p. 297

page 292

Mr Hoover ... stopped it   Gentry, p. 386

I never ... again   Gentry, p. 451; Liddy, p. 175

Don't ... the week   Powers (1987), p. 304

page 293

not because ... culpable ones   Benoit, p. 175

Usual liberal complaint against McCarthyism   Von Hoffman, p. C2

page 294

[Hoover] was ... of its ends   Toledano, p. 289

page 295

Black-bag jobs   Theoharis (1991), p. 129

reporting ... drugs   Theoharis (1995), p. 99

Leftists and whores with VD   Theoharis (1995), p. 100

that ... Bureau   Theoharis (1991), p. 287

Stevenson as homosexual?   Gentry, p. 403

page 296

Powell's career, dealings with Rankin, dealings with Hoover   Fenton, *passim*

page 297

No-one ... fun   Cooke (1977), p. 172

We're ... soap flakes   Reeves, p. 143

page 298

Recordings of JFK and Arvad   Reeves, p. 56

You don't fire God   Gentry, p. 472

JFK's clandestine marriage   Theoharis (1995), pp. 86–87

worst ... made   DeLoach, p. 59

page 299

He ... fireplug   Reeves, p. 321

Listen ... White House   Reeves, p. 154

They ... government   Reeves, p. 474

his ... about it   DeLoach, p. 303

page 300

Horace Hampton   Gentry, p. 634n

never ... like   DeLoach, p. 11

page 301

June 1969 revelation on Bobby Kennedy   Garrow, p. 81; Stern and Harwood, pp. 780–781

Look ... time   Branch, p. 250; Meacham, p. 62

King the opiate of post-Christian America's masses   Gottfried, pp. 29–31; Kimball, p. 8

page 302

In ... this matter   Garrow, pp. 22, 233

would ... ensue   Garrow, p. 24

page 303

My ... feelings   King (1963), pp. 88, 98–99

page 304

King's copyright control   Pappas, p. 140

Southerners ... preaching   King (1965), p. 79

page 305
DeLoach advises ... as given   DeLoach, pp. 204–205
I'm ... tonight!   Branch, p. 207; Meacham, p. 62
page 306
some sable Typhoid Mary   Stix, p. 42
Had the ... public figure   McKnight, pp. 6–7
That the ... omniscient   McKnight, p. 146; Pappas, p. 83
page 307
Kirk's recommendation   Powers (1987), p. 395
Wallace and Alabama Klansmen   Carter, p. 259; O'Reilly (1989), p. 172
page 308
I'd rather ... pissing in   Dallek, p. 126
Anonymous letter and tape to King   Garrow, pp. 125–126, Theoharis (1995), p. 98
Sullivan's fatal hunting accident   Ungar, pp. 35–36
page 309
lacking aggressiveness   Gentry, p. 616
Nixon circle on Hoover's intellectual powers   Oudes, p. 217
building outhouses in Peoria   Hodgson, p. 105
Black suit and Supreme Court verdict   Theoharis (1991), pp. 153–154
page 310
At some ... unreasonable   Summers, p. 387
Liddy and Leary   Liddy, pp. 108–115
Hoover ... through   Liddy, pp. 176–177
DeLoach and Hoover's privileges   DeLoach, p. 412
page 311
Nichols' picture in Tolson's obituary   Gentry, p. 736
It was ... jugular   Demaris (1975), p. 329
page 312
The other ... since   Theoharis (1995), p. 72
page 313
Damages to homosexuals   Theoharis, Poveda, Rosenfeld and Powers, pp. 135–137
3,135 McVeigh documents   Gibbs, p. 26
Maintenance and destruction of Donovan files   Gentry, pp. 734–735
page 314
Powers citing Cato's lament   Powers (1999), p. 159

bibliography

Chapter 1

BOSSY, John (1991a), *Giordano Bruno and the Embassy Affair*, New Haven, Connecticut: Yale University Press

BOSSY, John (1991b), 'Surprise, Surprise: An Elizabethan Mystery', *History Today* (September): pp. 14–19

CAMDEN, William (1688), *Annales Rerum Anglicarum et Hibernicarum Regnante Elizabetha*, London: R. Bentley

CARAMAN, Philip (1964), *Henry Garnet, 1555–1606, and the Gunpowder Plot*, London: Longmans

CECIL, Lord David (1973), *The Cecils of Hatfield House*, London: Constable

FRASER, Antonia (1994), *Mary Queen of Scots*, London: Weidenfield & Nicolson

HALL, C. (1989), 'Some Perspectives on the Use of Torture in Bacon's Time and the Question of his "Virtue"', *Anglo-American Law Review* (October–December), pp. 289–321

HAYNES, Alan (1989), *Robert Cecil, Earl of Salisbury, 1563–1612: Servant of Two Sovereigns*, London: Peter Owen

HAYNES, Alan (1992), *Invisible Power: The Elizabethan Secret Services, 1570–1603*, Stroud, Gloucestershire: Sutton Publishing

HAYNES, Alan (1996), *The Gunpowder Plot: Faith in Rebellion*, Stroud, Gloucestershire: Sutton Publishing

HIBBERT, Christopher (1991), *The Virgin Queen: The Personal History of Elizabeth I*, London: Viking

HUME, Martin (1912), 'The So-Called Conspiracy of Dr Ruy Lopez', *The Jewish Historical Society of England Transactions*: pp. 32–35

HUNTLEY, Frank L. (1964), '*Macbeth* and the Background of Jesuitical Equivocation', *Proceedings of the Modern Language Association* (Vol. 79): p. 390

IRWIN, Margaret (1960), *That Great Lucifer: a Portrait of Sir Walter Raleigh*, London: Chatto & Windus

JARDINE, Lisa, and STEWART, Alan (1998), *Hostage to Fortune: The Troubled Life of Francis Bacon, 1561–1626*, London: Victor Gollancz

KAMEN, Henry (1999), *Philip of Spain*, New Haven, Connecticut: Yale University Press

LACEY, Robert (1971), *Robert Devereux, Earl of Essex: An Elizabethan Icarus*, London: Constable

LEE, Sir Sidney (1880), 'The Original of Shylock', *Gentleman's Magazine* (February): pp. 185–200

LLOYD, David (1670), *State-Worthies, or, The Statesmen and Favourites of England Since the Reformation*, London: Samuel Speed

MacCAFFREY, Wallace T. (1981), *Queen Elizabeth and the Making of Policy, 1572–1588*, Princeton, New Jersey: Princeton University Press

MARCUS, L.S., MUELLER, Janet, and ROSE, Mary Beth (eds.) (2000), *Elizabeth I: Complete Works*, Chicago: University of Chicago Press

McNEILL, J.M. (ed.) (1959), *Bacon's Essays*, London: Macmillan

PETRIE, Sir Charles (1963), *Philip II of Spain*, London: Eyre & Spottiswode

PLOWDEN, Alison (1984), *Two Queens in One Isle: The Deadly Relationship of Elizabeth I and Mary Queen of Scots*, Brighton, Sussex: Harvester Press

PLOWDEN, Alison (1991), *The Elizabethan Secret Service*, Hemel Hampstead, Hertfordshire: Harvester Wheatsheaf

READ, Conyers (1975), *Mr Secretary Walsingham and the Policy of Queen Elizabeth*, 3 vols. New York City: AMS Press

SESSIONS, W.A. (ed.) (1990), *Francis Bacon's Legacy of Texts: The Art of Discovery Grows With Discovery*, New York City: AMS Press

SINGH, Simon (1999), *The Code Book: The Evolution of Secrecy from Mary Queen of Scots to Quantum Cryptography*, New York City: Doubleday

SITWELL, Dame Edith (1966), *The Queens and the Hive*, Harmondsworth, Middlesex: Penguin

SMITH, Alan Gordon (1936), *The Babington Plot*, London: Macmillan

SMITH, Alan Gordon (1934), *William Cecil*, London: Kegan Paul

SMITH, Lacey Baldwin (1986), *Treason in Tudor England: Politics and Paranoia*, London: Jonathan Cape

SOMERSET, Anne (1991), *Elizabeth I*, London: Weidenfeld & Nicolson

WAUGH, Evelyn (1953), *Edmund Campion*, Harmondsworth, Middlesex: Penguin

WEIR, Alison (1998), *The Life of Elizabeth I*, New York City: Ballantine Books

WILLIAMS, Penry (1979), *The Tudor Regime*, New York City: Oxford University Press

WILLIAMS, Penry (1998), *The Later Tudors: England 1547–1603*, New York City: Oxford University Press

Chapter 2

BAILLY, Auguste (1936), *The Cardinal Dictator: A Portrait of Richelieu*, London: Jonathan Cape

BERNARDIN, Édith (1964), *Jean-Marie Roland et le Ministère de l'Intérieur, 1792–1793*, Paris: Société des Études Robespierristes

BOSHER, J.F. (1989), *The French Revolution*, London: Weidenfeld & Nicolson

BUISSON, Henry (1968), *Fouché, Duc d'Otrante*, Bienne, Switzerland: Panorama

CARLYLE, Thomas (1934), *The French Revolution*, New York City: Modern Library

CHATEAUBRIAND, François Auguste René, Vicomte de (1951), *Mémoires d'Outre-Tombe*, 4 vols. Paris: Gallimard

CHURCH, Clive H. (1981), *Revolution and Red Tape: The French Ministerial Bureaucracy, 1770–1850*, Oxford: Oxford University Press

COBB, Richard (1970), *The Police and the People: French Popular Protest 1789–1820*, Oxford: Clarendon Press

COLE, Hubert (1971), *Fouché: The Unprincipled Patriot*, London: Eyre & Spottiswode

DARNTON, Robert (1982), *The Literary Underground of the Old Régime*, Cambridge, Massachusetts: Harvard University Press

DEACON, Richard (1990), *The French Secret Service*, London: Grafton Books

DOYLE, William (1989), *The Oxford History of the French Revolution*, Oxford: Clarendon Press

FLETCHER, Ian, and COOK, Andy (1994), *Fields of Fire: Battlefields of the Peninsular War*, London: Sarpedon Publishing

FORSSELL, Nils (1928), *Fouché: The Man Napoleon Feared* (trans. Anna Barwell), London: George Allen & Unwin Ltd

FOUCHÉ, Joseph (1912), *Mémoires*, New York City: Sturgis & Walton Co

GODECHOT, Jacques (1968), *Les Institutions de la France sous la Révolution et l'Empire*, Paris: Hachette

HILT, Douglas (1975), *Ten Against Napoleon*, Chicago: Nelson Hall

HUXLEY, Aldous (1941), *Grey Eminence: A Study in Religion and Politics*, London: Chatto & Windus

JORDAN, David P. (1989), *The Revolutionary Career of Maximilien Robespierre*, Chicago: University of Chicago Press

LA CLÈRE, Marcel (1973), *Histoire de la Police*, Paris: Librairie Plon

LOOMIS, Stanley (1965), *Paris in the Terror: June 1793–July 1794*, London: Jonathan Cape

MACAULAY, Thomas Babington, Baron (1889), Barère, *The Miscellaneous Writings and Speeches of Lord Macaulay*, London: Longmans, Green, and Co: pp. 285–342

MADELIN, Louis (1920), *Fouché, 1759–1820*, 2 vols. Paris: Librairie Plon

MANSELL, Philip (1981), *Louis XVIII*, London: Blond & Briggs

PALMER, R.R. (1989), *The Year of the Terror: Twelve Who Ruled France, 1793–1794*, Oxford: Basil Blackwell

RAPPORT, Michael (1998), 'Napoleon's Rise to Power', *History Today* (January): pp. 15–19

RICE-OXLEY, L. (1924), *Poetry of* The Anti-Jacobin, Oxford: Basil Blackwell

RICHARDSON, Frank (1972), *Napoleon, Bisexual Emperor*, London: William Kimber

SCHOM, Alan (1997), *Napoleon Bonaparte*, New York City: HarperCollins

SINGER, B.C.J. (1986), *Society, Theory, and the French Revolution*, New York City: St Martin's Press

TULARD, Jean (1998), *Joseph Fouché*, Paris: Fayard

ZWEIG, Stefan (1930), *Joseph Fouché: The Portrait of a Politician* (trans. E. and C. Paul), New York City: Viking Press

Chapter 3

ALBATS, Yevgenia (1994), *The State Within A State: The KGB and Its Hold on Russia, Past, Present and Future* (trans. Catherine Fitzpatrick), New York City: Farrar, Straus & Giroux

ANDERSON, M.S. (1978), *Peter the Great*, London: Thames & Hudson

ANDREW, Christopher, and GORDIEVSKY, Oleg (1990), *KGB: The Inside Story of its Foreign Operations from Lenin to Gorbachev*, London: Hodder & Stoughton

ANDREW, Christopher, and MITROKHIN, Vasili (1999), *The Mitrokhin Archive: The KGB in Europe and the West*, London: Allen Lane

ANON (2001), 'World Gets A Peek At KGB's Darkest Secrets', *The Australian* (11 April): p. 11

BLUM, Alain (1994), *Naître, vivre et mourir en URSS 1917–1991*, Paris: Librarie Plon

BROMAGE, Bernard (1956), *Man of Terror: Dzherzhynski*, London: Peter Owen

CHURCHILL, Sir Winston (1948–53), *History of the Second World War* (6 vols.), Boston: Houghton Mifflin

CONQUEST, Robert (1968), *The Great Terror: Stalin's Purge of the Thirties*, London: Macmillan

COURTOIS, Stéphane (ed.) (1999), *The Black Book of Communism: Crimes, Terror, Repression* (trans. Jonathan Murphy and Mark Kramer), Cambridge, Massachusetts: Harvard University Press

CUSTINE, Astolphe, Marquis de (1951), *Lettres de Russie*, Paris: Gallimard

DALRYMPLE, Dana G. (1964), The Soviet Famine of 1932–34, *Soviet Studies* (January): pp. 250–64

DANILOV, V.P., and BERELOVICH, Alexis (1994), 'Les documents de la VCK-OGPU-NKVD sur la campagne soviétique, 1918–1937', *Cahiers du Monde Russe* (Été): pp. 671–676

DEACON, Richard (1987), A *History of the Russian Secret Service*, London: Grafton

DOBRYUKHA, Nikolai (2001), 'Conversations with a Former KGB Chief', *Moscow Times* (16 March): p. 6

FREMANTLE, Brian (1982), *KGB*, London: Michael Joseph

FUEGI, John (1994), *The Life and Lies of Bertolt Brecht*, London: HarperCollins

GREY, Ian (1973), *Boris Godunov: The Tragic Tsar*, New York City: Scribner's

HARCAVE, Sidney (1964), *First Blood: The Russian Revolution of 1905*, New York City: Macmillan

HELLER, Mikhail, and NEKRICH, Aleksandr (1985), *Utopia in Power: The History of the Soviet Union from 1917 to the Present* (trans. P.B. Carlos), London: Hutchinson

HINGLEY, Ronald (1970), *The Russian Secret Police: Muscovite, Imperial Russian and Soviet Political Security Operations, 1565–1970*, London: Hutchinson

HINGLEY, Ronald (1973), *The Tsars: Russian Autocrats, 1533–1917*, London: Corgi

JAMES, Clive (1982), *From the Land of Shadows*, London: Jonathan Cape

KNIGHT, Amy (1995), *Beria: Stalin's First Lieutenant*, Princeton, New Jersey: Princeton University Press

KNIGHT, Amy (1997), *Spies Without Cloaks: The KGB's Successors*, Princeton, New Jersey: Princeton University Press

KNIGHT, Amy (1999), *Who Killed Kirov? The Kremlin's Greatest Mystery*, New York City: Hill and Wang

KOHLER, John O, (1999), *Stasi: The Untold Story of the East German Secret Police*. Boulder, Colorado: Westview Press.

KRIVITSKY, Walter (1939), *I Was Stalin's Agent*, London: Hamish Hamilton

KUPFERMAN, Fred (1979), *Au Pays des Soviets: Le Voyage Français au Union Soviétique 1917–1939*, Paris: Gallimard

LEGGETT, George (1981), *The Cheka, Lenin's Political Police*, New York City: Oxford University Press

LINDEMANN, Albert S. (1997), *Esau's Tears: Modern Anti-Semitism and the Rise of the Jews*, New York City: Cambridge University Press

LYONS, Eugene (1937), *Assignment in Utopia*, New York City: Harcourt, Brace and Company

MACDONALD, Ian (1990), *The New Shostakovich*, Boston: Northwestern University Press

MANDELSTAM, Nadezha (1974), *Hope Abandoned*, London: Collins Harvill

MASSIE, Robert K. (1968), *Nicholas and Alexandra*, New York City: Knopf

MAZOUR, Anatole G. (1960), *Rise and Fall of the Romanovs*, Princeton, New Jersey: Van Nostrand

MEDVEDEV, Roy (1972), *Let History Judge* (trans. Colleen Taylor), Oxford: Basil Blackwell

MEDVEDEV, Roy (1983), *All Stalin's Men*, Oxford: Basil Blackwell

MEDVEDEV, Zhores (1984), *Andropov: His Life and Death*, Oxford: Basil Blackwell

347

MUGGERIDGE, Malcolm (1933), 'The Soviet War on the Peasants', *The Fortnightly Review* (1 May): pp. 18–26

PENKOVSKY, Oleg (1965), *The Penkovsky Papers* (trans. P.S. Deriabin), London: Collins

PLATE, Thomas, and DARVI, Andrea (1981), *Secret Police: The Inside Story of a Network of Terror*, London: Robert Hale

PLOWDEN, Alison (1991), *The Elizabethan Secret Service*, Hemel Hampstead, Hertfordshire: Harvester Wheatsheaf

RUUD, Charles A., and STEPANOV, Sergei A. (1999), *Fontanka 16: The Tsar's Secret Police*, Montréal: McGill-Queens University Press

SAFIRE, William (1991), 'Pour It On', *The New York Times* (2 September): p. 11

SCHEBEKO, L.G. (1890), *Chronique du mouvement socialiste en Russie, 1878–1887*, Paris: SPB

SOBRAN, Joseph (1997), 'The Forgiven Holocaust', *Sobran's* (July): pp. 3–4

SQUIRE, P.S. (1968), *The Third Department: The Establishment and Practice of the Political Police in the Russia of Nicholas I*, Cambridge: Cambridge University Press

STADEN, Heinrich von (1967), *Land and Government of Muscovy*, Stanford, California: Stanford University Press

STICKLE, D.M. (ed.), (1992), *The Beria Affair: The Secret Transcripts of the Meetings Signalling the End of Stalinism*, Commack, New York State: Nova Science Publishers

TAYLOR, Edmond (1963), *The Fall of the Dynasties*, London: Weidenfeld & Nicolson

USTINOV, Sir Peter (1983), *My Russia*, London: Macmillan

VAKSBERG, Arkadii (1994), *Stalin Against the Jews* (trans. Antonina W. Bouis), New York City: Knopf

VOLGOKONOV, Dmitri (1990), *Stalin: Triumph and Tragedy* (trans. Harold Shukman), New York City: Grove Weidenfeld

ZAWODNY, J.K. (1962), *Death in the Forest: The Story of the Katyn Forest Massacre*, Notre Dame, Indiana: University of Notre Dame Press

Chapter 4

BAKER, Robert (1998), 'A Theory of International Bioethics: Multi-culturalism, Postmodernism, and the Bankruptcy of Fundamentalism', *Kennedy Institute of Ethics Journal* (September): pp. 201–231

BENTLEY, James (1984), *Martin Niemöller*, Oxford: Oxford University Press

BROOK-SHEPHERD, Gordon (1996), *The Austrians: A Thousand-Year Odyssey*, London: HarperCollins

BROWDER, George C. (1990), *Foundations of the Nazi Police State: The Formation of Sipo and SD*, Lexington, Kentucky: University of Kentucky Press

BRISSAUD, André (1972), *The Nazi Secret Service* (trans. Milton Waldman), London: The Bodley Head

BROWDER, George C. (1996), *Hitler's Enforcers: The Gestapo and the SS Security Service in the Nazi Revolution*, New York City: Oxford University Press

BURLEIGH, Michael (2000), *The Third Reich: A New History*, New York City: Hill and Wang

BRYSAC, Shareen Blair (2000), *Resisting Hitler: Mildred Harnack and the Red Orchestra*, New York City: Oxford University Press

CRANKSHAW, Edward (1956), *Gestapo: Instrument of Tyranny*, London: Putnam

CRANKSHAW, Edward (1971), *The Habsburgs*, London: Thames & Hudson

DORPALEN, Andreas (1964), *Hindenburg and the Weimar Republic*, Princeton, New Jersey: Princeton University Press

DOUGLAS, Gregory (1996–99), *Gestapo Chief: The 1948 Interrogation of Heinrich Müller*, 3 vols. San José: R. James Bender Publishing

FREI, Norbert (1993), *The Führer State, 1933–1945* (trans. Simon B. Steyne), Oxford: Basil Blackwell

GELATELLY, Robert (1990), *The Gestapo and German Society: Enforcing Racial Policy, 1933–1945*, Oxford: Oxford University Press

GILL, Anton (1994), *An Honourable Defeat: A History of the German Resistance to Hitler*, London: William Heinemann Ltd

GISEVIUS, Hans-Bernd (1947), *To the Bitter End* (trans. Richard Winston), Boston: Houghton Mifflin

HAMILTON, Charles (1984), *Leaders and Personalities of the Third Reich: Their Biographies, Portraits, and Autographs*, 2 vols. San José: R. James Bender Publishing

HILLENBRAND, F.K.M. (1995), *Underground Humour in Nazi Germany 1933–1945*, London: Routledge

HOFFMANN, Peter (1995), *Stauffenberg: A Family History, 1905–1944*, Cambridge: Cambridge University Press

IRVING, David (1989), *Göring: A Biography*, New York City: William Morrow & Company

KERSHAW, Ian (1996) *Hitler: 1889–1936, Hubris*, New York City: W.W. Norton

KERSHAW, Ian (2000), *Hitler: 1936–1945, Nemesis*, London: New York City: W.W. Norton

KLEMPERER, Klemens von (1992), *German Resistance Against Hitler: The Search for Allies Abroad, 1938–1945*, Oxford: Oxford University Press

LATTIMER, John K. (1999), *Hitler and the Nazis: A Unique Insight Into Evil*, Shepperton, Surrey: Ian Allan

MASUR, Gerhard (1971), *Imperial Berlin*, London: Routledge & Kegan Paul

PADOVER, Saul K. (1967), *The Revolutionary Emperor: Joseph II of Austria*, Hamden, Connecticut: Archon Books

PETRIE, Sir Charles (1952), *Monarchy in the Twentieth Century*, London: A. Dakers

SCHWARZ, Ted (1992), *Walking With the Damned: The Shocking Murder of the Man Who Freed 30,000 Prisoners from the Nazis*, New York City: Paragon House

SEWARD, Desmond (1992), *Metternich: The First European*, New York City: Viking

SINGH, Simon (1999), *The Code Book: The Evolution of Secrecy from Mary Queen of Scots to Quantum Cryptography*, London: Viking

SNYDER, Louis L. (1990), *Hitler's German Enemies: The Stories of the Heroes Who Fought the Nazis*, New York City: Hippocrene Books

TAYLOR, A.J.P. (1966), *From Sarajevo to Potsdam*, London: Thames & Hudson

TAYLOR, Edmond (1963), *The Fall of the Dynasties*, London: Weidenfeld & Nicolson

TOLAND, John (1976), *Adolf Hitler*, Garden City, New York State: Doubleday and Co. Inc

WHITING, Charles (1999), *Heydrich: Henchman of Death*, London: Pen and Sword Books

Chapter 5

ANTHONY, Carl Sferrazza (1998), *Florence Harding: The First Lady, the Jazz Age, and the Death of America's Most Scandalous President*, New York City: William Morrow & Co

BENOIT, Gary (ed.) (2000), *Twentieth-Century Heroes*, Appleton, Wisconsin: American Opinion Publishing Inc

BRANCH, Taylor (1997), *Pillar of Fire: America in the King Years, 1963–65*, New York City: Simon & Schuster

BUCKLEY, William F. (2000), 'Is The FBI Mad At You?', *National Review* (20 March): pp. 62–63

CARTER, Dan T. (1995), *The Politics of Rage: George Wallace, the Origins of the New Conservatism, and the Transformation of American Politics*, New York City: Simon & Schuster

CHALMERS, David M. (1965), *Hooded Americanism: The First Century of the Ku Klux Klan*, New York City: Doubleday

COOKE, Alistair (1988), *America Observed: The Newspaper Years of Alistair Cooke*, London: Reinhardt Books

COOKE, Alistair (1980), *The Americans: Letters from America, 1969–1979*, Harmondsworth, Middlesex: Penguin Books

COOKE, Alistair (1978), *Six Men*, Harmondsworth, Middlesex: Penguin Books

DALLEK, Robert (1998), *Flawed Giant: Lyndon Johnson and his Times, 1961–1973*, New York City: Oxford University Press

DeLOACH, Cartha (1997), *Hoover's FBI: The Inside Story by Hoover's Trusted Lieutenant*, Washington DC: Regnery Publishing

DEMARIS, Ovid (1974), 'The Private Life of J. Edgar Hoover', *Esquire* (September): pp. 71–78, 160–165

DEMARIS, Ovid (1975), *The Director: An Oral Biography of J. Edgar Hoover*, New York City: Harper's Magazine Press

ERNST, Morris (1950), 'Why I No Longer Fear the FBI', *Reader's Digest* (December): pp. 135–139

FENTON, Matthew McCann (1998), 'Shaking Up the House: The Colorful, Controversial Adam Clayton Powell, Jr.', *Biography* (January): pp. 44–48

GARROW, David J. (1981), *The FBI and Martin Luther King, Jr.: From 'Solo' to Memphis*, New York City: W.W. Norton

GELLMAN, Irwin (1995), *Secret Affairs: Franklin Roosevelt, Cordell Hull, and Sumner Welles*, Baltimore: Johns Hopkins University Press

GENTRY, Curt (1991), *J. Edgar Hoover: The Man and the Secrets*, New York City: W.W. Norton

GIBBS, Nancy (2001), 'Botching the Big Case', *Time* (21 May): pp. 24–30

GILJE, P.A. (1996), *Rioting in America*, Bloomington, Indiana: Indiana University Press

GOTTFRIED, Paul (1997), 'Martin Luther King, Jr., as Conservative Hero', *Chronicles* (April): pp. 29–31

HAMILTON, Nigel (1992), *JFK: Reckless Youth*, London: Century

HERZSTEIN, Robert Edwin (1989), *Roosevelt and Hitler: Prelude to War*, New York City: Paragon House

HODGSON, Godfrey (1980), *All Things to All Men: The False Promise of America's Presidency*, New York City: Simon & Schuster

HOWE, Irving, and COSER, Louis (1962), *The American Communist Party*, New York City: Præger

KIMBALL, Roger (1999), 'The Elephant in the Gallery, or, The Lessons of "Sensation"', *The New Criterion* (November): pp. 4–8

KING, Martin Luther (1963), *Strength to Love*, New York City: Harper & Row

KING, Martin Luther (1965), 'The Unchristian Christian', *Ebony* (August): pp. 77–80

LEWIS, Rupert (1988), *Marcus Garvey: Anti-Colonial Champion*, Trenton, New Jersey: Africa World Press

LIDDY, G. Gordon (1980), *Will: The Autobiography of G. Gordon Liddy*, New York City: St Martin's Press

LYNN, Robert, and WRIGHT, Elliott (1971), *The Big Little School: Two Hundred Years of the Sunday School*, New York City: Harper & Row

MAAS, Peter (1993), 'Setting the Record Straight', *Esquire* (May): pp. 56–58

McCULLOUGH, David (1992), *Truman*, New York City: Simon & Schuster

McKNIGHT, Gerald (1998), *The Last Crusade: Martin Luther King Jr., the FBI, and the Poor People's Campaign*, Boulder, Colorado: Westview Press

MEACHAM, Jon (1998), 'The Middle of the Journey', *Newsweek* (18 January): p. 62

MURRAY, Robert K. (1964), *Red Scare: A Study in National Hysteria, 1919–1920*. New York City: McGraw-Hill

NIXON, Richard (1978), *The Memoirs of Richard Nixon*, London: Macmillan

O'REILLY, Kenneth (1983), *Hoover and the Un-Americans*, Philadelphia: Temple University Press

O'REILLY, Kenneth (1989), *'Racial Matters': The FBI's Secret File on Black Americans, 1960–1972*, New York City: Free Press

OUDES, Bruce (1989), *From The President: Richard Nixon's Secret Files*, New York City: Harper & Row

PAPPAS, Theodore (1998), *Plagiarism and the Culture War: The Writings of Martin Luther King Jr. And Other Prominent Americans*, Tampa, Florida: Hallberg Publishing Corporation

POWERS, Richard Gid (1987), *Secrecy and Power: The Life of J. Edgar Hoover*, London: Hutchinson

POWERS, Richard Gid (1999), 'Hoover, J. Edgar', *American National Biography*, New York City: Oxford University Press, Vol. 11: pp. 156–160

REEVES, Thomas C. (1991), *A Question of Character: A Life of John F. Kennedy*, New York City: Free Press

ROBINS, Natalie (1992), *Alien Ink: The FBI's War on Freedom of Expression*, New York City: William Morrow & Co

STERN, Laurence, and HARWOOD, Richard (1969), A Dirty Business, *Nation* (23 June): pp. 780–781

STIX, Nicholas (1997), 'The Black Nationalism of George S. Schuyler', *Chronicles* (November): pp. 41–43

SUMMERS, Anthony (1993), *Official and Confidential: The Secret Life of J. Edgar Hoover*, New York City: G.P. Putnam's Sons

THEOHARIS, Athan (1991), *From the Secret Files of J. Edgar Hoover*, Chicago: Ivan R. Dee

THEOHARIS, Athan (1995), *J. Edgar Hoover, Sex and Crime: An Historical Antidote*, Chicago: Ivan R. Dee

THEOHARIS, Athan, and COX, John Stuart (1988), *The Boss: J. Edgar Hoover and the Great American Inquisition*, Philadelphia: Temple University Press

THEOHARIS, Athan, POVEDA, Tony G., ROSENFELD, Susan, and POWERS, Richard Gid (1999), *The FBI: A Comprehensive Reference Guide*, Phœnix: Oryx Press

TOLEDANO, Ralph de (1974), *J. Edgar Hoover: The Man in His Time*, New Rochelle, New York State: Arlington House

TUCKER, Richard K. (1991), *The Dragon and the Cross: The Rise and Fall of the Ku Klux Klan in Middle America*, Hamden, Connecticut: Archon Books

UNGAR, Sanford J. (1979), 'The Bureau', *The New Republic* (13 October): pp. 35–36

UNGER, Robert (1997), *The Union Station Massacre: The Original Sin of J. Edgar Hoover's FBI*, Kansas City, Missouri: Andrews McMeel

VON HOFFMAN, Nicholas (1996), 'Was McCarthy Right About the Left?', *The Washington Post* (11 April): pp. C1–C2

WELLES, Benjamin (1997), *Sumner Welles: FDR's Global Strategist*, New York City: St Martin's Press

WHITEHEAD, Don (1957), *The FBI Story*, London: Frederick Muller Ltd

WHITEHEAD, Don (1970), *Attack on Terror: The FBI Against the Ku Klux Klan in Mississippi*, New York City: Funk & Wagnall

index